Flyfisher's Guide to
# Northern California

## Titles Available in This Series

Flyfisher's Guide to Alaska

Flyfisher's Guide to the Florida Keys

Flyfisher's Guide to Idaho

Flyfisher's Guide to Northern California

Flyfisher's Guide to Montana

Flyfisher's Guide to Michigan

Flyfisher's Guide to Wyoming

Flyfisher's Guide to Northern New England

Flyfisher's Guide to Washington

Flyfisher's Guide to Oregon

Flyfisher's Guide to Colorado

Flyfisher's Guide to Pennsylvania

Flyfisher's Guide to Minnesota

Flyfisher's Guide to Utah

Flyfisher's Guide to Texas

Flyfisher's Guide to New York

Flyfisher's Guide to Virginia

Flyfisher's Guide to Freshwater Florida

Flyfisher's Guide to Wisconsin

Flyfisher's Guide to Chesapeake Bay

On the Fly Guide to the Northern Rockies

On the Fly Guide to the Northwest

Saltwater Angler's Guide to Southern California

Saltwater Angler's Guide to the Southeast

Flyfisher's Guide to

# Northern California

**Seth Norman**

Wilderness
Adventures
Press

Belgrade, Montana

This book was made with an easy opening, lay flat binding.

*Published by Wilderness Adventures Press, Inc.™*
*45 Buckskin Road*
*Belgrade, MT 59714*
*800-925-3339*
*Website: www.wildadv.com*
*email: books@wildadv.com*

Printed in the United States of America

ISBN 1-932098-15-1 (pbk.)

*This book is dedicated to three generations of leading ladies:*

*to The Soph, that she may someday go to a decent trade school;*

*to Sophie's Mom, Lisa Jungclas, Ph.D., who is upstairs singing to The Soph at this moment, proving that even people called Doctor remember verses to songs featuring marching ants, twinkling stars, farm animals, and "Hands, shoulders, knees and toes, knees and toes";*

*and to my Mother, Enid Norman, who has strongly suggested that I not sing at all, under any circumstances, but who has supported other efforts in all sorts of important ways.*

# Table of Contents

# Foreword

## The Authors

This state is blessed with waters and an incalculable quantity of talent. Northern California is a hub for America's — even the world's — most passionate, experienced, committed, and opinionated flyfishing innovators, guides, tyers, tacticians, and experts. Settling for a finite number of sources leaves out countless others with invaluable information; the hard fact is that for every single venue covered there are other people who could have imparted insight and wisdom. Would that it were possible to put all these together, even to entertain the vigorous disputes they would indulge. It is not.

## The Waters

Everybody wants to know the best places to go and be alone when they get there. None of the rivers described here are well kept secrets. They are among the finest in California, where many or most flyfishers will someday visit. It's the intent of this book to help prepare fishers for that time.

For those from out of state or country, welcome. Odds are you will be surprised at how good this gets.

The idea of "destination" guided the selection process for venues, and the winnowing was neither arbitrary nor subject to a set of absolute rules. "Northern California" is defined by the division established in the DeLorme *Gazetteer*, all are trout rivers or streams — mostly wild trout — including several where steelhead and rainbows run together, if not to the sea. Authors and editor walked some fine lines, making decisions subject to question: should a writer mention a tributary that cannot tolerate much pressure? Identify access inch by inch, or more generally? Insist on a detailed hatch chart for a particularly unpredictable river? Strive for uniform organization and emphasis, or adapt a structure that fit personal style and the requisites of the river described?

Answers to the above: no; depends; the most relevant to fishers; "yes."

Ultimately the editor relied a great deal on the writers' judgments and on the nature of the waters they fish. For example, Fall River access is so limited that a single page about it would suffice, while the upper Sacramento required an exit-by-exit guide. Hat Creek insects are discussed in detail because the educated trout there often demand exact imitation; that's not usually the case on the lower Owens.

Most often the river ruled, and the writer.

The same "writer rule" applied to tactics. Those described in these chapters are important enough that there is an index of "how to." Often the approach of individual authors was at variance, occasionally in conflict — no single indicator setup serves every place every time, and there are several styles of fishing soft hackles, at least. A reader would be well advised to examine each approach carefully, if they have not already done so, experiment, then develop a repertoire with which he or she is comfortable.

## Chapter Organization

Each of these chapters contains a brief overview; a map; discussion of influential factors such as water flow and runoff; identification of the trout found there; a description of the fishery; location of access sites, and boat ramps if applicable; advisories about wading; a presentation of the hatches and feed writers considered most important, along with recommended fly patterns, tackle and rigging suggestions, and tactics. (Many of the latter are listed in the Index to Techniques.)

"Stream Facts" summarizes important points made in the text.

The services section follows Stream Facts, providing information about accommodations, restaurants, fly shops, guides, hospitals, campgrounds, airport, and auto rental if available. These are designed to assist anglers in planning a trip as well as on the road. Much of this information relates to a "hub city" or cities — those nearest a venue and large enough to provide for most traveling needs. (Some hub cities have three places to stay, one closer to 300.) Authors were asked to recommend favorite places to eat and stay; in some cases the editor added to these. This book is not *The Michelin Guide.*

## Accommodations

Accommodations are identified by the rating system below. Note that doubles are sometimes the same price as singles, or close, so that an establishment identified as $$ may be a bargain for two or three people. Special features — "allows small pets" — were included when that information was available.

$ – $40 and under for a single
$$ – $40 – $75
$$$ – above $75

## Restaurants

A similar rating system was used for restaurants, although menu prices vary more than room tariffs. For comparison only:

$ – Fast food, diner, or bargain
$$ – Dinner and a beer for $10 or less.
$$$ – Fine dining or seriously overpriced

## Fly Shops

An effort was made to be as inclusive as reasonable: fly shops are noted at hub cities, on routes to venues, and within 20 miles of airports in several transit cities (major metropolitan areas with commercial air service). Finding every one of these was problematic: writers, two large computer search programs, the mailing lists of three manufacturers and an advertising index were used to gather this information. Dedicated flyfishing stores were given priority. General tackle shops are mentioned in areas where they were the only source or when an author believed they served flyfishers' needs well.

A later edition may extend the range of this survey. To any shop that fit the protocol above and was inadvertently left out, we offer a sincere apology and a promise to remedy the omission next time.

Note: a sincere attempt was made to list guides for these venues. There are several thousand licensed guides in California, however, 14 percent are cranky and have weapons permits; 37 percent guide Fall River; 18 percent avow expertise on every liquid body between Mexico and the Canadian border; nine percent stake claims extending from Argentina to the Arctic — the latter are probably exaggerating.

In short, the attempt failed, so the only guides mentioned are the authors, when that is their business. Note that this is not the author's fault, since every single one of them recommended many or all of their competitors. Fishers who would like guides — always an excellent idea — are advised that word of mouth is a good way to find a good one; that most shops have guides or contacts with them; and that many independents advertise in *California Fly Fisher*, a magazine in which the editor happens to have a vested interest.

Campgrounds are identified, individually or generally, with information on how to find out more about them. Hospitals are listed, as are airports and commercial carriers, if any, auto rentals (usually through airports), and auto mechanics when authors had a recommendation, which wasn't very often. Biographical sketches are also included. (The editor encouraged authors to toot their horns. When several proved tone deaf, he may have added accompaniment.)

## About Camping in State Parks

As of this writing, all state parks are working on a first-come, first-served basis. The state does, however, plan to use another company for bookings. They expect to retain the 800-444-PARK number or to have a referral set up on that line.

## Regulations

It is simply imperative that anglers check regulations — they may change several times in a year. To receive a copy of California's regulations, call 916-653-7664 or write the Department of Fish and Game Headquarters, Box 944209, Sacramento, CA 94244-2090.

# Introduction

California's fortune in waters is vast, diverse, complex, and changeable. We are lucky for the abundance except when it comes to guidebooks, which are necessarily compromises — a "comprehensive" work would require 20 volumes. As I approached this book, the important question was simply what *kind* of compromise I might choose to make.

The quick-sketch approach to venues has value and had been done. Instead, I contemplated a careful examination of rivers, a set of close studies offering to flyfishers the kind of mysteries special waters often keep secret, each presented by anglers who are themselves, through experience and insight, also treasures.

Done, I hope. With this caveat:

This book does not "represent" California flyfishing. It considers only moving water, and omits the sort of smaller venue that cannot tolerate exposure, hundreds of thousands of places where streams run and fish rise. It includes many of the best known destinations (and one or two that should be famous), as seen through the eyes and through the years by someone who can offer advice on the ways of trout *here* — specific observations, lessons, and a set of realistic expectations.

About the authors: some of these writers are widely published, others had never written professionally. As a group, they proved people of great goodwill, wisdom, and generosity. On paper, each has his or her own voice; while it was my intent to meddle as rarely as possible, it was also my job to ease the reading process. At times that meant deconstructing precious metaphors and omitting philosophical meanderings vaguely related to Kant and Thoreau. To their credit, no author insisted, "You Kant Thoreau that part out."

*Mea culpa.* And many thanks.

# Major Roads and Rivers of Northern California

# California Facts

3rd largest state in the union
163,707 square miles
72,964,480 acres
250 miles across
770 miles north to south

**Elevations:** –282 feet near Death Valley to 14,494 feet on Mt. Whitney
**Counties:** 58
**Population (1990 census):** 33,871,648

12 Indian Reservations
6 National Parks
2 National Recreation Areas
14 National Forests
29 Wilderness Areas
36 State Parks
28 State Recreation Areas
2 Regional Parks

**Nicknames:** "The Golden State"
**State Motto:** Eureka (I have found it)
**Primary Industries:** Agriculture, Manufacturing, Services, Trace
**Capital:** Sacramento
**Bird:** California valley quail
**Flower:** Golden poppy
**Tree:** California redwood
**State song:** *I Love You, California*

# Fall River: Wide Skies

## by Andy Burk

It's tempting to think of Fall River in religious terms: for a long time Heaven was easier to access; the trout sometimes seem to practice Zen meditation while your fly drifts past; and the reaction of anglers so frustrated is frequently blasphemous. All this plays out under an ocean of sky pierced by the startling cone of Mount Lassen, along glides of crystalline water waltzing angel's hair of weeds. As the afternoon wind begins to build from a whisper, so do the prayers of fisher folk begging for a *hexagenia* hatch *tonight*, when all hell will break loose.

### Overview

One of California's largest and most productive spring creeks, Fall River emerges from the area known as Thousand Springs, winding 17 miles down to pen stocks that empty into the Pit River. At its uppermost reaches, the land is wild enough for wolverines, but most of the Fall's run courses a rich, open, and long-settled valley. After its first few miles Fall stops tumbling and glides along reed beds, hurrying a little on the outside of the bends where its undercut banks make lies for big browns. Serene, is the Fall.

And a pleasure for observers of nature: Fall Valley is a popular nesting site for waterfowl, as well as a stopover for migrations of cinnamon teal, mallards and wood duck, among others. Eagle and osprey fish the river, along with several species of heron and the occasional sandhill crane. Ermine and weasels hunt the shore; muskrats dig elaborate burrow systems into banks. Also common here is a marmot of such size that at least one angler has insisted that he's seen "a big brown monkey, two feet tall, tearing leaves off a bush beside Spring Creek Bridge."

One reason this wildlife thrives is that virtually the entire river passage is private, lined by old, established ranches and farms. For decades owners fenced clear across the river to keep outlanders away. It's probably not true that one of these constructions was electrified, but the story represents a prevalent attitude.

A lawsuit fixed the fence problem, but it took Cal Trout's purchase of a ribbon of land off Island Road to let the public onto the water anywhere close to the premium water of the middle stretch, within reach of the upper section. Though parking is somewhat limited (the wise arrive early) from here you may launch any manually or electrically powered water craft light enough to carry along a short path. The only other public access site is farther downriver, on Pacific Gas & Electric (PG&E) property at the intersection of Glenburn and McArthur Roads. There are also several private operations.

That's it. Virtually no bank access anywhere, and between weeds, reeds and the nature of the river's channel, Fall River would be difficult to fish from shore if there was. Some sort of watercraft is simply a must.

For our purposes the river may best be divided into three sections: the upper

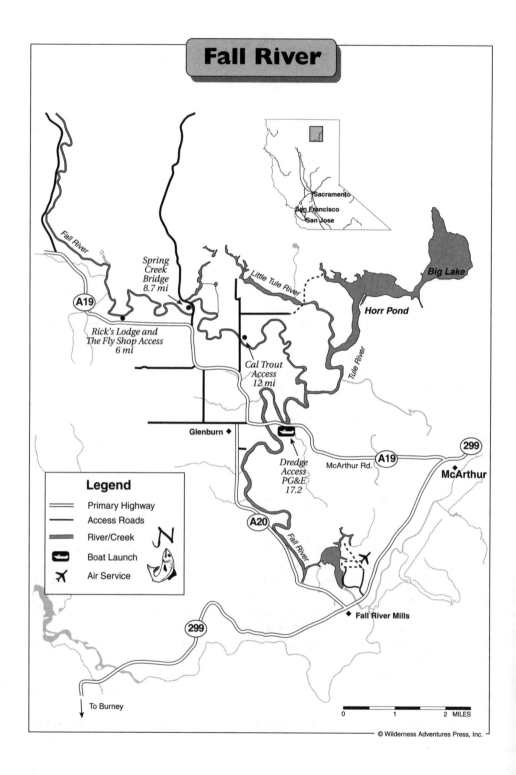

Fall River

Spring
Creek
Bridge
8.7 mi

A19

Rick's Lodge and
The Fly Shop Access
6 mi

Fall River

Little Tule River

Big Lake

Horr Pond

Cal Trout
Access
12 mi

Tule River

Glenburn ◆

Dredge
Access
PG&E
17.2

McArthur Rd.

A19

299

McArthur

A20

Fall River

Legend

═══ Primary Highway
─── Access Roads
━━━ River/Creek
🛥 Boat Launch
✈ Air Service

N

Fall River Mills

299

To Burney

0        1        2  MILES

© Wilderness Adventures Press, Inc.

Sacramento
San Francisco
San Jose

reach, from origins at Thousand Springs down to the Spring Creek Bridge; the Middle section, from the bridge to the mouth of the Tulle river; and the lower Fall, from the confluence of Tulle to the pen stock on the Pitt River at Powerhouse #1. All three sections have excellent fishing in their season.

Season is important here. While river flow is relatively consistent, fishable during all but the highest periods of spring runoff, weather is far less predictable. Especially in springtime, the well-prepared angler will be ready for both balmy temperatures and cold rain. Summertime days will reach 100 degrees, but afternoon winds usually provide relief. Like spring, autumn may bring warm days or cold, with drenching rain. While one may certainly argue that such vagaries are common anywhere in Northern California, and that a key to fishing comfortably is to prepare for change, this is particularly important when you're exposed in a pram or canoe with small chance of finding cover and no refuge on shore.

Odds are, however, that you'll find fair conditions here the majority of the time. Even on marginal days you may wish to push the limits of endurance. The average size of Fall rainbows is between 13 and 17 inches, with 18- to 22-inch fish common enough that a skilled angler may hook into one or two a day. Truly large fish here run to 27 inches and generally succumb only to perfect presentations.

All of these are wild. While the scarcer browns run to the buttery yellow colors of their tribe, the rainbows are somewhat unusual. Along with their classic, vivid red stripe and olive back, they shimmer with a deep and subtle golden color — a treat that often surprises first-time Fall fishers. Though anglers may at this writing legally kill two fish under 14 inches, few do so. Catch-and-release is not the law; it is, however, the rule.

### Fishing The Fall

Fishing the Fall can be difficult, given the clarity of water and the selective nature of fish that see many flies over a season. The river has a reputation for humbling anglers. However, the very numbers of fish, as well as the tactics that have evolved here, give fishers better than excellent opportunities. For those not familiar with Fall River, the best option is to hire a guide on the first outing. A good one will teach you more about the river than would many trial-and-error outings.

Here are two general points that a good guide might make. In the spring, Fall rainbows tend to concentrate in the upper river's upper section, spawning or preparing to spawn in creeks like Bear and Spring (siltation may be changing this pattern, however). This means launching in the morning at the Cal Trout Access, then rowing, paddling, or electric-motoring upstream for several miles. You can drift back with the current in the afternoon.

Second, pay close attention to weeds on Fall River — the fish certainly do: lacking other significant cover, Fall fish orient to weed beds and the luxuriant growth is where they find abundant food. In the early season especially, when weed growth is sparse, look for what patches are available — these hold fish.

*Lengthy casts and long, light leaders are required on the Fall River.*
*(Photo: Mike Mercer)*

## Tackle

Fall is best fished with a four- or five-weight rod between 8.5 and 9 feet long. A moderate action will provide some cushion for the light tippets necessary, and a reel with a smooth drag will provide more protection. The latter should have plenty of backing. Make sure that you carefully examine all gear before your trip — the Fall is no place for mistakes.

Leaders are a subject of debate among river regulars, with many of the wise advising lengths to 20 feet in order to keep the more visible fly line well out of the trout's window of vision. However, 13 to 16 feet is probably enough if you stick to spring creek tapers. Expect to add either 5X, 6X or 7X tippet, depending on conditions. Some subsurface fishing will require heavier 4X or 5X tippet.

A floating line is standard and indispensable all year on this mostly shallow river, in weight forward or double taper. Add to this a type-two density, full-sinking line, and perhaps another with a 13-foot, high-density sink-tip and you're covered.

## Tactics

As indicated earlier and reiterated in the sidebar, tactics on the Fall include one "must-know," a downstream presentation that insures that fish see your fly before seeing line or leader. Casts should be made well above a feeding fish, and the line fed out with shakes of the rod — some favor a side-to-side action, most use up-and-down. If it is necessary to reposition the fly, do so by raising the rod tip and drawing the fly into the lane — make sure the latter stage of the drift is natural. If no take occurs, avoid dragging the fly upstream through the fish's window of vision. Instead, swing it off to the side and retrieve carefully, creating as little wake as possible.

This downstream presentation should be used with dry flies during hatches. It's also advised with the nymph and indicator rig that is the most common and effective method of fishing the Fall. Set-up for the latter is relatively simple: place a small strike indicator of your choice — a pinch-on, lil' corkie or yarn — between one and three feet above your fly. Using 6X or 7X tippet will allow the nymph to move more naturally in the current. Apply a microshot 10 inches above the fly to make sure it gets down.

Striking with this rig takes some practice — another area where a guide may be of help — and some anglers opt for a sideways pull when the indicator pauses or dips under. Whatever motion you use, remember your fragile tippet. It's a challenge, but there are fishers who employ no tactic but this one on the Fall and catch fish with it every day of the season. Others go to sinking lines and sinktip presentations on days when little surface feeding is observed or when inclement weather makes a delicate approach difficult. Cast across stream and feed slack as line and fly sink. When the line is well down and downstream, apply tension to swing through the hole or slot you've chosen. Pay particular attention to undercut banks. Retrieve the fly slowly at the end of the swing; strikes at this time may be savage.

Dry fly fishing on the Fall may be spectacular at any point in the season (more on this in the next section). Once again, proper presentation in the downstream model is critical. Strive to get your fly exactly into the feeding lane with a drag-free drift. As a rule, any fault will mean failure.

### Hatches and Flies

Fall River is a diverse ecosystem with prolific hatches. The prepared angler is better rewarded — either a guide or a conversation with local fly shop staff will be helpful. The following offer a general identification of major hatches, their timing, and the section of river where you're most likely to find them:

*Pale morning dun* (*Ephemerella infrequens*), known better as PMDs, are the prevalent mayfly species on the upper and middle sections of Fall River. They begin hatching as early as April and continue through the end of the season, with one peak of activity in May and June, then another in September and October. The emergence starts around 10:30AM most mornings and may last until 3:00PM. Trout key in on all stages of the hatch.

➤ **Recommended Nymphs**
   Burk's Hunchback Infrequens #14-18
   Mercer's Poxyback PMD #16-18
   Pheasant Tail Nymph #14-16

➤ **Recommended Dries**
   Burk's Silhouette Dun #14-18
   Harrop's No Hackles #16-18
   Lawson Thorax Dun PMD #16-18

Transitional Dun CDC #16-18
Rusty Sparkle Quill Spinner
Quigley's Cripple #16-18

Another important hatch on the upper and middle Fall in early spring and autumn is the **blue winged olive** (*Baetis* species). These are primarily early morning risers and precede the PMD hatch. Prepare to fish tiny flies on very light tippets.

➤ **Recommended Nymphs**
Pheasant Tail Nymph #18-20
Mercer's Poxybacked Baetis Dark and Light #18-20
Burk's Legged Nymphs, Natural and Olive #18-20

➤ **Recommended Dries**
Lawson's Thorax BUN BWO #18-20
No-Hackles #18-20
Dark Olive Paradun #18-20
CDC Emergent BWO #18-20
Rusty Quill Spinner #18-20
Parachute Adams #18-22

Another diminutive insect, most common in the late summer months throughout the entire river, is *Tricorythodes*, or Tricos. While most often fished in the spinner stage, nymph and dun can both provide excellent angling.

➤ **Recommended Nymphs**
Mercer's Poxy-backed Trico Nymph #20-24

➤ **Recommended Dries**
A.K.s ParaTrico #20-22
Sparkle Quill Spinner, Male and Female #20-24

For most experienced Fall fishers, few hatches compare to the **Hex mayfly** riot in the hours before dark on the middle and lower sections, in June and July. *Hexagenia limbata* is the largest of its tribe in the western United States and draws to the surface the biggest fish that will ever come up. Come up they do, hoping to wolf down as many of these beasts as they can in an evening feast. You will hear rising fish you can't see in falling light, though it will be tempting to think "Man, that must be a beaver."

Hex nymphs may fish extremely well prior to the late hatch, in an across-and down swing. Hughes and Hafele recommend imitating the naturals' smooth swimming action by pulsating the rod tip. By the time the duns are coming off, however, you won't want to waste time rerigging by flashlight. Have your dry fly ready on another rod, tied to stout tippet — 5X or even 4X — on a leader of 9 or 10 feet. Of course, the big flies can't be handled with the delicacy of your other Fall presentations, but between the reduced visibility and the sudden greed of fish quite finicky only minutes before, anglers often have an advantage. Half an advantage, anyway. Make the best of it, and do float home carefully in the dark.

# The Fall River Twitch

Simply to say "Fall River" is to suggest to veterans a particular fishing tactic, written in full as "the Fall River Twitch." It's best to describe this in the context of an early spring outing, when many fish have moved to the upper section of river in order to spawn at Bear or Spring Creek.

Begin with an early morning's motor or row upstream from the Cal Trout launch site, past fields so green they seem to glow in the dawn light. You begin to ease into the place by watching the undulations of water weeds. If the light is good—or your eyes are—you'll soon see the fish as well, perhaps not all of the five or six thousand per mile, but so many more than you expect that the first gasps of "look there!" will eventually fade to a kind of constant crooning.

The weak will stop before they intended to, tying off sideways to the flow with a pair of anchors. The strong will take enough time to stare down a moment, partly to admire the water clarity, mostly to watch for mayfly nymphs struggling toward the surface to hatch. Perhaps you see only a few at first. Then, as a hatch begins or your vision adjusts, half a million more. If the moment is right, you'll see also the bulging of trout swirls within your range—downstream, that means...

Select a fly to match the emergers you've been watching (those who did not take time to examine the water will tie on based on the suggestions included here). Already you've decided between a leader of 20 feet, as some experts suggest, or selected Burk's best bet of an Umpqua Spring Creek model in the 13- or 16-feet lengths. You've also carefully considered whether to go with 5X tippet, which is appropriate to the size of fish you may encounter, or with 6X or 7X, which will allow your nymph to move more naturally, thus drawing more takes.

Either way, you've also applied an indicator, one to three feet up from the fly, and pinched on a microshot to get it down. Thus rigged—and with a fish still rising in reach downstream—you proceed to begin the Twitch, the downstream presentation that insures your fly reaches a fish before your line or leader.

It's so simple in description. Make a short cast into the feeding lane well upstream from the fish. If necessary, reposition the fly by skating it and the indicator one direction or another. Lower the rod tip and immediately begin shaking out line, using an up-and-down or side-to-side wobble. Throw the slack quickly enough to let the fly slide down without a trace of drag, while keeping the line tight enough to strike when the indicator dodges suddenly or disappears.

It will disappear. Odds are good it will react to a fish between 10 and 50 times a day if you've done most of the above correctly. Best yet, this tactic works all season here, on a stream with a flow so controlled that it's rarely ever unfishable—not even in early season when Mt. Lassen is white to the base, nor in the hot days of summer when the fields are brown.

➤ **Recommended Nymphs**
Burk's Hexagenia Nymph #4-8

➤ **Recommended Dries**
Hex Paradrake #6-8
Quigley's Hex Cripple #6-8
Yellow Humpy #6-8

The last of the Fall's major mayfly hatches is found only on the upper river, and even there it is elusive. Look for *green drakes, Drunella grandis,* on drizzly, overcast days in the early spring and fall months. If you find them, expect excellent fishing.

➤ **Recommended Nymphs**
Black A.P. nymph #8-10
Mercer's PoxyBacked Green Drake Nymph #10-12
Burk's Olive Leg Nymph #12-14

➤ **Recommended Dries**
Thorax Green Drake #10-12
Lawson's Green Drake Paradrake #10-12
Quigley's Green Drake Cripple #10

*Caddis* do play a major part in the Fall's food chain and may provide good fishing in the evenings, beginning in late June and lasting into early September. While hatches may be sporadically heavy on the upper river, they are especially prolific on the middle and lower sections. Fine fishing may sometimes be had on dries, but consider swinging a pupae imitation on a sinking or sink-tip line.

➤ **Recommended Nymphs**
Mercer's Z-wing Caddis #14-18
LaFontaine Sparkle Pupae #1214

➤ **Recommended Dries**
Elk Hair Caddis #14-20
Henryville Caddis #16-20

There are *other useful Fall River flies,* and it sometimes pays to experiment with different patterns and techniques. A selection of miscellaneous flies for this venue might include the following:

➤ **Recommended Flies**
Woolly Buggers #6-12
Zug Bugs #12-16
Burk's Water Boatman #12
Mercer's Poxyquill Nymph's #14-18;
Burk's Bloodsucker #8
Burk's Bugeye Damsel, Olive #12
Mercer's Poxybacked Callibaetis #16-18
Burk's Bullethead Streamers, Silver and Gold #6

# Stream Facts: Fall River

### Location
- 70 miles east of Redding on Highway 299, left on Glenburn Road or McArthur Roads (see Cal Trout and PG&E access).

### Seasons
- Last Saturday in April through November 15.

### Special Regulations
- 2 fish, minimum size 14 inches, artificial lures with barbless hooks only.

### River Characteristics
- The Fall is a broad spring creek, weedy by June, with reed banks. The best sections are accessible only by watercraft, either from the Cal Trout access or from launches at one of the private lodges. Early in the season fish spawning on the upper river, and up tributaries of the Bear and Spring. The trout disperse as the season progresses; the rainbows are particularly attracted to the heavier weed growth. The rarer browns take advantage of undercut banks, and the deep edges of bend pools.

### Trout
- Predominantly rainbows, mostly 13 to 17 inches, to 25, and a few browns even bigger.

### River Miles
- 17

### Boat Ramps
- For manually and electric powered craft only, Cal Trout Access. The simplest way to find this is to take 299 through Fall River Mills to McArthur, turn left on Glenburn Road for six miles, then turn right on Island Drive for 1.5 miles. Cross the bridge; the Cal trout access is on your right. Parking is limited here, so arrive early. You will need to carry your craft down a short path.
- There is also a PG&E launch site for small boats on the lower river, where Glenburn and McArthur roads meet. Make sure to check on current status of this before you come, either at one of the fly shops, or with PG &E at 916/386-5164.

### Campgrounds
- Pit River Campground, Bureau of Land Management, 10 sites, no fee, 3.5 miles west of Fall River Mills on US 299, then one half mile south on Pit River Powerhouse Road.
- McArthur Burney Falls Memorial State Park, Highway 89 between Burney and McCloud, 128 sites (in summer, you will probably need a reservation — call 800-444-PARK), 24898 Highway 89, Burney, CA 96013, park telephone: 916 335-2777.

### Hub Cities
- Fall River Mills, Burney (for Burney, see Hat Creek).

## FALL RIVER MAJOR HATCHES

| Insect | A | M | J | J | A | S | O | N | Flies |
|---|---|---|---|---|---|---|---|---|---|
| Pale Morning Dun<br>*Ephemerella infrequens* |  | █ | █ | █ | █ | █ | █ |  | Nymphs: Mercer's Poxy-Back PMD #16–18; Burk's Hunchback Infrequens #14–18; Pheasant Tail Nymph #14–16<br>Dries: Harrop's No Hackles #16–18; Transitional Dun CDC #16–18; Quigley's Cripple #16–18; Burk's Silhouette Dun #14–18; Lawson Thorax Dun PMD #16–18; Rusty Sparkle Spinner #16–18 |
| Blue Winged Olive<br>*Baetis, pseudocloeon* |  | █ | █ | █ | █ | █ | █ |  | Nymphs: Pheasant Tail Nymph #18–20; Mercer's Poxybacked Baetis #18–20; Burk's Legged Nymphs #18–20<br>Dries: No-Hackles #18–20; Lawson Thorax Dun BWD #18–20; Dark #18–20; Rusty Quill Spinner #18–20; CDC Emergent BWD #18–20; Parachute Adams #18–22 |
| Tricos<br>*Tricorythodes* |  |  |  |  | █ | █ |  |  | Nymphs: Mercer's Poxybacked Trico Nymph #20–24<br>Dries: A.K.S. Paratrico #20–22; Sparkle Quill Spinner, Male and Female #20–24 |
| Hexagenia |  |  | █ | █ |  |  |  |  | Nymphs: Burk's Hexagenia Nymph #4–8<br>Dries: Quigley's Hex Cripple #6–8; Hex Paradrake #6–8; Yellow Humpy #6–8 |
| Green Drakes<br>*Drunella grandis* |  | █ | █ | █ |  | █ | █ |  | Nymphs: Black A.P. Nymph #8–10; Mercer's Poxybacked Green Drake Nymph; Burk's Olive Leg Nymph #10–12<br>Dries: Thorax Green Drake #10–12; Lawson's Green Drake Paradrake #10–12; Quigley's Green Drake Cripple #10 |
| Caddis |  |  |  |  |  | █ |  |  | Nymphs: Mercer's Z-Win Caddis; La Fontaine Sparkle Pupae<br>Dries: Henryville Caddis #16–20; Elk Hair Caddis $14 |

Also: Woolly Buggers #6–12; Zug Bugs #12–16; Burk's Water Boatman #12; Mercer's Poxyquill Nymph #14–18; Burk's Bloodsucker #8; Burk's Bugeye Damsel, Olive #12' Burk's Bullethead Streamers, Silver and Gold #6

# Fall River Mills

## Elevation – 3,400 • Population – 6,000 (entire valley)

*See also the private lodges section and Burney in the Hat Creek section.*

### ACCOMMODATIONS

Several private facilities offer accommodations on or very near Fall River Mills:

**Fall River Hotel & Restaurant**, 24860 Main Street, Fall River Mills, CA 96028 / 916-336-5550 / Built in 1930s, with 1930s theme; no phones; color TV; some rooms share bath; fishing package — $99 room for two, dinner for two, breakfast for two, box lunch; can contact local guides / $–$$

**Hi Mont Motel**, Hwy 299 East, Fall River Mills, CA 96028 / 916-336-5541 / $$

### RESTAURANTS

**Fall River Hotel & Restaurant**, 24860 Main Street, Fall River Mills, CA 96028 / 916-336-5550 / $$–$$$

**Hal & Kathy's Cook House**, Fall River Mills, CA 96028 / 916-336-6098 / $$– $$$ / Variety soups, salads, all you can eat specials — hearty American

**Bleachers Pizza**, Hwy 299 East, Fall River Mills, CA 96028 / 916-336-5353 / $

### SPORTING GOODS AND FLY SHOPS

**Shasta Angler**, 43503 Highway 299 East, Fall River Mills, CA 96028 / Full service shop; 7 days a week during season

*In Burney:*

**Trout Country**, 38247 Hwy 299 East, Burney, CA 96013 (PO Box 58, Cassel) / 916-335-5304 / Full service shop; open 7AM to 6PM, April through June, 8AM to 5PM July through November; closed during winter

**Vaughn's**, 37307 Main St., Burney, CA 96013 / 916-335-2381 / All tackle shop with fly section, licenses; open 8AM to 6PM Monday through Saturday, 9AM to 3PM Sunday; mid-April to mid-October: 8AM to 5PM Tuesday; mid-October to mid-April: 8AM to 5PM Tuesday through Saturday, 9AM to 3PM Sunday

*In Cassel:*

**Clearwater House in Cassel**, 21568 Cassel Road, 96016 / 530-335-5500 / A full-service shop (see Clearwater House description in Hat Creek section)

### HOSPITALS

**Mayers Memorial Hospital**, Burney, CA, 96013 / 916-335-3222

### AIRPORTS

**Fall River Mills County Airport**, capable of handling prop planes and small jets / 916-336-5966 / No commercial flights

## AUTO RENTALS

Sometimes through airport — make sure to call first / 916/336-5966

## PRIVATE LODGES

Access on Fall River is limited, as are accommodations nearby. The only places to stay on the river are private and as follows:

- **Spinner Fall Lodge**, Glenburn Star Route, Fall River Mills, CA 96028 / April-November 916-336-5826 / *Rates:* Single $60, Double $85, includes breakfast / *Directions:* Highway 299 East from Redding 55 miles, to Highway 89, left there, heading north 17 miles to County Road A-14, right 7.5 miles to lodge / *Amenities:* tackle, food, guides, boat rental, cocktails and dining, 18 hole golf course nearby. Spinner Fall Lodge is a well known lodge located within two miles of Fall River's headwaters. The nearest point of public access is 17 miles downstream.
- **Valentine and Susan's Fall River Fishing Get-Away Cabin** / 415-731-4385 or 415-777-31995 / $100 per night, two night minimum / *Directions:* 299 to Fall River Mills, left on Glenburn Road, the first house past the Cal Trout access on Island Road / *Amenities:* This cabin is elegantly appointed with an eye to the views, it sleeps two, and has a kitchen and patio. Valentine Atkinson is one of flyfishing's finest photographers.
- **Riverside**, booked through The Fly Shop, 4140 Churn Creek Road, Redding, CA 96002 / 800-669-FISH / *Rates:* $800 for a two-night, three-day package, up to $1500 for a four-night, five-day package / *Amenities:* A four bedroom, 2.5 bath private house on the center section of the river, with amenities: jacuzzi, deck, dish and clothes washers, stereo, TV with satellite dish, propane barbecue and three 14-foot johnboats with electric motors.
- **The Whipple Ranch**, 28076 Spring Creek Road, Fall River Mills, CA 96028 / 916-336-6750 / *Rates:* $175 for up to three people per night, $25 extra per person; boat rentals (with electric motor) $50 per day, $30 per half day / *Directions:* Highway 299 East to Fall River Valley, pass golf course on right, left on Glenburn Rd., jog right, then turn left on McArthur at the Glenburn Church; drive three miles to Spring Creek Rd., take right, proceed .1 mile, take right onto Whipple Ranch Lane / *Amenities:* Part of a 280-acre site, the two-bedroom guesthouse sleeps four (two beds per room) and stands toward the upper middle portion of the river, with a deck just off the stream. The owners also have a launch site on the upper section. House is fully equipped, including all cooking utensils, linens, et al.
- **Lava Creek Lodge**, booked through Fishing International, Santa Rosa CA 95405 / 800-950-4242 / *Rates:* Operated on an American plan, with three meals provided – $85 per person, double occupancy, standard room or cabin; $95 deluxe, $60 extra per person per room; midweek and three-day discounts; boat rental fees for Fall River are $50 per half day, $75 (with electric motor), or $12 per hour; also boat and canoe rentals on Eastman Lake; guides available / *Directions:* The lodge is 100 feet from the entrance to Ahjumawi State Park, an area known for its wildlife / *Amenities:* Located off Eastman Lake, part of the feeder system for

the Fall River, Lava Creek Lodge has standard and deluxe rooms in the lodge, and cabins nearby. The dining room and bar look out over the lake.

- **Circle 7 Guest Ranch**, 27663 Island Road, Fall River Mills, CA 96028 / 916-336-5827 / *Rates:* For whole house (sleeps 11): weekdays, $100 for one person, $75 per person for two people, $65 per person for three people, $50 per person for four or more; weekends and holidays, two-day minimum stay, $200 per day for up to four people, $50 per additional guest / *Amenities:* 650-acre guest ranch with large homes, fully furnished, satellite TV, washers/dryers, decks on the river, boat docks with rentals.

## FOR MORE INFORMATION

Fall River Chamber of Commerce
Box 475
Fall River Mills, CA 96028
916-336-5840

# The Trinity: A River for All Seasons

*by Herb Burton*

New seasons bring change to the rugged and remote Salmon-Trinity Alps. Resident rainbow and brown trout of the Trinity River adapt to weather and flows, and anadromous fish continue cycles that once led to runs of legendary status.

But time changes the Trinity in larger ways. Completion of Trinity and Lewiston Dams in the 1960s severed the main stem, cutting off hundreds of miles of spawning habitat while drastically reducing flows below. What had been a great wild river was transformed into a controlled, rich, and fertile tailwater. In this different water a new generation of young flyfishers has discovered a very respectable — and often unpredictable — trout fishery, which complements what's left of the salmon and steelhead returns.

### Overview

The headwaters of the main Trinity River originate deep in the Salmon-Trinity Alps Wilderness. Fifty-three high mountain lakes nestle in these mountains, and over 1,600 miles of streams contribute to a massive network of 41 tributaries and secondary rivers, including the North Fork Trinity River, New River, and South Fork Trinity River.

This watershed still feeds the main stem of the Trinity, now roughly 120 miles long, measuring from the base of Lewiston Dam near the historic town of Lewiston, to the confluence with the famed Klamath River at the junction of Weitchpec. The river's upper reaches are most controlled: flows are placid and closely resemble a quality spring creek with many long tapering glides interspersed by gentle riffles. This is desirable and tempting water that lends itself to a variety of trout fishing methods. Many anglers are quite satisfied simply getting to know the upper river and to meet its resident trout.

As the river begins to change course, turning northwesterly around Dutch Creek bend, it gains velocity from descent and volume from tributaries. All the later support fish populations of one sort or another, mostly anadromous stock, although the uppermost sections hold year-round trout. At last, below the North Fork, as the Trinity flows through the upper Big Bar/Big Flat Canyon, it turns back to wild river, with rapids rated to class III, making this a salmon and steelhead stretch best left to serious young anglers. Below Big Flat the river settles down to Class I and II, in an area more traditionally fly water, until it cascades again down the radical Burnt Ranch/Grays Falls gorge. Except for a few limited trails at Burnt Ranch, Grays Falls, and China Slide, this area is accessible only to those with the will, skill, and equipment to face Class 5 and 6 waters.

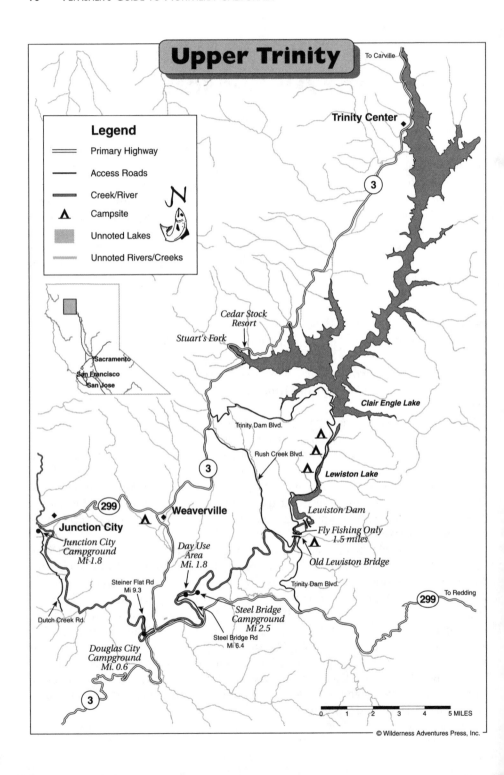

**Upper Trinity**

To Carville

Trinity Center

**Legend**

Primary Highway

Access Roads

Creek/River

Campsite

Unnoted Lakes

Unnoted Rivers/Creeks

N

Sacramento

San Francisco

San Jose

Cedar Stock Resort

Stuart's Fork

Clair Engle Lake

Trinity Dam Blvd.

Rush Creek Blvd.

Lewiston Lake

Weaverville

Lewiston Dam

299

Junction City

Fly Fishing Only 1.5 miles

Junction City Campground Mi 1.8

Day Use Area Mi. 1.8

Old Lewiston Bridge

Steiner Flat Rd Mi 9.3

Trinity Dam Blvd.

299 To Redding

Dutch Creek Rd.

Steel Bridge Campground Mi 2.5

Steel Bridge Rd Mi 6.4

Douglas City Campground Mi. 0.6

3

0  1  2  3  4  5 MILES

© Wilderness Adventures Press, Inc.

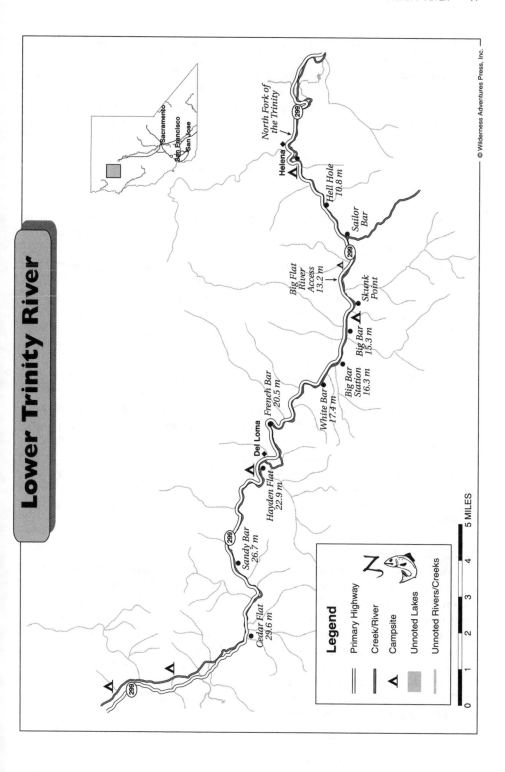

Lower Trinity River

Legend

Primary Highway
Creek/River
Campsite
Unnoted Lakes
Unnoted Rivers/Creeks

N

0 1 2 3 4 5 MILES

North Fork of the Trinity

Helena

Hell Hole
10.8 m

Sailor Bar

Big Flat River Access
13.2 m

Skunk Point

Big Bar
15.3 m

Big Bar Station
16.3 m

White Bar
17.4 m

French Bar
20.5 m

Del Loma

Hayden Flat
22.9 m

Sandy Bar
26.7 m

Cedar Flat
29.6 m

Sacramento
San Francisco
San Jose

© Wilderness Adventures Press, Inc.

In Hoopa Valley the Trinity flattens out across a broad bed. This is transition water, with migrating salmon and steelhead, and provides some of the river's finest opportunities for flyfishers seeking these species. Beyond the Valley, the Trinity rushes through Weitchpec Canyon, at last joining the Klamath.

The entire Trinity watershed has a mean reputation as a difficult venue that hides secrets well. No quality fishery is easy, and the Trinity is no exception: you must learn her. Even then, the yield in numbers is seldom high. But those who put forth the time and effort and who have the good fortune to experience some of the rare and magical sessions that Trinity produces will never be the same.

### Fishing the Trinity

The upper river supports a resident trout population consisting of rainbow and brown trout and is visited by ocean-run browns, Loch Levens (This is the subject of some debate: if the browns are sea run, they should receive protection under current Fish and Game policies, yet they do not.) While the overall trout population rates well below other fine watersheds, the river has an ability to nurture fish of exceptional size — particularly brown trout, the more prevalent of the larger fish. These often exceed 5 pounds, with occasional fish above 10. The rainbow population consists of hatchery and wild stocks that are annually flushed into the system during high-water release periods from the lakes above. As elsewhere in California coastal streams, rainbows measuring over 16 inches are managed as steelhead.

In the Trinity's diverse fishery, anglers tend to separate by preference: those who fish for resident trout and those who angle for anadromous species. Though the river is open all year, the former usually prefer to fish the general trout season (last Saturday in April through November 15th, though the flyfishing only section closes September 15), and the latter tend to arrive after the closure to fish on through the winter until the whole river shuts down March 14. (Spring and summer runs warrant fishing year-round.) Preferences aside, the opportunity to pursue trophy brown and rainbow trout on such a scenic river — along with steelhead, Chinook, and coho salmon — has prompted some to refer to the Trinity River as "a poor man's New Zealand."

### Trinity Trout Access

Although resident and some migratory trout can be found distributed throughout the river, the majority tend to favor the upper reach, from Junction City on up to Lewiston, roughly 20 to 30 miles. Peak concentrations of fish reside at the uppermost fishable boundary in the "flyfishing only" waters (see regulations in Stream Facts) directly below Lewiston Dam. These provide anglers with the most consistent action. Resident trout populations thin out drastically downstream from Douglas City; below that the fish tend to take on migratory behavior patterns. That means that while the documented numbers of browns in the middle and lower river are low, catches of large fish are reported annually from the mouth of the Klamath at Recqua to Del Loma and Big Bar, and on upriver.

*The ever-popular flyfishing-only section below Lewiston Dam. Grab a ticket and get in line. (Photo: Seth Norman)*

### Access to Flyfishing Only Water

The Upper Trinity's flyfishing water is located approximately 40 miles west of Redding, off Highway 299. This section of quality river is only 1.5 miles long, running from 250 feet below Lewiston Dam down to the Old Lewiston Bridge. Despite its short length, this is by far the most popular destination on the river for flyfishers. It is also the heart of the Trinity River anadromous fishery, sanctuary for spring and summer run salmon, and for steelhead "holding over" prior to spawning. For these reasons a special season is in effect from the last Saturday in April through September 15th. Only single, barbless hooks are allowed; the limit is zero.

Access is well defined and easy to follow. A major ingress point is Hatchery Road off Trinity Dam Boulevard, which heads upstream from the east side of the upper bridge. Pullouts along the left side of the road lead to paths, and anglers can walk along the bank to the upper reach of the river. (Note: the river is closed to fishing all year from the dam downstream 250 feet.)

Another means of reaching this water from the west side of the stream is by crossing the bridge (instead of turning right on Hatchery Road) and following Trinity Dam Boulevard for half a mile as the road curves (and rises) north toward Lewiston Lake. Watch for a turnoff to the right (a hard right) and if you reach the entrance to Mary Smith Campground, you've missed it. This rough gravel road drops down to the river, backtracking downstream to a point across from the Trinity River hatchery.

Reaching the river below the upper bridge requires more effort. This section receives about half the attention as the upstream water and is generally well worth visiting. Although the streamside vegetation is dense, an angler can head downstream from either side of the bridge. During lower flows the water is wadable along the sides of the channels. A private access to this area is through River Oaks Campground/Trailer Park.

The lower boundary for the flyfishing only area is Old Lewiston Bridge. From Lewiston, this can be reached by taking a left from Trinity Dam Boulevard just past the Plug 'n Jug, where the sign reads "National Historic Town of Lewiston (Turnpike Road)" a short drive down a narrow, windy lane to a bent Y. Straight on is the bridge, to the right is Old Town, where several of the hotels and restaurants are located. (The Old Lewiston Bridge can also be reached from the upper bridge on the opposite side of the river, via Rush Creek Road: see map.)

There is a short stretch of public access on the west side of the river beside the bridge riffle above, a large pool and productive tailout below. Upstream access is somewhat limited — though you are generally fine below high water — but is possible by heading a few hundred yards into town, between River Oaks and the Old Lewiston Hotel.

Taken altogether, the flyfishing only water includes a broad spectrum of water types that are sure to please any angler. Flows range from a mere 300 cubic feet per second minimum during late summer to a raging 4,000–5,000 cfs at the height of early spring runoff. The river fishes best between 450–1,500 cfs, levels that anglers can expect to find by late May or June in years with normal rain and snowpack.

### Fishing the Fly Only Water

During high water flows and the early season, streamer fishing and deep-water nymphing is without a doubt the most productive approach. Streamer patterns — woolly buggers, zonkers, leeches, muddlers, and patterns that simulate juvenile salmon, steelhead, rainbow, and brown trout — can provoke strikes when fished down and across on 2X or 3X tippet. Nymphs such as golden stones, burlaps, rubberlegs, Prince, Birds Nest, and suggestive soft hackles are all effective. Early season dry fly opportunities are subject to the dictates of weather and water releases. Insect activity can include adult stoneflies, PMDs, Baetis, Callibaetis, and yellow sallies. Fishing midday, when air and water temperatures are highest, is usually best.

Once summer settles in, early and late fishing are the tickets to success. By late August or early September, just prior to the closing, spring-summer chinook salmon, steelhead, and migratory brown trout will all gather in this little piece of prime flyfishing water. These newcomers can provide the occasional "bonus" catch to those prepared for them.

### Below Old Lewiston Bridge

The Trinity provides some high quality trout opportunities downstream from the designated flyfishing only section, also. Below Old Lewiston Bridge the season is open

*The Trinity River downstream from Old Lewiston Bridge. (Photo: Seth Norman)*

for all fishing styles from the last Saturday in April through March 14th. (Bag limits here change often — anglers must closely review California Department of Fish and Game regulations for gear and harvest restrictions.) Access can be had by hiking in from the bridge access or by floating the river to downstream takeouts. Three excellent road access points are at Rush Creek, Cemetery Road, and at Cemetery Access (which isn't the same as Cemetery Road: see map). All three reach short stretches of quality water bounded by private property.

To get to the Cemetery Road access, follow Rush Creek Road (on the west side of the river) just past the Old Bridge RV Park, then take an immediate left on Cemetery Road. This deadends at an old Fish and Wildlife stations a few hundred yards in. There are some well defined riffles and a large holding pool.

To reach the Rush Creek Access, continue on Rush Creek Road beyond the Cemetery Road turnoff, heading west, then take a left where a sign indicates Bureau of Land Management property.

Cemetery access is on the opposite side of the river, off Goose Ranch Road, which can be reached by either Turnpike Road or Viola Lane. The turnout will be about a half mile down, on the right. The pool near the parking area is usually dominated by conventional tackle anglers pursuing summer and fall salmon or steelhead, but a flyfisher willing to invest time and effort can find some excellent water both above and below this.

From these three spots downstream the accessible banks are mostly private, but not everywhere. The river touches national forest lands in several places. Take care about trespassing. When in doubt, stop and ask.

Angling pressure develops on this stretch during the early season, but the water here also fishes exceptionally well in winter months and offers anglers off-season trout access with traditional steelhead fishing. Deep, wet fly techniques are most effective during high water periods; dry fly activity picks up in low water years. Look for midday hatches of Baetis, PMDs, and Callibaetis on those flatwaters receiving plenty of southern exposure. Most of the fish will be browns or the dominant steelheads; fish up to 10 pounds on dries are possible if all conditions come together.

The next major area of access is off Steel Bridge Road, reached from Highway 89, six miles west of the Lewiston turnoff. Although the road winds through much private property, it deadends into a rough campground, where a trail heads upriver and provides access to quality trout waters.

Another access, perhaps the last on the good trout water on the upper river, is also of 89, two miles below Douglas City at Steiner Flat Road. Steiner parallels the river through area that offers a variety of options — again, for those willing to put a little more time and effort into getting away. The trout here are sparse, but the primary holding lies will sometimes support a double-digit fish receptive to deepwater nymphing and "heavy meat" streamers.

### Tackle

If an angler had to live and die with a single rod to fish the Trinity, it should be a 9-foot, 6-weight outfit. This is not the magic stick for all conditions, especially in winter, but it will suit most trout situations. A lightweight outfit such as an 8.5- or 9-foot, 3- or 4-weight would also lend itself to summer and early fall conditions and fish dry flies well during hatches. Then, since there's nothing worse than to be undergunned, anglers might also carry a 9-9.5 foot, 8-weight outfit to meet the challenge of early spring and winter water flows and to dredge larger than average flies.

Any of the above outfits should be complemented by a dependable reel with at least 35 yards of backing — less could be trouble and result in the loss of a Trinity trophy, a la spooled the core. Floating lines, weight forward with double taper, will do 90 percent of your fishing, but a high speed sinktip is necessary during high water and to get down in major holding waters. Since Trinity can be clear as gin without tonic, leaders should be no less than 10 feet in length, better to use a 12-footer. Carry a selection of tippets appropriate for the flies you will cast, from 3X on down to 6X.

Trinity's waters are downright cold year-round, and in the fly-only section right below the dam seldom rises to 58 degrees. Anglers can always wear neoprene waders, although lightweights are a relief during the heat of summer and early fall seasons. Boots need felt soles or some other kind of traction to help minimize slipping. A wad-

*The Giants may have lost, but this kid is happy with a Trinity River rainbow.*
*(Photo: Herb Burton)*

ing staff is a valuable third leg — a must in high velocity waters and during the messy conditions of the late season.

Weather patterns in the Trinity Alps are forever changing, so anglers should prepare for all possibilities. We often experience a 50-degree variance between summer nighttime and daytime temperatures. Be ready to add or peel layers; take rain gear and suntan lotion, sunglasses, hat/visor, etc. It often pays to call in advance (see Trinity Fly Shop).

# Trinity in Time

### by Seth Norman

In 1963 Trinity River became just another river dammed. Despite Congress' insistence that the river be managed to "do no harm" to the legendary anadromous fishery, and despite specific instructions directing the Secretary of the Interior "to adopt appropriate measures to insure the preservation and propagation of fish and wildlife," the real power in play, the Bureau of Reclamation, diverted the "surplus" water they saw as "wasting" to sea.

Trinity's fishery collapsed almost immediately. Sport and commercial operations were devastated, canneries closed, hotels, restaurants, and guides all lost business. The Bureau's promises of protection and Congress' statutory provision were safely ignored while the Department of the Interior stood by.

In 1981 Interior Secretary Andrus ordered a 12-year flow study, noting that "since the Trinity River Division was placed into operation, salmon and steelhead runs in the Trinity River system have undergone severe declines." But that study was delayed three years, until 1984, when Congress enacted legislation to support the effort, based on a "drastic reduction" in fish populations.

Finally, in 1991, Secretary Lujan mandated the Trinity River's flow be increased from 10 percent of the pre-dam flow all the way to 30 percent (drought level before the dam, lowest since 1911). In the meantime, what was to have been a 12-year study will now be at least 13. The Central Valley Project Water Association has already outlined ways and methods by which they can delay or set aside the order for this minimum release — never mind that Congress, three times since 1984, has mandated that Trinity flows be increased above Lujan's interim figure beginning in 1997.

It is Secretary of the Interior Bruce Babbitt who will ultimately decide.

Trinity's fish have always had a few advocates. For the last four years their voices have been joined in an organization originally promoted by flyfishers: Friends of the Trinity River, a coalition of sport and commercial fishers, kayakers and rafters, local business owners, and the Hoopa Indian tribe. Created by long-time steelhead fisher Byron Leydecker (who consulted with Trinity locals like Herb Burton, author of this section), Connor Nixon of the Old Lewiston Inn, guide Don Johnson, lodge owner Joe Mercier, and others. Friends' leaders aggressively pursued the interest of fish — wild fish — with the express goal of getting back the water promised, mandated, and ordered; then to releasing this on a schedule designed to enhance the survival of those species to which "no harm" would come.

Friends' actions have been both aggressive and effective. Under Leydecker's direction, the coalition has been in near constant contact with politicians, state and federal agencies, resource management groups, bringing to bear significant pressure while suggesting — relentlessly — that a committed contingency is watching, holding accountable, and insisting that actions taken serve the river's interests before those downstream — the ones which now pump most of Trinity's water over a mountain.

Right now it can be argued that Friends and those in favor of fish are winning — more water. The mechanics of that process are complex, however, and the jeopardy immediate.

In contrast, however, what's needed from anyone who values runs of salmon and steelhead is quite simple. A form letter is supplied at the back of this book. If this letter represents how you, as a flyfisher, feel about this fishery, copy it, sign it, and send it .

*One big Trinity brown, and he's hooked for life.*
*(Photo: Herb Burton)*

## Stream Facts: Trinity River

There are 16 sections of the California Sport Fishing Regulations dedicated to the Trinity River (listed under Klamath River Regulations). Note that the stretch popularly known as "flyfishing only" is technically open to all artificials with single, barbless hooks. Regulations for that section are straightforward, as are those below for anglers who fish catch-and-release.

### Seasons
- Flyfishing only section, from 250 feet downstream of Lewiston Dam to Old Lewiston Bridge, last Saturday in April through September 15.
- Old Lewiston Bridge to Cedar Flat: last Saturday in April to March 14.
- Below Cedar Flat, see regulations.

### Special Regulations
- Flyfishing only section, from 250 feet downstream of Lewiston Dam to Old Lewiston Bridge, 0 limit.
- Old Lewiston Bridge to Cedar Flat: check changeable regulations or call your lawyer.

### Trout
- Rainbows (difficult to distinguish from steelhead) and browns to 10 pounds or more. Some of the latter are probably sea-run — no reliable counts. Overall, the trout per mile is lower than in most venues, but they are mixed with an abundance of anadromous fish.

### River Characteristics
- The upper section of the Trinity's main stem is now a tailwater with a mix of deep channels, riffles, runs, and pools, heavy riparian growth and abundant aquatic insects. It is mostly a medium size stream, safely wadable with reasonable precautions — and very pretty.

### River Miles
- 1.5 miles of no-kill "flyfishing only" stretch, about 20 more with good to fair trout fishing.

### River Flows
- To 5,000 cfs at flood. The river fishes best between 450 and 1,500 cfs.

### Boat Ramps
- No paved ramps but inflatables and drift boats may put in at Old Lewiston Bridge and take out at Rush Creek. Local information is a must.

### Hub City
- Lewiston, some services in Weaverville.

# TRINITY RIVER MAJOR HATCHES

| Insect | J | F | M | A | M | J | J | A | S | O | N | D | Flies |
|---|---|---|---|---|---|---|---|---|---|---|---|---|---|
| Salmonfly *Pteronarcys californica* | | | | █ | | | | | | | | | Nymphs: Black Rubberlegs #6–8, Kaufman's Stone #6–8, TFS Black Pheasant Stone #6–8<br>Dries: Orange Sofa Pillow #4–8, Orange Stimulator #4–8, TFS Ex-Body Stone #4–8 |
| Golden Stone *Hesperoperla pacifica* | | | | | █ | | | | | | | | Nymphs: TFS Burlap Golden Stone #8–12, Pheasant Tail Golden Stone #8–12, Bird's Nest #8–12<br>Dries: Golden Stimulator #8–12, Madame X #8–12, TFS Ex-Body Stone (T-Bone) #8–12 |
| Golden Stone *Calineuria californica* | | | █ | | | | | | | | | | Nymphs: Burlap Golden Stones #8–12, TFS Olive Stone #8–12, Bird's Nest #8–12<br>Dries: Olive Stimulator #8–12, Olive Sofa Pillow #8–12, TFS Ex-Body Stone (T-Bone) #8–12 |
| Little Yellow Stone *Isoperla* | | | | | | █ | | | | | | | Nymphs: Bird's Nest #12–16, Sulfur Emerger #12–16<br>Dries: Yellow Humpy #12–16, Sulfur Parachute #12–16, PMD Parachute #12–16, Yellow Elk Hair #12–16 |
| Blue Wing Olive *Baetis* | | | █ | █ | | | | | | █ | █ | | Nymphs: Pheasant Tail #16–20, TFS Baetis Nymph #16–20<br>Dries: Adams Parachute #16–20, Adams #16–20, TFS Baetis Series #16–20 |
| Pale Morning Dun *Ephemerella infrequens* | | | █ | █ | | | | | █ | █ | | | Nymphs: TFS Sulfur Emerger #14–18, Bird's Nest #14–18, Hare's Ear #14–18<br>Dries: TFS Sulfur Paradun #14–18, Parachute #14–18, Paranymph #14–18, Light Cahill Quigley's Cripple #14–18 |

## TRINITY RIVER MAJOR HATCHES (cont.)

| Insect | J | F | M | A | M | J | J | A | S | O | N | D | Flies |
|---|---|---|---|---|---|---|---|---|---|---|---|---|---|
| Speckled Wing Dun *Callibaetis* | | | | | ▓ | ▓ | | | | | | | Nymphs: Pheasant Tail #12–16, TFS Callibaetis Shellback #12–16, Hare's Ear #12–16, TFS Callibaetis Paranymph #12–16<br>Dries: TFS Paradun #12–16, Parachute #12–16, Punk Rocker #12–16, Buglite #12–16, Hendrickson #12–16, Quill Body Dun #12–16 |
| Midges | ▓ | ▓ | ▓ | ▓ | ▓ | ▓ | | | | | ▓ | ▓ | Griffiths' Gnat #18–20, TFS Polyback Emerger #18–20, Palamino Midge (Black) #18–20 |
| Caddis *Hydropsychid Rhyacophila* | | | | | | ▓ | ▓ | ▓ | ▓ | ▓ | | | Nymphs: Bird's Nest #12–16, Hare's Ear #12–16, Sparkle Pupa #12–16<br>Dries: Elk Hair Caddis (Tan/Olive) #12–18 |
| October Caddis *Dicosmoecus* | | | | | | | | | ▓ | ▓ | | | Nymphs: TFS Rusty Caddis Pupa #6–10, Rust Pheasant Tail #6–10<br>Dries: TFS Greased Liner #6–10, Sofa Pillow #6–10, Stimulator #6–10 |

Aquatics and hatch time frames are quite similar to other northern California waters. The Trinity's locale as well as the unique tailwaters of Trinity and Lewiston dams create quality off-season aquatic hatches, will be of interest to those seeking winter opportunities for both brown trout and steelhead on drys in open waters but less desirable to those focusing on the upper river.

# Lewiston

## Elevation – 1,850 ft. • Population – 1,000

The town of Lewiston is right on the "fly only" water and has a variety of accommodations and services. What can't be had here may be found in Weaverville.

## ACCOMMODATIONS

*Excellent lodging is available at:*

Old Lewiston Inn, P.O. Box 688, Lewiston, CA 96052 / 800-286-4441 / A B&B with huge breakfasts, antiques, hot tub, a sense of humor, and a back yard on the "flyfishing only" water. Triples near price of single. Wide variety of flyfishing packages, with or without all meals. Connor Nixon, the owner, has fought the good fight for the river / $

Lewiston Valley Motel, P.O. Box 324, Lewiston, CA 96052 / 916-778-3943 / Pool, AC, onsite restaurant and mini-mart, big rooms / $$

Indian Creek Motel, On the river / 916-623-6294 / 1, 2 or 3 bedrooms, housekeeping units / $$

Lakeview Terrace Resort, On Lewiston Lake / 916-778-3803 / Housekeeping cabins, RV park, pool, rental boats for lake, cabins for single to 10 or more guests / $

## CAMPING

There is little public camping available on the upper river near the flyfishing only section (Rush Creek is closed as of this writing).

There are four campgrounds on nearby Lewiston Lake, however, off Trinity Dam Boulevard, beginning with **Mary Smith Campground**, close to the dam. For information call Trinity Alps Wilderness, Trinity National Forest, in Weaverville / 916-623-2121

For a private campground on the flyfishing only stretch, try **River Oaks Resort**, 800-693-3474. RV hookups, tent sites, restroom with showers.

Another private campground in the area is **Trinity Island Resort** (camping/RVs), 916-623-5798, P.O. Box 237, Douglas City, CA 96024.

There is also a no-fee **Bureau of Land Management campsite** at Steel Bridge, 25 miles east of Douglas City on Highway 299 (or about six miles west of the Lewiston turnoff), then 1.5 miles north on Steel Bridge (aka "Steelbridge") Road.

## RESTAURANTS

*In Lewiston:*

Mama's Restaurant, Trinity Dam Boulevard / 916-778-3177 / Breakfasts and great hamburgers / $

Duew's and Nonnies, Old Lewiston Road near corner of Trinity Dam Blvd / Good hamburgers and diner food / $

**Lewiston Hotel Restaurant**, Deadwood Road in historic district / 916-778-3823 / $$ / Full menu, full bar; excellent steaks and (huge) prime rib (the latter enough for two)

**Serendipity** / 916-778-3856 / $$ / Limited entrees averaging $10, all excellent; fresh baked bread, homemade desserts; beer and wine

*In Weaverville:*

**La Grange Restaurant**, on Highway 299 west leaving Weaverville heading toward Eureka / 916-623-5325 / $$–$$$ / Award-winning food, excellent wine list, microbrews and cocktails

## SPORTING GOODS AND FLY SHOPS

**Trinity Fly Shop** (Owner: Herb Burton), P.O. Box 176, Lewiston, CA 96052 / 916-623-6757 / The only dedicated fly shop in the area / From 299 west, turn right at sign for Trinity Dam/Lewiston Lake; drive 4 miles to Lewiston, at sign for Trinity shop, make left on Lewiston Road, 4.5 miles to store

Most of the convenience stores in Lewiston have general tackle sections with flies.

## MEDICAL

**Trinity County Hospital**, Weaverville / 916-623-5541

**Trinity Family Medical Group**, Trinity / 916-623-5011

## AIR SERVICE

In Redding for commercial flights (see Lower Sacramento services)

Weaverville has a day-use strip for private plans and an arrangement with a taxi company within earshot of the airport. Call in advance. They will hear you land, pick you up and deliver you to either Lewiston or Weaverville / Taxi: 916-623-5400

## AUTO RENTAL

**Rent-a-Wreck** (in Redding, see Lower Sacramento services), Hartnell Avenue / 916-222-8304

## FOR MORE INFORMATION

Weaverville Chamber of Commerce
317 Main
Weaverville, CA, 96093
916-623-6101

# Hat Creek: The Pilgrimage

## by Dick Galland

Hat Creek is California's version of the chalk streams of southern England where flyfishing was born. The water flows smooth and clear over a silt and gravel bottom dense with aquatic vegetation. The constant temperature, clarity, and volume of water combine to make Hat Creek a giant aquarium. Other than the seasonal changes in vegetation and slight variations in temperature, Hat Creek in December looks much the same as Hat Creek in June.

Carefully managed and heavily fished, Hat Creek is home to California's most sophisticated trout. The Wild Trout section is just over 3 miles long, beginning at Hat Creek Powerhouse 2, and ending at the fish barrier just above the confluence of Hat Creek with the Pit River in Lake Britton. The upper 2 miles are classic spring creek flatwater, while the lower mile is a continuous series of riffles and runs.

### Overview

Hat Creek rises from springs and snowmelt on the eastern slope of Mount Lassen Volcanic National Park. It loses elevation rapidly as it drops north out of the Park, a noisy little freestoner cutting miniature gorges in the lava flows that define this part of northeastern California. It remains a freestone stream, charging over its rocky bed until it levels out across the ranch lands in the upper end of the Hat Creek Valley, undercutting its banks and branching repeatedly to flood-irrigate pasture lands.

Hat Creek is used up on the ranches in the Hat Creek Valley. But it is the nature of water in this part of the world that there are parallel underground flows. One branch of the underground river comes to the surface in Rising River Lake, two miles above its confluence with Hat Creek, reborn at this confluence in the waters of Rising River. Here it becomes the Hat Creek celebrated by anglers: the Hat Creek of the Cassel Flats Baum Lake and the Hat Creek Wild Trout Project. This is an area rich in pioneer history and in the history of California trout fishing. Here, on the banks of Hat Creek, wild trout management was inaugurated in California and California CalTrout was born.

Lower Hat Creek was the home of the Ilmawi and Atsuge native peoples who lived on the abundant fish, game, and plants. With the arrival of European settlers in the 1870s, much of the land was taken up in farms. By 1920, Pacific Gas and Electric Company had bought up all the lands along lower Hat Creek and the Pit River Valley and begun construction of a complex system of dams and powerhouses. Lake Britton Dam was completed in 1926 and its warm waters encouraged populations of squaw fish and suckers. The movement of these nongame fish up into Hat Creek, combined with angling pressure on the native rainbows, led to a severe decline in trout populations.

In the mid 1960s, a group of concerned anglers and fisheries biologists from Pacific Gas and Electric Company and the Department of Fish and Game conceived

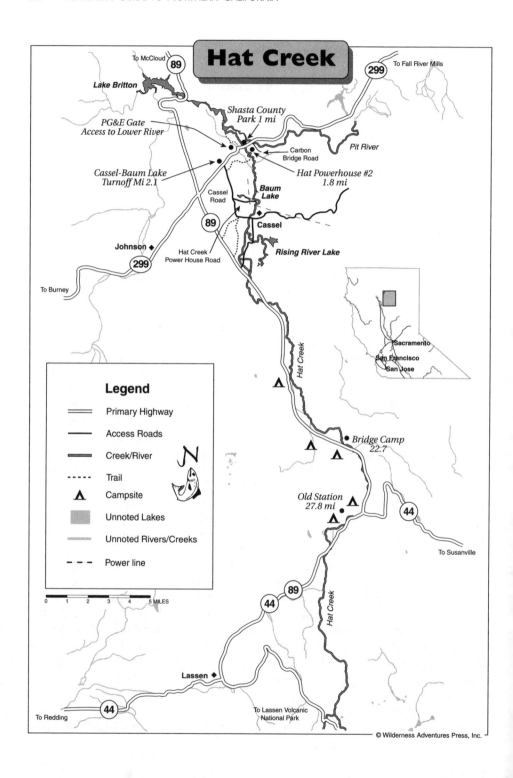

© Wilderness Adventures Press, Inc.

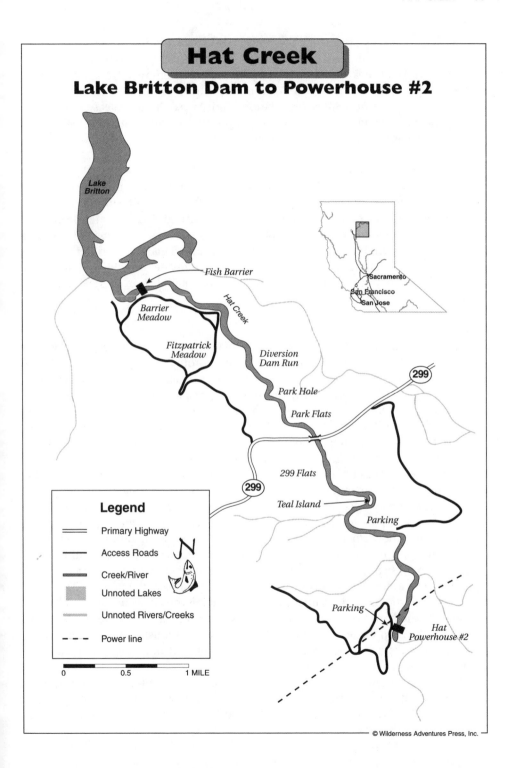

# Hat Creek
## Lake Britton Dam to Powerhouse #2

Lake Britton

Fish Barrier

Hat Creek

Barrier Meadow

Fitzpatrick Meadow

Diversion Dam Run

Park Hole

Park Flats

299

299 Flats

299

Teal Island

Parking

**Legend**

Primary Highway

Access Roads

Creek/River

Unnoted Lakes

Unnoted Rivers/Creeks

Power line

0     0.5     1 MILE

Parking

Hat Powerhouse #2

Sacramento
San Francisco
San Jose

© Wilderness Adventures Press, Inc.

a radical plan for rehabilitating the creek. The trout were captured, the stream poisoned to remove all remaining fish, and a fish barrier was built just above the confluence of Hat Creek with the Pit River. Restocked with brown trout and Pit River rainbows, Hat Creek became, in 1967, the first fishery in the West to be managed exclusively for wild trout. Special regulations and the catch-and-release ethic of the anglers who fish Hat have resulted in a hugely productive, self-sustaining fishery that is 85 percent rainbow trout and 15 percent browns.

### Fishing the Two Hat Creeks

Hat Creek is two distinct fisheries: flatwater and fast water. The entire wild trout project is just over 3 miles long. There is a 400-yard section of fastwater just below Powerhouse 2 that is highly productive and heavily fished. The flatwater begins just below this fastwater and extends two miles to the beginning of the lower fast-water section, north of the Hat Creek Park and Highway 299. This mile of riffles and runs culminates in the Barrier Pool, a 100-yard section of flatwater immediately above the Fish Barrier, a 6-foot tall wooden dam which keeps rough fish from moving up into the creek.

### The Flatwater

Hat Creek's flatwater section is a magical place, one of the most beautiful waters in the state. The broad, placid stream meanders through grassy meadows that rise gently to a mixed forest of pine and cedar and oaks. Ducks and geese are common. Broad-winged hawks crisscross the meadows looking for mice. Golden eagles scan for jackrabbits while osprey patrol the ribbon of water for unwary trout. Averaging 100 feet wide and four feet deep, Hat Creek flows at a constant 450 cubic feet per second of water all year long. Smooth surface flows and complex currents are characteristic of this water, calling for an angler's best efforts.

The occasional high bank offers an excellent view of fish feeding or fish holding against the light bottom and around the weed beds. You can see big fish holding in the deeper, less accessible slots on the bends and under the overhanging oaks and alders. The weed beds are a wonder; vast carpets of elodea; the familiar aquarium plant myriophyllum, known locally as coontail; and ranunculus, an aquatic with pretty little yellow-centered white flowers that poke through the water's surface in summer.

Grassy banks edge the meadow water, sloping gently and providing easy access. But a word of caution: muskrats find Hat Creek as appealing as the trout do. They have burrowed into the banks in numerous places making the edges unstable. Take care as you walk the banks searching for fish. More than one angler has been surprised, even injured, when his leg disappeared to the knee in a muskrat hole concealed by meadow grass. It's easy to be distracted by the sight of 100 trout rising to the profusion of insects characteristic of a Hat Creek hatch.

There is some surface activity every day of the season, often three or four species hatching simultaneously. The flatwater is reckoned to have as many as 6,000 fish per mile. When a hatch is on, it's a sight to behold and enough to make even a spring

*Nymphing Hat Creek during fall. (Photo: Mike Mercer)*

creek veteran's hands shake. The average trout is perhaps 12 inches, although there are lots of 14- and 15-inch fish and enough 16- to 20-inchers to keep the big fish angler happy.

Catch rates are difficult to predict. Even guides and experienced spring creek anglers can have a 15-fish evening followed by a three-fish day. Many variables mark spring creek fishing: weather, hatch intensity, and feeding activity. The highest overall probability of catching a trout lies in fishing the Powerhouse Riffle with nymphs. The highest with a dry fly lies in the evening caddis hatch in June from the Powerhouse Riffle down to Hat Creek Park at Highway 299.

### Flat-water Fishing Strategies

Spring creek trout demand careful presentations. You'll need good casting skills: the ability to put your fly in a 2-foot circle at 30 feet. In addition, learn the Hat Creek skate and the Fall River twitch, outlined in this section. Combine these skills with careful planning. Call the local fly shops to discuss seasonal fishing conditions and hatch activity, then plan your first trip to coincide with a particularly good hatch. Buy your flies at a local fly shop; these patterns will work best. You'll want to allow yourself as much time as possible at Hat Creek; a day and a half of fishing can prove frustrating. Weather, wind, and coincidence all play a critical part in hatch activity. An evening with a profuse hatch, with fish up everywhere eagerly feeding, can be followed by an evening with a sporadic hatch and little surface feeding. The appeal of spring creek fishing that everyday begins as a puzzle: which pattern and presentation will attract the fish today? Clarity of water, smooth surface flow, and the abundance — not to say profusion — of insects, allow fish the luxury of being exceedingly selective.

### Selectivity

These trout are, above all, opportunists. Their lives are a balancing act of energy expended vs. food taken. Fish search for those bugs, or those stages in the bug's development that are easiest for them to capture. Nymphs in the weeds are easily taken. During prehatch periods, when nymphs leave their weedy homes to swim weakly to the surface, they are not just easy to take but safer for the trout than coming to the surface and exposing themselves to predators. Once they are in the surface film, many insects are unable to fully emerge from their nymph skin. Trout recognize these crippled bugs and key on them. Even mayflies that fully emerge must spend several minutes on the surface stiffening up their wings before they can fly.

### Choosing a Fly

Asked to choose a single dry fly to begin with on Hat Creek, the best selection would be a parachute hackled mayfly dun pattern. Tied in sizes 16 through 22 in light olive, orange, brown, black, and tan, this fly will match virtually every mayfly hatch an angler encounters on the stream. Mayflies hatch every day of the season, from the pale morning duns of May through the *Baetis* of November.

The caddis is the easiest dry fly for catching fish on Hat. Beginning in spring and peaking in midsummer, the evening caddis hatch is as close to a sure thing as you'll get. A size 20 brown elk hair caddis is the bug of choice for this fast and furious fishing, usually beginning at dusk and peaking near dark. Success stems from the quick emergence of the naturals and from the failing light. Fish have less time to detect a poor presentation.

### Tackle

Spring creek fishing puts a premium on presentation. Don't handicap yourself with a short rod. Long casts and line control after the cast require a long rod. Nine feet is perhaps ideal. You can aerialize plenty of line and pick line up off the water to adjust your drift after the cast has been made. Some anglers even go to a nine-and-a-half or ten-foot rod. But take care not to bring a "gun," a stiff powerful casting rod that will pop your 6 or 7X tippet the moment you hook up. You'll want a rod with a more moderate action to protect light tippets and big fish. Line weights are best on the light side: 3 to 6. Be certain that your line is in good condition, clean and well-dressed. A few minutes at the beginning of each day with the line dressing kit will pay tremendous dividends in casting efficiency. A reel with a smooth drag or an exposed rim will complete your outfit.

Clear water and small bugs demand fine terminal gear. Tippets of 5, 6, and 7X are most commonly used on the flatwater and fastwater. Tapered leaders from 7.5 to

9 feet, culminating in 5X, allow the addition of 6 or 7X tippets to suit whatever hatch or presentation situation you may encounter. Make certain your tippet is fresh.

### Vest Essentials

Besides a line dressing kit, floatant powder for treating your dry flies is essential. Spring creek patterns are small. Many are tied with CDC feathers. A paste floatant is useless. Powder is exceptional for drying and waterproofing these tiny dries. The key to flatwater is matching the hatch: you must be able to determine exactly which bugs are hatching. A small aquarium net and a pair of magnifying glasses or a hand lens will allow you to collect samples. Get into the river and put your head close to the water's surface. If you pick up bugs with your net as they drift by, often you will find two or three different kinds. Choose the most abundant one as your starting point. Since many of the best hatches are evening emergences, carry a flashlight that can attach to your hat brim or to some part of your vest, leaving your hands free for the knots. By all means stay until dark — the big guys come out as the last light fades. When you can no longer see your fly, cut back your leader to 5X and knot on a woolly bugger. Swing it across and down, rod tip in the water, stripping fast on the retrieve. And hold on!

### Hat Creek Skate

The Hat Creek skate is a presentation strategy that can give you a perfect drift even if you don't manage a flawless cast. Position yourself slightly above and several feet off to the side of the rising fish. Bear in mind that the ring left by the rise drifts downstream with the current and that fish are usually holding a bit upstream of where the rise first appears. In other words, take care that your cast is far enough upstream not to spook the fish. I find it helpful to draw an imaginary line from myself, through the spot where the rise first appears, and on to some object on the opposite bank. This ensures that my cast lands well above the fish's holding position.

Cast 10 feet above and two or three feet beyond the rise. Immediately raise your rod tip and draw the fly toward you until it is exactly in the center of the trout's feeding lane. Drop your rod tip and point it at the fly. Don't mend. Follow your fly with your rod tip as it drifts over the fish and five or six feet beyond. If you don't get a take, lift your fly gently off the water and recast.

You may have to drift dozens of times before a fish comes up. Stay focused on that fish until you catch it, put it down, or it becomes clear that the fish won't take your fly. This technique gives you a very high probability of success. You have located the fly at the exact center of the trout's feeding lane without drag and given the trout everything he wants in his meal: a right-looking bug, behaving properly and easily taken.

### Fall River Twitch

Besides the Hat Creek skate, another style of presentation should be in your spring creek repertoire. Locally, it's called the Fall River Twitch. It takes its name

*Nymphing the prime, deep Powerhouse 2 riffle on Hat Creek.*

from the magnificent spring-fed river 20 minutes east of Hat Creek. Fall can only be fished from a boat — typically a pram with an electric motor, anchored 40 or 50 feet above the feeding fish. The fly is cast downstream to land above the last rise. Line is fed out so the fly drifts directly down over the rise (see Fall River, techniques and sidebar).

To achieve a similar presentation from shore or while wading, begin by having adequate loose line stripped from your reel. Cast downstream, stopping your rod so the fly lands well above the rising fish. Adjust the fly and line so they are exactly in the fish's feeding lane. Drop your rod tip to the water's surface. With your line hand, strip a loop of the extra line and put it in front of the forefinger of your casting hand. At this point you have a loop of about five feet of line between your line control finger and the first stripping guide of your rod. With your wrist, flip your rod tip up and let it drop down to the surface again. Surface tension on the line already on the water will pull the extra line out your rod tip.

Repeat the process: feed a loop with your line hand to your line control finger, flip your tip up and let it drop. Feed and flip. Feed and flip. Stay ahead of the current, taking care not to move your fly. Dead drift the fly into the rise and 10 feet beyond. If you don't get a take, point your rod tip off to one side and retrieve your line quietly. Repeat the process. The virtues of this presentation are that the trout sees the fly first, not the leader or tippet, and it is completely without drag when done right.

## Flatwater Etiquette

Hat Creek is a popular fishery, so a word about angling etiquette is appropriate here. In all such matters, be guided by a combination of the Golden Rule and polite inquiry. A carefully-phrased question will not only represent you as a considerate person, but will reveal the temperament of your fellow angler, allowing you to draw your own conclusions about how to fish in proximity to him or her. Give your fellow anglers lots of fishing room, particularly in the direction they seem to be headed.

During a hatch when lots of fish are surface feeding, give other anglers 100 feet on either side. With lots of targets, no one will need to move much to find fish to cast to. When no hatch is on and one is obliged to fish nymphs or streamers, allow more water for the angler to travel searching for fish.

Float tubes and boats are not appropriate on Hat. The flatwater is neither long enough nor wide enough for bank and wading anglers to coexist peacefully with tubers. Much of the flatwater is wadable. Excellent flatwater tubing opportunities exist a few minutes away on Baum Lake. The lower fastwater on Hat is too fast to tube.

A note about flatwater wading: Don't, unless you absolutely have to. If you must, step in carefully; the water is always deeper than it looks. Pick up your feet as you walk to avoid shuffling, which disturbs the bottom. Avoid stepping on weed beds; they are bug condominiums. Squashing their homes reduces their numbers and ultimately affects trout.

## Fastwater Fishing: The Powerhouse Riffle

The fastwater section of Hat begins with the Powerhouse Riffle, a highly productive stretch of water, two to three feet deep and extending downstream from the Powerhouse for about 200 yards. No part of Hat Creek gets as much fishing pressure, and yet offers so high a probability of a good catch. It's not the place to commune with nature. On any day of the season, you'll likely find other anglers; on some days, many of them. Fishing here is straightforward; the trout are accustomed to booted feet shuffling among them. They move out of the way to let boots pass and then resume their feeding positions. The Powerhouse Riffle's remarkable productivity lies in the fact that the riffle itself is rich with bugs and the deeper flatwater just below is loaded with fish moving up into the fastwater to feed. During intense hatches in particular, the riffled water masks poor presentations. Most riffle fish are small; 8 to 12 inches. But there are enough 15- to 18-inch fish to encourage even the experienced Hat Creek angler to come back, particularly when the little yellow stones come off on June evenings or when the Trico hatch is in full swing in July, August, and September.

## Powerhouse Riffle Etiquette

With the concentration of anglers in a relatively short section of water, normal rules of etiquette don't apply. The basic rule is not to fish so close to another angler that your lines tangle. Don't wade across another angler's water; cross above. Wade where the water is the shallowest, not through deeper water, the prime holding lies.

When in doubt about how to approach another angler, inquire politely. Polite behavior on your part will generally elicit the same from your fellow anglers. It is amazing that so many people can share a small piece of river without conflicts.

When you hook a fish, play and land it as quickly as your tippet will allow. Nothing will annoy your fellow anglers faster than playing a fish to the point of exhaustion. Doing the "San Juan Shuffle" to stir up the streambed and attract fish is absolutely frowned upon. It is unnecessary and destructive. There are plenty of bugs in the drift to satisfy the trout.

### The Lower Fastwater

The mile above the Fish Barrier deserves careful exploration. You can start at the Barrier and work your way up, park at the Foundation and fish up or down, or park at the fence at the upper end and fish either direction. There are fewer fish per mile in the fastwater because of higher water velocity and lack of holding areas. However, in spring, when salmonflies and golden stones are hatching, and again in the fall when October caddis emerge, there are enough good fish to make it worthwhile. This lower fastwater section reveals its secrets to those who take the time to learn. It is a mile of riffles and runs, mostly wadable, with ledges and depressions that harbor larger fish.

Once discovered, these prime holding areas can be relied upon to produce regularly. This is water for chest waders and a wading staff. The bottom is cobble, with some larger rocks set firmly in a concreted base of ash and sand. Near the Foundation, CalTrout placed boulder clusters in the mid-80's, hoping to provide additional holding water. While fish are regularly caught around these boulders, the project has generally been a disappointment, a case of not enough structure. The boulders have caught the fine sand that Hat carries and caused bars to develop. These sand bars in turn have provided footing for aquatic vegetation, homes for those aquatic insects who live in weeds, and more food for fish. The most attractive quality of the lower fastwater is the beauty of the stream, with its forested banks of oak and pine and cedar; the quality of sunlight dappling the rushing water, and a sense of solitude so different from standing room crowds at the Powerhouse Riffle.

### Fastwater Fishing Techniques

The principal skill for fastwater success on Hat Creek is shortline nymphing. Relatively simple to master, shortlining begins with a long rod: the 9-footer again serves perfectly. A floating line and a leader about the length of the rod complete the tackle.

Choose a fly from the suggested nymphs. If there is a hatch on, pick one that imitates the nymph form of that bug. Tippets of 5X would be the heaviest advisable; 6X is preferable. Place the weight about 10 inches above the fly. Add an indicator if you wish. A small bit of bright poly yarn combed out and tied in with an overhand knot at about twice the depth of the water is easiest to spot.

*Dick Galland demonstrates short-line technique.*
*(Photo: R.Valentine Atkinson)*

Most of Hat's fastwater measures two to four feet deep and has a very constant velocity, so once set up you have little need to change your rig, except for flies. Just make sure you're on the bottom. If you don't feel your weight touching down every couple of drifts, add more.

Shortline nymphing is typically done facing across the current flow. Casts are short, rarely more than two rod lengths. Lob the weight upstream, lift the extra line off the water and lead the drifting line down in front of you, moving your rod tip at the same rate the current is moving. This technique relies on careful wading and water reading to search out the slots, weedbeds, submerged rocks, depressions, and other underwater features that offer the trout current relief.

Hat Creek trout are used to wading boots, by the way, so you will catch fish very close to yours. Just wade and fish slowly across the stream or down promising seams.

High stick, dry fly fishing in the fastwater is very productive when a good hatch is taking place. Use the same rod, leader and tippet. Make short casts and lift everything but the leader off the water. Fish close and carefully with elk hair caddis, little yellow stones, salmonflies, and well-dressed paraduns. You'll find many willing fish.

## Weather

Hat Creek flows at an elevation of 2,600 feet for most of its length. There are distinct seasons in this part of eastern Shasta County. Springtime — late April and much of May — typically offers cool nights and warm days: 40s to high 70s. Expect the chance of rain through the end of May. Summer begins in earnest around the beginning of June. This usually marks the end of rains for the summer months. Expect clear skies, hot days, and balmy nights, with temperatures ranging between the 60s and 90s.

Fishing activity becomes more concentrated in the mornings and evenings in late August and early September. In mid-September, the first fall storm will break the grip of summer heat and begin a long Indian summer. Night temperatures begin to dip into the 30s, days peak in the 70s. Oaks and sycamores and maples take on the brilliant colors of fall. Often this balmy weather will continue right through closing day, November 15th. But closing day can just as easily be snow storms as shirtsleeves, so be prepared for unsettled weather after mid-October.

## Access

Lands surrounding the Wild Trout water on Hat Creek are owned by Pacific Gas and Electric, which provides access to these lands through a series of roads. Occasionally, gates on these roads are closed for short periods for specific management purposes, but generally all roads listed in the mileage log below are open throughout the fishing season, late April to mid-November. All access to the wild trout water on Hat Creek is north or south off Highway 299, about midway between Burney and Fall River Mills.

## Mileage Log

**0.0** Begin mileage at the junction of Highway 89 and 299. Proceed east on highway 299.

**2.2** Cassel Road turnoff to south. Take Cassel Road 2.1 miles south to Crystal Lake State Fish Hatchery Road, turn east and go 1.1 miles to reach Baum Lake.

**2.8** Hat Creek Powerhouse 2 road turnoff to the south. Follow this paved road two miles to the powerhouse parking area. The trail system for the entire section of Hat Creek between Highway 299 and the powerhouse begins here.

**3.6** Barrier Pool Road turnoff going north. This two mile dirt road loop will take you to the fish barrier, the barrier pool, and to several access points along the lower fastwater. Suitable for passenger cars except in times of heavy rain.

**3.9** Hat Creek Park turnoff to the north. This attractive roadside park offers fishing, ample parking, toilets, and picnic tables under tall pines at the water's edge. Trails lead from the Park downstream on the west side to the barrier and upstream on the west side to the Powerhouse. This is the most suitable place along Hat Creek for disabled anglers. Crossing the Highway 299 bridge at the Park, trails lead up and downstream on the east side of the stream.

**4.2** Carbon Bridge Road turnoff going south. Follow this dirt road 1.4 miles to a parking area at the site of a wooden bridge that spanned the creek in the early 1900s. This is the principal access point to the flatwater's middle section, about an equal distance between the Powerhouse and Hat Creek Park. Suitable for passenger cars, although it can be muddy and rutted in the spring and fall.

### Catch-and-Release Ethic

Much of the success of the Hat Creek Wild Trout Project lies in the attitude of the anglers who fish it. For years, regulations required the use of barbless artificial flies (and lures) and allowed two fish per day over 18 inches to be kept. Anglers concern for the fishery, however, created a de facto catch-and-release ethic. A keepable trout is a prime spawner, and the future of Hat Creek depends on these fish being put back. Always play trout as quickly as possible, landing with a net so they are never held out of the water, and release gently when fish are able to swim away on their own. If you wish to keep something for dinner, go to Baum Lake or to Hat Creek in the tiny community of Cassel. Both waters are heavily stocked, and you will catch plenty of silvery rainbow trout with the stubby, worn-down fins characteristic of hatchery fish. These fish rarely overwinter. Eat them!

### Hat Creek Fly Box

The Hat Creek fly box has only a few patterns — those that match specific hatches. There is no need for attractors or other generalized imitations. You may wish to substitute your own favorite mayfly dun or caddis pattern, but if you arrive on the stream with the following selection, you'll be able to fish any hatch with confidence any day of the season. Remember the basic premise: it's not what you throw but how you throw it!

➤ **Paraduns**
   Green Drakes #10-12 (green)
   Mahogany Dun #14 (brown)
   Pale Morning Dun #16 (pale olive)
   Pale Evening Dun #16 (creamy orange)
   Blue Winged Olive #18 (green)

*Solitude can be found on mountain streams. To Fish Hat Creek, you should probably like company. The Powerhouse 2 riffle is the most heavily fished water on Hat Creek. (Photo: Mike Mercer)*

Baetis and Caenis #18-22 (tan)
Trico #20-22 (black)
Midge #20-24 (black)

➤ **Cripples**
Pale Morning and Evening Duns #16 (olive marabou)
Baetis #18-20 (maroon marabou)
Tricos #20-22 (black marabou)
Midges #20-24 (black marabou)

➤ **Spinners**
Pale Morning and Evening Duns#16-20 (rusty)
Mohogany Dun #16-20 (rusty)
Blue-winged Olives #16-20 (rusty)
Baetis #16-20 (rusty)
Trico #20-22 (black)

➤ **Elk Hair Caddis**
October caddis #8 (orange)
Tan #14-16 for lower Hat
Tan #20 for the flatwater

➤ **Stimulators**
Western Salmonfly #6 (orange)
Golden Stonefly #8 (dark yellow)
Little Yellow stone #14 (yellow)

➤ **Nymphs**
Pheasant Tail #12-20

➤ **Birds Nest**
Gray, Black, Brown, Olive, and Rust #12-16

➤ **AP Nymph**
Black #16-18

➤ **Prince Nymph**
#10-16, with and without beads

➤ **Rubberlegs**
Black #6-10

➤ **Streamers**
Woolly bugger #2-12 (black, brown, and olive)

➤ **Monroe leech**
#10 in black and brown

### Notes on Fly Tying for Hat Creek

If you are a fly tier, you know that proportion is the key to a good fly. To better construct the patterns in this list, buy a professionally-tied sample of each one that's unfamiliar and practice until you have it mastered. If you don't live near a fly shop, call one of the major shops in the state and tell the person who takes your order that you need patterns as samples for tying your own. Ask them to select particularly well-tied examples for you.

# STREAM FACTS: HAT CREEK

### River Characteristics
The slow water part of Hat offers premier spring creek conditions — smooth, clear water with complex currents, luxuriant weed growth, terrific hatches, and trout that can do higher math. The average fish here is bigger than in the riffles, perhaps 12 inches, with many 14 to 16, and some to 20. Watch for larger fish in difficult to reach lies near bends and under the banks.

The fast water piece of Hat Creek here is characterized by wide riffles rich with insect life and smaller fish in the eight to 12-inch range. Larger trout to 18 inches do move up to feed. These sections are often crowded, but riffles mask awkward presentations and may be the best place for beginners.

### Getting There
From Redding, take Highway 299 east 50 miles to the town of Burney and continue on about eight miles to the sign for Powerhouse 2.

### Season
First Saturday in April until November 15

### Special Regulations
Flies and lures only, with single barbless hooks. Two fish over 18 inches may be kept and never are—see section in this chapter on catch-and-release ethic.

### Fish
85 percent rainbows, 15 percent browns

### River Miles
3.6 in wild trout section described here

### Flows
450 cfs, regulated and steady

### Boat Ramps
none

### Hub Cities and Towns
Burney, Cassel (hospital and airport in Fall River Mills)

## HAT CREEK MAJOR MAYFLY HATCHES

| Insect | A | M | J | J | A | S | O | N | Time | Flies |
|---|---|---|---|---|---|---|---|---|---|---|
| Pale Morning Dun<br>*Ephemerella infrequens* | | ■ | | | | | | | M<br>M / A | #16 Pale Olive Paradun<br>#16 Rusty Spinner |
| Pale Evening Dun<br>*Ephemerella inermis* | | | ■ | | | | | | A<br>M / A | #16 Creamy Orange Paradun<br>#16 Rusty Spinner |
| Green Drake<br>*Ephemerella grandis* | | ■ | | | | | | | A | #10 Green Drake Dun |
| Small Western Green Drake<br>*Ephemerella flavinea* | | ■ | | | | | | | A | #12 Green Drake Dun |
| Trico<br>*Tricorythodes minutus* | | | | | ■ | ■ | | | M | #20 Trico Spinner |
| Mahogany Dun<br>*Paraleptophlebia bicornuta* | | ■ | | | | | ■ | | A | #16 Mahogany Paradun |
| Tiny Western Olive<br>*Pseudocloeon turbidum* | | | | ■ | ■ | | | | A<br>A | #20 Bright Olive Floating Nymph<br>#20 Bright Olive Paradun |
| Little Western Iron Blue Quill<br>*Baetis parvus* | | | ■ | | | | ■ | | A<br>A<br>M / E | #20 Olive Tan Floating Nymph<br>#20 Tan Paradun<br>#20 Tan Spinner |
| Little Western Iron Blue Quill<br>*Baetis propinquus* | | | ■ | | | ■ | | | A<br>A<br>M / E | #22 Olive Tan Floating Nymph<br>#22 Tan Paradun<br>#22 Tan Spinner |

HATCH TIME CODE: M = morning; A = afternoon; E = evening; D = dark; SF = spinner fall; / = continuation through periods.

## HAT CREEK MAJOR CADDISFLY & STONEFLY HATCHES

| Insect | A | M | J | J | A | S | O | N | Time | Flies |
|---|---|---|---|---|---|---|---|---|---|---|
| Little Western Weedy Water Sedge *Aminocentrus aspilus* | | ██ | ██ | | | | | | E<br>E | #16 Green Sparkle Pupa<br>#16 Henryville Special |
| Giant Orange/October Caddis *Dicosmoecus atripes* | | | ██ | ██ | | | | | A<br>A | #8 Yellow Caddis Larva<br>#8 Orange Bucktail Caddis |
| Spotted Sedge *Hydropsyche californica & occidentalis* | | | ██ | | | | | | E<br>E | #14 Brown / Yellow Sparkle Pupa<br>#16 Henryville Special |
| Spotted Sedge *Hydropsyche cockerelli* | | ██ | ██ | | | | | | M<br>M | #14 Brown / Yellow Sparkle Pupa<br>#16 Henryville Special |
| Little Sister Sedge *Cheumatopsyche campyla* | | ██ | ██ | | | | | | All Day<br>A | #16 Green Sparkle Pupa<br>#16 Henryville Special |
| Salmon fly *Pteronarcys californica* | | ██ | | | | | | | All Day<br>A | #6 Black Rubber Legs<br>#6 Improved Sofa Pillow |
| Golden Stonefly *Acroneuria californica* | | ██ | | | | | | | All Day<br>A | #8 Burlap Nymph<br>#8 Golden Stimulator-dry |
| Little Yellow Stone *Alloperla pacifica* | | | ██ | ██ | ██ | ██ | | | All Day<br>A | #14 Little Yellow Stone Nymph<br>#14 Little Yellow Stone-dry |

HATCH TIME CODE: M = morning; A = afternoon; E = evening; D = dark; SF = spinner fall; / = continuation through periods.

will likely need reservations. McArthur Burney Falls Memorial State Park, 24898 Highway 89, Burney, CA 96013; park telephone: 916-335-2777. For reservations call 800-444-PARK.

There are numerous **USFS campgrounds** along Hwy 89 south of Hwy 299. They are all sited on upper Hat Creek, a boisterous little freestone stream, heavily stocked.

**The Hat Creek Hereford Ranch** has a campground with Hat Creek running through it. Ponds stocked with trout.

**Unimproved casual camping** possible throughout the USFS lands in this area. You will need a campfire permit, and a map to make certain you're not on private timberlands, of which there are a great many hereabouts. Campfire permits are easily obtained at the CDF office in Johnson Park, or at USFS Hat Creek Work Center, a few miles south of Hwy 299 on Hwy 89.

## RESTAURANTS

The author recommends for general ambiance and food:

**Arts Outpost**, 37392 Main, Burney, CA 96013 / 916-335-2835 / Food and service are good; ambiance is pleasant; generous portions; no smoking; bar with cable TV; an attractive and comfortable dining room with a measure of privacy

**The Rex Club**, 37143 Main, Burney, CA 96013 / 916-335-4184 / Good food; OK ambiance; smoking allowed in the adjacent bar, which drifts over into the dining area; salad bar; good filet mignon

**BJs Coffee Hut**, 37314 Main, Burney, CA 96013 / 916-335-4909 / The local cafe; open for breakfast, lunch, and dinner; country food; great breakfast; acceptable dinners

**Half Time Pizza**, Burney Shopping, Burney, CA 96013 / 916-335-3998 / Salad bar, big screen TV

**Clearwater House on Hat Creek**, 916-335-5500 / Superb entrees and desserts served family-style in the relaxed atmosphere of the author's fishing lodge; reservations a must for those not staying at Clearwater House

*Also in Burney:*

**Alpine Drive In**, 37148 Main, Burney, CA 96013 / 916-335-2211 / $
**Alvarez Mexican Cafe**, 37063 Main, Burney, CA 96013 / 916-335-2998 / $

## FLY SHOPS AND SPORTING GOODS

As you might expect, there are many good fly shops in this area. Their hours vary by seasons, however, and some close in winter.

*In Cassel:*

**Clearwater House in Cassel**, 21568 Cassel Road, 96016 / 916-335-5500 / a destination shop at the author's lodge (see Clearwater House description)

# Burney

### Elevation – 3,100 • Population – 3,200

Eastern Shasta County is the wild trout center of California. Within a 60-mile radius of Burney are the five finest wild trout rivers in the state, plus several smaller streams and excellent stillwaters. These waters include Hat Creek, Fall River, the Pit River system, the McCloud, the upper and lower Sacramento, Burney Creek, Baum Lake, Manzanita Lake, and Eastman and Big Lake. The best fishing coincides with the general trout season: the last Saturday in April through the 15th of November. Stillwaters are open all year.

Burney is a full service community with several motels, cafes, restaurants, banks, gas stations and garages, grocery stores, fly shops and other major services. The next little community, Johnson Park, two miles east of Burney, also has a fly shop, service stations, and restaurants.

## ACCOMMODATIONS

**Clearwater House on Hat Creek**, 21568 Cassel Road, Cassel, CA 96016 / 916-335-5500 / $$–$$$

**A Fly Fisher's Inn on Hat Creek**, in Cassel, minutes from Baum Lake and the Wild Trout Water / 7 bedrooms with private baths; excellent meals and service; guides for all area waters; California's only Orvis endorsed lodge

*Burney motels in order of author's preference:*

**Shasta Pines**, 37386 Main, Burney, CA 96013 / 916-335-2201
**Burney Motel**, 37448 Main, Burney, CA 96013 / 916-335-4500
**Charm**, 37363 Main, Burney, CA 96013 / 916-335-2254
**Green Gables**, 37385 Main, Burney, CA 96013 / 916-335-2264
**Sleepy Hollow Lodge**, 36898 Main, Burney, CA 96013 / 916-335-2285

## CAMPGROUNDS

There are four types in the area: US Forest Service, State Parks, PG&E, and private. The most conveniently located for fishing Hat Creek is the **PG&E Cassel Campground** in Cassel. Walk to fishing on the Cassel Flats or Baum Lake. Running water, pit toilets, fee. About 15 campsites set in pines and oaks. Pleasant. Cassel General Store nearby for limited groceries. First come/first served. Fills up in the summer.

**McArthur Burney Falls State Park** is 6 miles north of Hwy 299 on Hwy 89. A wonderful little park. Nice campsites. Little store. Fee. Swimming in Lake Britton. Fishing and sightseeing around the falls of Burney Creek. The creek above the falls is stocked weekly and open to bait fishers. Below the falls is artificials only, 14-inch max. All wild trout. A beautiful place and a must-see in the area: 100' falls with over one million gallons of spring water per day pouring over and out of the side of the cliff. Cool even in August. Nature trail. A five-minute drive to Lake Britton dam on the Pit for good angling. 128 sites, but in summer, you

*In Burney:*

Trout Country, 38247 299 E Burney, CA 96013 (PO Box 58, Cassel) / 916-335-5304 / Full service shop; closed during winter

All Tied Up Fly Fishing Company, 37026 Main St. Burney, CA 916-335-4732

## Hospitals

Mayers Memorial, Fall River Mills, CA (17 miles east of Burney) / 916-336-5151 / An emergency room and physicians on duty; helicopter ambulance service is available to the regional hospital in Redding

## Airport

Horizon Air / 800-547 9308

United Express / 800-241-6522

Fall River Mills County Airport / 916-336-9948 / Accommodates prop planes and small jets; no commercial flights

Redding Municipal Airport / 916-224-4320 / Anglers can fly commercially into Redding and drive the 1.5 hours to Hat Creek; the Redding airport is served several times a day from the north and south by United Express, Horizon Air and others; major rental car agencies have desks at the airport

An often overlooked option for traveling to the intermountain area is to fly into Reno, Nevada, and rent a car for the 2.45 hour drive to Burney. It's a beautiful passage from desert to mountains. Flight schedules and fares from out-of-state points can be more attractive than those to Redding.

## Auto Rentals

It is often possible to arrange to rent a late model car through the airport operator in Fall River Mills (check in advance — not available as of this writing). Auto rentals are available at Redding Airport:

Avis / 916-221-2855

Budget / 916-221 8416

Hertz / 916-221-4620

## Auto Mechanic

Al's Engine Rebuilding, Johnson Park / 916-335-4251 / Favorite auto mechanic in the Burney area: Al Vaught

## For More Information

Burney Chamber of Commerce
37088 Main Steet
Burney, CA 96013
530-335-2111

## Other Activities in the Area

Not to be missed sights/activities/etc. in the Hat Creek area:

1. Crystal Lake State Fish Hatchery. See where the greatest portion of your license dollars go. Interesting, particularly at feeding time. Call to find out when that happens. 916-335-4111
2. Lassen Volcanic National Park. Beautiful. Steam vents, boiling mud, great views, etc. Step across Hat Creek. Walk to Hat Lake, its source. Walk up Lassen Peak. See forever. 595-4444
3. McArthur-Burney Falls State Park. A must-see, as noted. Take the two mile nature trail around the falls. 916-335-2777
4. Fort Crook Museum. Pioneer history and native American artifacts, photos. Fall River Mills. 916-336-5110
5. The Fall River Golf Course. Those who play consider this one of the state's great ones. Cheap. 916-336-5555
6. Thousand Lakes Wilderness. A 25-square-mile pocket wilderness halfway between Burney and Lassen Park, west of Hwy 89. Several pretty lakes. Easy to walk into. Good fishing for smallish fish, mostly rainbow and brookies. Some larger ones in Lake Eiler, the closest to the trailheads. Cool in summer. Permits at the USFS office at Hat Creek. 916-335-4103; or in Fall River 916-336-5521

# McCloud: The River Cathedral

## by Frank Holminski

Monsignor Jack Beattie once gave a mass at the banks on the McCloud River. With a gesture meant to include the lush wild canyon and shadowed green water of this most beautiful freestone stream, he said, "Of all the cathedrals throughout the world where I have said, attended, or presided over services...this is by far the most beautiful."

The author also worships here and is certain that this river has everything a trout stream should have: difficult access, beautiful scenery, and best of all, big, native and wild trout — a place where each cast has the potential of hooking a fish of a lifetime. But there is much more to the McCloud and its environs, enough to cause those who wander down the canyon's narrow paths to wonder about the life surrounding them and perhaps to think of those who have come before.

### Overview

Located in Siskiyou County just south of Mount Shasta, the McCloud River is one of the primary cold water tributaries to the Sacramento River system. Rugged anglers have traveled here for more than a hundred years — since long before Shasta dam cut off the once-famous salmon and steelhead runs. That dam construction left the river to native rainbows and Dolly Varden, soon joined by stocked German and Loch Leven browns.

Unhappily, whether from the influence of the dam or competition from non-native immigrants, the Dolly Varden fail to thrive; none have been caught for many years. Of those species of fish extant when people arrived, only the rainbow survive.

Other aspects of the ancient McCloud remain, if not untouched, wild nonetheless. Parts of the river course a steep-sided canyon with few trails or none at all, where the footing is treacherous and poison oak abundant. While no anglers in recent memory have fallen prey to the mountain lions, black bears, and rattlesnakes that still prowl these reaches, there have been close calls, especially with rattlers. Even when wading the river, an angler should take extreme caution, for the irregular bottom and strong currents combine to create the kind of unforgiving conditions where a mishap can leave one "skunked and dunked," at least. But for the careful and clever, the McCloud can be more than worthwhile.

### Trout

Previous to California's long drought in the late 1980's and early 1990's, the ratio of rainbows to browns in the McCloud was 8 to 1. Low water reversed that dominance. Then, once Lake Shasta filled again, the balance swung back to rainbows.

Rainbows are the trout most anglers will catch here, and these are special fish. *Oncorhynchus mykiss* ssp., the McCloud River rainbow, has colonized much of the trout fishing world. California's first hatchery was built on this river, and many of the

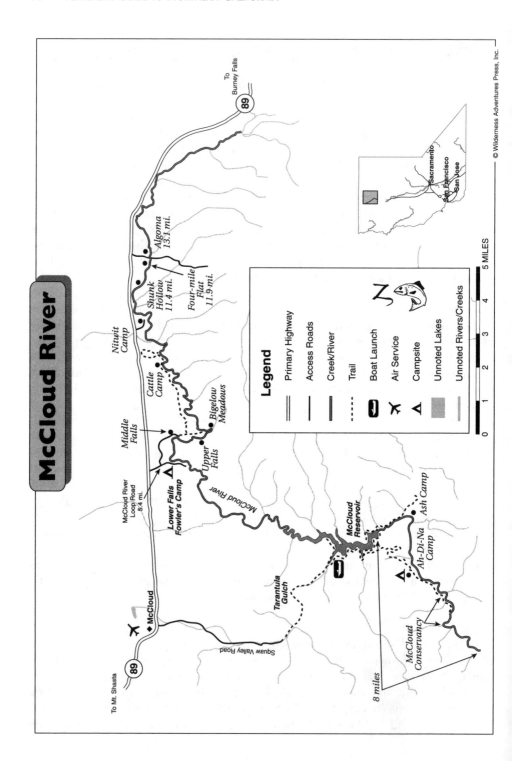

# McCloud River

To Mt. Shasta

89

To Burney Falls

89

Algoma 13.1 mi.

Shunk Hollow 11.4 mi.

Four-mile Flat 11.9 mi.

Nitwit Camp

Cattle Camp

Bigelow Meadows

Middle Falls

Upper Falls

McCloud River Loop Road 5.4 mi.

Lower Falls
Fowler's Camp

McCloud River

McCloud

Squaw Valley Road

Tarantula Gulch

McCloud Reservoir

Ash Camp

Ah-Di-Na Camp

McCloud Conservancy

8 miles

© Wilderness Adventures Press, Inc.

Sacramento
San Francisco
San Jose

## Legend

| | |
|---|---|
| Primary Highway | |
| Access Roads | |
| Creek/River | |
| Trail | |
| Boat Launch | |
| Air Service | |
| Campsite | |
| Unnoted Lakes | |
| Unnoted Rivers/Creeks | |

0  1  2  3  4  5 MILES

*A lush, McCloud River canyon. (Photo: Ken Morrish)*

fish introduced to the Sierra are descendants from these. Ultimately, their eggs were shipped across oceans.

It was partly the McCloud strain's hardiness and beauty that led to such widespread dissemination. In *Sierra Trout Guide*, Ralph Cutter suggests another feature of their genetic personality: that they are less likely to run toward the sea. That tendency had proved unfortunate with previously exported species: "...it was found, to the dismay of many, that once the trout approached maturity, they would migrate to the ocean and disappear."

In a peculiar irony, the McClouds now share their river with a species often anadromous: *Salmo trutta*. Both Germans and Loch Leven browns inhabit the river. The latter are particularly well known for their spawning run up from Lake Shasta. That event is a much anticipated but unpredictable affair. It can make a memorable trip when you catch it, but if you don't, remember that there are resident browns in the river all year long.

Some are enormous. Most of the trout anglers will catch here, however, range from nine to 14 inches. Intermediate and advanced anglers willing to spend the time often catch fish between 16 and 24 inches; and it's possible, though difficult, to hook trophy browns of 25 to 30. The three-foot long Loch Levens are rarely seen or landed.

## Fishing the McCloud Seasons

The McCloud is legally open for fishing from the last Saturday in April until November 15. The climate and conditions on the river suggest three more-or-less distinct seasons within that frame: spring, the author's favorite, from May 15 to July 15; summer, from July 25 to September 15; and fall, a good second choice to spring, from September 15 to November 15.

Flows in the river are normally highest in spring. Snow melt and the end of the rainy season will determine when these begin to diminish. If winter hangs on, it is best to delay a visit until the days lengthen and heat up. Though the McCloud is rarely unfishable, April and early May can be cold and unproductive.

By mid-May, opening day crowds have thinned. If the weather has started to warm, bugs begin to come off, and complex evening hatches happen with some consistency. These may feature several species of caddis and mayflies (including brown drakes) coming off at the same time. Because it is difficult to anticipate precisely when these hatches will occur, it's unwise to leave the water before dark. Of course, that means you can easily spend as much as four hours, or as little as 10 minutes, fishing with dries. That's one reason the author carries woolly buggers and rubber legs during this time (and throughout the year); another is the fact that both stone and salmonflies are active now, and Dobson fly hellgrammites move toward the shallows.

Summer is hot on the McCloud, with lots of bright sun on the water most of the day. Kids are out of school, and campgrounds are full of vacationing fishers and families. The fish become cautious. Mornings and evenings are best, before the sun hits the water and after it sets. Chase shade as long as you can; fish fast or deep water when it's gone. Keep an eye open for hatches of midges, little yellow sallies, blue winged olives, and caddis. Keep in mind that the brown trout migration may have started, so when other fishing is unproductive, working streamers on a sink tip or fullsink line is an alternative with possibilities.

Fall cools the air in October. The change of season brings out magnificent colors — the scenery is incredible — with deciduous trees in full flame. Migrating browns have usually entered the river in force, the October caddis hatch. A fisher may sometimes find solitude, except on weekends or when word gets out that the browns and caddis are happening.

## Tackle

Rods of 4- to 6- weight will serve on the McCloud, from 8 to 10 feet long. In addition to floating line, it's wise to carry both a fastsink sinktip and a fullsinking line. The floater is for dries, obviously, and for nymphing with an indicator. The sinktip is useful for making short casts in fast water, probing with nymphs or streamers; the fullsink is for longer casts to fish streamers in slower sections.

Three lines allows for the many fishing styles you may want, or need, to employ here. Before discussing techniques in detail, consider several general suggestions:

- On this river the better fish hold in water that is at least waist deep. Though large fish are sometimes found in the shallows, the odds for anything over 14 inches get better deeper.

- As noted and worth repeating, chase shadows when light is on the water at mid-day;

- Employ a methodical approach to a selected spot. Begin with a half-dozen flies in mind. Fish each through an area several times. If none produces, adapt your style, add weight or extend tippet.

### Fishing Dry Flies

For long casts in big water, the author prefers a braided leader constructed by the following formula: eight feet of braid, one foot of 4X tippet, three feet of 5X — a total of 12 feet. A nine-foot leader will suffice for short casts on smaller water: five feet of braid, one foot of 4X, three feet of 5X. When tiny flies are required, use a lighter tippet.

The advantage of braided leader is that it is supple enough to cast accurately and consistently. It must be dressed with silicon paste before it's wetted. So treated, it floats better than mono.

### Nymphing

Perhaps the single most important rule for nymphing on the McCloud can be contained in two words: work deep. Caddis do beat their way to the surface here, mayflies swim up, emerge and drift; terrestrials fall in. By all means, take advantage of these. But remember that the vast majority of life hugs the bottom. The majority of fishers, on the other hand, often end up working some middle part of the water column by failing to properly weight nymphs or by sweeping streamers too shallow. Though this tendency is true in many venues, it might be more prevalent on the McCloud for an historical reason: many fishers learned this river during the drought, when flows were slighter than normal. Thus, in the very same place where, in 1989, they caught this fish using that fly, rigged just so…they hope for an encore. Except this time the offering that once bumped a brown's nose sails above him, well beyond comfortable reach. The following rigs and tactics will help reduce that error:

To the end of a nine-foot 0X leader (you may wish to try this first with six feet) tie a polypropylene yarn strike indicator with an improved cinch knot. A 0X is lighter and floats better than fly line, so is less affected by surface currents; it's harder to see, but easier to mend. In a pinch, 1X or 2X material can be used, but it won't have the strength to turn over a bulky nymphing rig.

Using a Trilene knot (this lasts much longer than an improved clinch knot) attach 4X tippet around this leader, sliding the knot down to the indicator before tightening. Leave an inch-long tag on the knot to help locate the end in tangles. Tippet length should equal the depth of the water you will fish, where your weight will hang, plus the distance from weight to fly — 3 to 18 inches.

*McCloud River pocket water. (Photo: Frank Holminski)*

There is a way to measure water depth in advance of final rigging. Attach several weights, then cast into your drift. When the weights catch bottom, gently raise your rod tip — the distance from the surface of the water to your indicator shows the depth and the length of excess tippet. Adjust accordingly.

This test does take a few moments, and the rig will need changing when you work different depths. But this is a more precise system than a rough approximation used in many parts of varying stream. Consider the time you spend getting it right as currency. In fishing also, you generally get what you pay for.

A last note about tippet; it is neither necessary nor advisable to step down tippet sizes or to use any taper from where it is tied to the 0X leader, as the difference in line diameters will effect sink rate and drag.

Weight is important in any nymphing system. For most water on the McCloud, a BB shot of .4 grams, or a AAA shot of .8 grams will get the fly down. In faster currents a #0 may be required. It's a balance: use enough weight to put the fly in the range of fish near the bottom, and only that, since the more weight a fish feels, the quicker it will drop your fly.

Of course, current makes the drift. Usually, moving water tends to stratify into three layers, with the fastest on top and the slowest at the bottom. That means that if your indicator and line are moving at surface speed, it might be towing your weight and fly along too quickly and lifting them from the bottom where they should be.

# "Fly Fishing the McCloud River" — The Game

"This game was not conceived as a substitute for actually being on the river," writes developer McDonald Horton in the instructions, no doubt looking to smooth neck hackles. After all, take away the rush of water against your waders, wild scents of water, and the feel of a rod loading in your hand — forget the lunge that whips you forward and startles your heart — what would you have left? Electronic pinball with fish?

Imagine that the question isn't rhetorical. Consider that Frank Holminski was the consultant who factored in some of the skills and variables discussed in "McCloud" and every other chapter of this book. Among these: reading water, figuring where fish hold and feed in different conditions — of light, time of day, season and weather, by species and size; recognizing bugs and beasts; understanding enough about their lives to pick and use correctly a fly that matches, given the variables above…

Add to these a challenge for hand-eye coordination when "setting" the hook — you get an eighth of a second — make landing a fish depend on how relentlessly you squeeze your mouse, and include demons that will throw the hook no matter what. Set up a moving representation of the pools, riffles, and runs of McCloud River locations; then for good measure, add a "shuffle" component, so that while fish will haunt the better water, they won't stick so close you can memorize exact spots — all played out to Vivaldi's "Four Seasons," with occasional interruptions from a peanut gallery.

By then you do have a game…and a learning tool with several levels of expertise, suggesting that at the very least it's unwise to guess at flies and best to consider the influences important to fish. In fact, teaching is clearly part of the scheme: players can select for entomology lessons, tips on strategy, and reading water.

Trying to compensate for rapid surface current by holding back the indicator on a taut line usually serves only to swing the fly up, as the water pushes downstream against the fly and tippet. You don't want your line to pull the indicator either backward or forward. Instead, mend line. "Stack mends," small roll casts, let you throw slack line upstream from the indicator — try for a foot or so. When your indicator catches up with the slack, mend again.

Heavy currents can make this process harder. It's often necessary to shorten your casts, which means you must wade closer to the lie. Just how close depends on the water surface. White water will allow an approach to within one and half rod lengths. At that distance you can keep most or all of your line and leader off the water and lift even the indicator, at times.

### Deep Nymphing

When working deep water, line control is easier but casting more difficult. At depths of more than eight feet, it's best to work from a perch on shore, throwing only as much line as you can control. Casting with a wind resistant indicator and a long tippet requires that you slow your rhythm, delaying longer between strokes. Landing a fish on a long-tippet setup — with the indicator stuck at your tiptop — can also be a challenge.

In deep water, takes are usually slow and subtle. Many come at the drift's mid-point, just as the fly begins to rise. Never terminate a drift until sure that your line and tippet have pulled taut.

### Streamers

Many flyfishers don't care to fish streamers on sinktip or fullsinking lines. They find casting and mending difficult, even tiring, and have too little success.

It's mostly a question of practice. There may not be a better river than the McCloud on which to make the effort.

The author prefers a full sink line with a level leader, three or four feet of 3X. Begin fishing a pool where the faster water ends and proceed all the way to the tailout. Use quartering casts. Stack-mend to get depth, then let the streamer swing. Hold on: not only can this tightline technique provide relief from watching an indicator bob, but the average fish will be bigger than those caught on nymphs or dry flies.

### Hatches and Patterns

It's a fact of life that hatches on the McCloud are unpredictable in all aspects — timing, duration, and volume. Parts of the river are different enough that their schedules vary, and heavy winter flows may change the nature of a section from year to year. Hatches you can expect to see during the season include little yellow sallies; many species of caddis, including October; mayflies from baetis in sizes 14 to 20; green drakes sized 8 to 12; and an assortment of midges, typically black and gray (invaluable in the summer). Insects that don't hatch off the water but can be fished with dries include the adults of stone and salmonflies, with imitations up to size 6, as well as terrestrials, including small ants, 16 and 18, beetles from 10 to 14, and hoppers size 8 to 12. Though the action can be terrific at times, the McCloud is not best known as a dry fly stream.

### Access

The McCloud River is broken into two segments by what is called Lake McCloud (or sometimes McCloud Reservoir). For easy reference hereafter, the river above the lake is upper, below the dam, lower.

### Upper River Access

The McCloud River headwaters are formed by the confluence of several small creeks near Colby Meadows. From here west toward Fowler Creek, Highway 89 parallels the river, with a series of unmarked dirt access roads leading south to what is mostly small water (during the drought the depth could be measured in inches). There is a campground on this section at Algoma, less than a quarter mile south of 89, off Stouts Meadow Road.

Inflows from tributaries and springs augment the river below. The "McCloud River Loop Road" provides the best access to the most fishable parts of the river. Actually the "Cattle Camp Road," now with a Forest Service alias, "The Loop," is identified by that name on two exits from Highway 89.

The first of these exits is just over six miles from the town of McCloud: pass it and go 4.8 miles to the second. Turn right (roughly south). The first track to the left will be Cattle Camp, where there is a nice campground. This is a good place to begin exploring: access to the river is easy, though brushy banks make wading worth the effort.

There are some good wild fish through here, though they are few and far between. Flows fluctuate above the Upper Falls and can drop enough to leave relatively little holding water. Still, this can be a good section to raise tiny natives to dry flies and occasionally hook a planter. You may eat the latter if so inclined: the upper river is stocked during the season and falls under the general regulations for the Sierra District — no gear restrictions and a daily limit of five fish.

From Cattle Camp, the Loop Road will run near to the McCloud for a total of about 5.5 miles before it reaches Fowler Camp and heads back toward 89. Within 500 yards of Cattle Camp, however, you will hit the first of a series of dirt pullouts leading to the river (on the left as you proceed from Cattle Camp). These roads are dusty and rough, manageable by trucks, sometimes by passenger cars. Use caution and good judgment. In general, bigger pools in this section are hit hard by bait fishers. Riffles and smaller pocket water can produce more small, wild fish on flies.

About 1.6 miles from Cattle Camp, the Loop Road moves away from the stream for about three quarters of a mile. At the next turnoff, you can hike up some part of that distance to fish water less stressed. A half mile beyond that turnoff, at the intersection of Cattle and Bigelow roads, a left will take you toward Bigelow Meadows — above here is some deep water with browns. As you drive toward Bigelow, you will encounter a road on the right (.25 miles) marked "Lakin Dam."

*Working it: A McCloud trout on the reel. (Photo: Frank Holminski)*

This road ends at a parking lot near a picnic area, with toilets and a platform over the river for handicapped fishers. Lakin is a marshy little reservoir with cool, deep water — an area worth exploring. Access from here to Upper Falls is now gated but can be walked, which makes it easy to follow the river between these two points.

There is a half mile of fishable water between Upper Falls and Middle Falls. During the drought this was poor; it has improved since then.

Loop Road continues on to Fowler Camp, last access of the upper river open to the public. You can follow the road into the campground, and from there work up toward the Middle Falls where there's substantial amounts of holding water. Or, you may bear right and drive until you reach a turnaround and parking area at the Lower Falls. Here you will find a paved trail that follows the river upstream through the campground. Hiking from the end of the trail to the Middle Falls requires wading or rock hopping. More adventurous fishers follow the hillside above the river, downstream, looking for scrambles down, but the river's freestone nature makes progress slow, and within several hundred yards you will reach private, posted property, the upper edge of the Wyntoon Estate.

The five miles from here to the lake is coveted by many a flyfisher. The fact is, how-ever, that there are probably more — and much bigger — fish below Lake McCloud.

### Lower River Access

From the base of the dam McCloud River flows for eight miles until bordered again by private property. Releases from the lake are set at a minimum of 50 cubic feet per second but managed in order to provide 200 to 210 cfs at the measuring point near Ah-Di-Na campground, about 3.5 miles below. By that point on the stream, a surprisingly large part of the river water is provided by inflows from lesser creeks. That means that the cfs outflow from the dam is not always a good indicator of levels lower down, especially during periods of heavy rain. (Note: by agreements between various parties, lake releases may be modified, so that during a drought, flows at Ah-Di-Na typically ranges from 160-180 cfs.)

Access to the lower McCloud is through the town of McCloud, at the main inter-section where Squaw Valley Road heads south toward Lake McCloud. Eight miles out of town — a pretty drive — the road forks. Left is the boat ramp; continue right. Two miles later you will see a right turn clearly marked by a Forest Service sign to Ah-Di-Na and the Nature Conservancy. Continuing left will take you to Spillway Pool and Ash Camp.

Toward Ash Camp, drive around the lake for four miles, cross the dam, and turn right on the dirt road. Within several hundred yards, you will see a gated (usually open) track on your right. It's an easy walk or drive to the pool at the bottom of the hill.

Most of this is difficult to wade — the amount of water release determines just how hard. The easiest place to fish is the arm at the bottom of the road. As it widens to 150 yards, it also gets deeper. Long-line techniques with nymphs or streamers can be effective, and keep an eye out for evening rises.

Continuing on from Spillway Pool, this road leads to Ash Camp, the last road access between this uppermost part of the river and the Ah-Di-Na area downriver.

Ash Camp is an unimproved site with room for five or six parties — bring water. From here it is possible to fish the section upstream between the camp and the dam, a bouldery stretch with good pockets and some riffles. Stay alert, especially when wading, and stay on the camp side of the stream for the safest route upstream. You can fish almost all the way to the dam without having to cross.

Again, stay alert. Releases from the dam, though usually steady, can produce a rapid and dangerous rise in the water level.

Just above Ash Camp is another kind of access point altogether. The footbridge found there is part of the Pacific Crest Trail (PCT), which follows the river about three miles, almost to Ah-Di-Na, before veering off to the west. The PCT offers another opportunity for flyfishers. Note first, however, that most of the trail heading down-stream is cut high above the river, and there are few established paths down. A fisher taking this route must be prepared to bushwhack, keeping clearly in mind the haz-ards of rugged terrain, especially poison oak. It's not easy by any means.

# McCloud River: Ethical Angling in the Bestiary

*by Seth Norman*

If you have never seined a stream before, the McCloud probably isn't a good place to start. At least not in spring. True, mayfly nymphs are abundant, the free-living caddis rappel on silken lines; golden stones are beginning to march in their elegantly patterned armor, and their giant cousins, the salmonflies, (*Pteronarcys californica*), also edge toward land to break with watery life, both species intending to break out of the papery husks they leave on rocks to frighten children. But heaven help the novice who meets his first his two- or three- year-old Dobson fly nymph — a true "hellgrammite" long as a finger, that stretches out in the net using gills that walk while grasping blindly with horny mandibles, eager to injure or eat whatever has disturbed it. High drama — their bites do hurt, but in many places anglers use them for bait. What's important for the fisher to know is that these creatures, and all the rest, are there.

If hatches on the McCloud are unpredictable, then the richness of underwater life is constant. Most concentrate on the bottom: crawling, hiding, losing hold and tumbling, hugging tight with claws or pectoral fins, building houses of stone and detritus, hunting, grazing, fleeing for life or twisting in jaws when flight fails.

Bestiary. All fertile waters are like this, but the fisher with experience on other streams will still marvel at the quantity of McCloud specimens, and at their size.

The latter speak loudly to fly selection, especially in the early season, but also later on. Though the bulk of creatures in the biomass will shrink in the heat, stone, salmon and Dobson fly nymphs often live several seasons; and come October, the caddis of that name caddis will emerge, sometimes an inch long or more.

Rubberlegs. Big APs, Kaufman's stone and stimulators. Take streamers for the sculpin and fry that grow fat here. Certainly, a 25-inch brown trout will take a 22 brassie if it drifts near enough. But for a nymph nearly three inches long, that fish will move.

So will small fry, however, which presents the fisher with a dilemma: stick a six-inch rainbow on a size 4 hook, and the wide gap may put the point out its eye or right through its brain.

There is an answer to this, and it only takes a little care. Tie or buy your big flies on hooks with smaller gaps and 3X or 4X shanks. The loss of hooking or holding characteristics will be modest, if any. And you're less likely to watch as some juvenile, failing to revive in your hand, slips dying down the stream, to make a meal for hellgrammites.

That said, here's one way to approach the river below. Cross the PCT bridge above Ash Camp and walk downstream for about 15 minutes. The trail will cut away from the river, then return to it. At the first point that you can clearly hear and see the stream, you will find a path on the left that descends to a rocky area near a pool. Fishing from here back to Ash Camp can take half a day, or a full one if you stretch it.

It is possible to continue downstream from this point, but once you leave the PCT conditions get difficult — there is no riverside trail working into the gorge. Brush is thick, the river banks bouldery, and the pools may be deep and steep on both sides. For exactly those reasons, this is one part of the river where a fisher will probably find solitude.

You can return to the PCT, continue downriver and drop down by bushwhacking — seriously difficult terrain.

In *California Trout Fishing*, Jim Freeman writes that he would sometimes have his wife drop him at Ah-Di-Na and pick him up at Ash Camp — that he would either do this in a day or sleep overnight on the stream. For this journey Freeman preferred spin/fly tackle in order to plumb depths along the way. A long, long, day hike, this is.

### Toward Ah-Di-Na Campground

Returning to the fork at the Lake, midway between this juncture and the dam: take the right turn, marked "Ah-Di-Na 7 miles; McCloud Preserve 8 Miles" (at the point where bearing left leads toward Ash Camp). While the road is unpaved, it can usually be negotiated in two-wheel drive vehicles if taken slowly and carefully where the surface is rutted or studded by rocks. (Typically it will run smooth enough to allow drivers to pick up speed, then suddenly turn rotten.) The climb is steep and takes you away from the river. The summit of the hill — a smallish mountain — is about the halfway mark.

At 6.5 miles the PCT crosses this road. (If you reach the turnoff to Ah-Di-Na Campground you have gone .5 miles too far.) This crossing is marked by a large turnout on the left side, just downhill is the trail. You can use the PCT to strike out for the river, hiking upstream to access the lower end of the gorge that begins near Ash Camp, but a better trail along the river's edge can be found .5 miles further on, near the entrance to Ah-Di-Na Campground.

The Ah-Di-Na campground turnoff is the first you will encounter that is clearly marked. As you near the entrance, but before proceeding into the campground, you will notice a spur that goes left leading to a trail upstream (the better trail mentioned above.) This can be driven for about a hundred yards, and fishers may park along it without paying the use fee in the campground. DO NOT park in the campground without paying that fee. The citation you may receive will be expensive by comparison, and more trouble.

There are two other options to entering the campground. Continue on the main access road instead of taking the turnoff, driving toward the Nature Conservancy's

McCloud River Preserve. You will find two other unimproved campground/day use areas on the way. The first (about .5 miles) is not marked and it has a steep, rough entrance road. High ground clearance is recommended, and a vehicle larger than a truck with camper shell could have problems getting in and out.

Another half mile along the road is a sign reading "River," with an arrow pointing left, and "Preserve" with an arrow pointing straight ahead. This left road leads to several pullouts and some short steep, rough access roads to the river.

At this writing the Ah-Di-Na campground is closed, its future a question of money and the politics it will take to get it. However, the river flowing through the campground is open all the way upstream Ash camp. Conditions on the stream are as good as in the Preserve water described below, and with the exception of opening week and the last weeks of the season, anglers will often find fewer people. Also somewhat fewer fish, because here the river is not protected by catch-and-release regulations.

### The Nature Conservancy and The McCloud River Preserve

The McCloud River Preserve is owned by the Nature Conservancy, a private, national organization that obtained the property in 1979. Part of the Conservancy's goal is to provide future generations with a look at what a completely wild country this once was, a "pristine river canyon" that is still the habitat of bear, osprey and puma. A small staff lives on the site year-round in order to manage, educate, and study. Their research projects include water quality monitoring and documentation of fish migrations.

While the Conservancy is under absolutely no obligation to open the Preserve to the public, they do allow hiking and fishing on the first 2.5 miles under carefully prescribed conditions. All fishing is catch-and-release, zero limit, single barbless hooks, with artificials only.

The property begins at the confluence of Lady Bug Creek. A quarter mile trail from the parking area at the end of the access road (too small for RVs; park at Ah-Di-Na campground instead) leads to a site with a manager's cabin, and a sponsor's cabin, a two-seat outhouse. There is a kiosk with a sign-in sheet, a display rack of information, and a guide to the nature trail. Anglers can usually find a map of the property that shows the trail system and the names given to each section of river.

Also at the kiosk are tags each angler must have in order to fish the Preserve: a total of 10 fishers are allowed on these 2.5 miles at any time. Five of these tags are reserved. Starting in February, people may call or write to the Conservancy's main office in San Francisco, (201 Mission Street, 4th Floor, San Francisco, CA 94105), specifying the date or dates they wish to visit. Usually all available days are taken in short order.

Five more tags are held for daily walk-ons, and anglers hoping to receive one of these line up at the kiosk early in the morning, sometimes before 5 a.m. (Do not fish this property without a tag. Do not take tags off the property to "come back later.")

*Seth Norman with a plump McCloud rainbow from the Nature Conservancy section.*

Two important notes about this process: many of the people who reserve days fail to show. Their tags are passed out at 10AM. If you do not arrive early enough to get one of the first five, you might return at this time. Also, a sizable number of anglers who do enter early leave the river early, by noon or 1PM, returning their tags to the kiosk. This can provide another opportunity to get on the water.

A last note: The McCloud Conservancy is more than a just another fishing destination. It is a place where anglers and others can enjoy relatively uncrowded conditions and use a trail system that gives fishers fairly easy access to great water. Unfortunately, there are anglers who ignore the Conservancy's request to stay on these trails; now there are noticeable "shortcuts" to certain pools, some in places so steep they are unsafe. The vegetation suffers here, erosion begins, and the angling community is placed in the position of literally trampling the wishes of its host.

Maintaining the McCloud River Preserve is costly — $30,000 a year must be raised from contributions. Yearly memberships in the Nature Conservancy and the McCloud River Preserve, which come with subscriptions to the *Nature Conservancy Magazine* and the quarterly California newsletter, begin at $35 — roughly the price of a medium quality fly line, or one-fourth the daily entry fee to most private waters.

The McCloud River Preserve's address is Box 409 McCloud, CA 96057.

# STREAM FACTS: MCCLOUD RIVER

## Seasons
- Last Saturday in April through November 15.

## Special Regulations
- Upper River: no special regulations.
- Lower River: McCloud Dam to Ladybug Creek, artificials only with barbless hooks, two fish any size.
- McCloud River Preserve: artificials only, barbless hooks, zero kill

## River Characteristics
- Upper River: small pretty water, mostly shallow, moderate gradient with meadows and some small wild fish that often rise to dries; also stocked fish, heavy summer traffic down toward the McCloud Loop.
- Lower River: a heavily wooded canyon, burly water with heavy flows, few classic riffles, mostly deep runs, pools, and pocket water. Difficult to challenging wading; the McCloud has few trails right along the river. Water temperature varies between 48 degrees in spring to a midsummer "high" of 52 degrees, then returns to 48 degrees by mid-fall.

## Trout
- Guesstimated at about 2000 fish per mile. Catch ratio of rainbows to browns, 8:1.
- Rainbows will average 14 inches, browns 16. The former range to 22, the latter to 36.

## River Miles
- Upper: approximately 18 miles
- Lower: approximately 8 miles

## River Flows
- Upper: stream fed, gentle, with some deep pools.
- Lower: Releases from dam are regulated to maintain the following minimums at Ah-Di-Na campground: 170 cubic feet per second from March to May 15; 200 cfs May 16 through August; 210 cfs September 1, until the end of season.

## Hub Cities
- McCloud, Mount Shasta

## McCLOUD RIVER MAJOR HATCHES

| Insect | A | M | J | J | A | S | O | N | Time | Flies |
|---|---|---|---|---|---|---|---|---|---|---|
| Golden Stone *Caleneuria californica* | | ■ | ■ | | | | | | D | Nymph: Golden Stone<br>Dry: Golden Stone |
| Little Yellow Stonefly *Alloperla pacifica* | | ■ | ■ | | | ■ | | | D | |
| Salmon Fly *Pteronarcys californica* | | | ■ | | | | | | D | Nymph: Stimulator<br>Dry: Stimulator; Rubber Legs |
| March Brown *Rhithrogena* | | ■ | | | | | | | LM – A | Nymph: Hare's Ear<br>Dry: Adam's Parachute |
| Little Olive | | ■ | | | | ■ | ■ | | LM – A | Nymph: Pheasant Tail<br>Dry: Little Olive Paradun |
| Green Drake *Drunella grandis* | | ■ | ■ | | | | | | LM – A | Nymph: Green Drake<br>Dry: Green Drake |
| Gray Sedge *Hydropsychid* | | ■ | | ■ | | | | | LM – A – E | Nymph: Byrd's Nest<br>Dry: Byrd's Nest |
| Spotted Sedge *Hydropsyche cockerelli* | | ■ | | | ■ | | | | M – A | Nymph: Byrd's Nest<br>Dry: Elk Hair Caddis |
| Pale Morning Dun *Ephemerella infrequens* | | | | ■ | ■ | | | | LM – A | Nymph: Hare's Ear<br>Dry: PM Comparadun |
| October Caddis *Dicosmoecus atripes* | | | | | | | ■ | | LM | Nymph: October Caddis<br>Dry: Stimulator |
| Midge | ■ | ■ | ■ | ■ | ■ | ■ | ■ | | LM | Dry: Griffith's Gnat |
| Tube Worm | ■ | ■ | ■ | ■ | ■ | ■ | ■ | | | San Juan Worm |

HATCH TIME CODE: M = morning; LM = Late Morning; A = afternoon; E = evening; D = dark

# MT. SHASTA

### Elevation – 3,554 ft. • Population – 3,700

The town of McCloud is closest to the McCloud River but has relatively few services. Mount Shasta, just off I-5, 10 miles from McCloud, has many more.

## ACCOMMODATIONS

**Best Western Tree House**, Box 236, Lake Street, Mt. Shasta, CA 96067, off I-5, central Mt. Shasta exit / 800-545-7164 / $$–$$$ / Indoor pool, restaurant, bar

**Finlandia**, 1612 S Mt. Shasta Blvd., Mt. Shasta, CA 96067 / 916-926-5596/ Some kitchen units / $

**Swiss Holiday Lodge**, S Mt. Shasta Blvd., Mt. Shasta, CA 96067, off I-5 McCloud exit / Pets OK, whirlpool, complimentary continental breakfast / $–$$

**Mount Shasta Ranch**, 1008 W A Barr Road, Mt. Shasta, CA 96067 / 916-926-3870 / B&B, full breakfast, also a cottage for rent / $$–$$$

**Mountain Aire Lodge**, 1121 S Mt. Shasta Blvd, Mt. Shasta, CA 96067 / 916-926-3411 / Pets allowed ($5), lodge, community kitchen, family units, pool table / $–$$

**Strawberry Valley Inn**, 1142 S. Mt. Shasta Blvd., Mt. Shasta, CA 96067 / 916-926-2052 / AAA and senior discounts, suites available w/sitting rooms, continental breakfast, jacuzzi, complimentary wine and beverages at 5PM / $$

## CAMPING

Most of this area is part of the vast Mt. Shasta Wilderness. On the upper river there is camping at Fowlers Camp, Cattle Camp, and Algoma.

To reach **Fowlers Camp**, drive 6 miles east of the town McCloud on Highway 89, then turn right at the *first* entrance of McCloud River Loop Road. The camp is about a mile south from the highway. This is the best choice for RVs.

To reach **Cattle Camp**, pass the first McCloud River Loop Road entrance and drive 4.8 miles to the second. Turn right; the first major dirt turnoff, about a quarter mile in, is Cattle Camp. RVs okay.

The **Algoma** site is off Highway 89, roughly 11 miles from the first Loop Road turn-off, then three-quarters of a mile half mile south on Stouts Meadow Road.

For camping on the lower river, there is an unimproved site at **Ash Camp**. From the town of McCloud, take Squaw Valley Road south toward Lake McCloud. Eight miles out of town the road forks. Left goes to the boat ramp. Stay to the right. Two miles later, go left at the turnoff to Ah-Di-Na Campground and the Nature Conservancy, drive around the lake, cross the dam, and turn right on the dirt road to Ash Camp, about two miles further. Trailers and RVs not advised. Bring water.

**Ah-Di-Na Campground** is closed at this writing but may open in 1997 (call Mt. Shasta Wilderness / 916-926-4511. To reach it, follow the directions above until you reach the fork to Ah-Di-Na. Stay on the sometimes steep and bumpy dirt road for 7 miles to the campground.

## RESTAURANTS

**Laurie's Mountain View Cafe**, 401 N Mt. Shasta Blvd., Mt. Shasta, CA 96067 / 916-926-4998 / $

**Bagel Cafe Bakery & Juice Bar**, 105 E Alma St., Mt. Shasta, CA 96067 / 916-926-1414 / $

**Black Bear Diner**, Mt. Shasta, CA 96067 / 530-926-4669 / $$ / Open 24 hours

**Howlin' Hound Restaurant**, Mt. Shasta, CA 96067 / 916-926-3419 / $$

**Lalos Mexican Restaurant**, 520 N Mt. Shasta Blvd., Mt. Shasta, CA 96067 / 916-926-5123 / $$

**Lily's**, 1013 S Mt. Shasta Blvd., Mt. Shasta, CA 96067 / 916-926-3372 / $$$ / Wonderful food

**Michael's Restaurant**, 313 N Mt. Shasta Blvd., Mt. Shasta, CA 96067 / 916-926-5288 / $$$

**Mike & Tony's Restaurant**, 501 S Mt. Shasta Blvd., Mt. Shasta, CA 96067 / 530-926-4792 / $$$ / Big meals, great fillets, fresh coffee beans, open early in the morning

**Piemont Restaurant**, 1200 S Mt. Shasta Blvd., Mt. Shasta, CA 96067 / 916-926-2402 / $–$$ / Italian, American, make their own pasta

**SAY Cheese Pizza**, 304 Maple St., Mt. Shasta, CA 96067 / 916-926-2821 / $$

**Serge's French Cuisine Restaurant**, 531 Chestnut St,. Mt. Shasta, CA 96067 / 916-926-1276 / $$$

**Tree House**, I 5 & Lake, Mt. Shasta, CA 96067 / 916-926-3101 / $$

**Poor Georges Restaurant**, 610 S Mt. Shasta Blvd., Mt. Shasta, CA 96067 / 916-926-4047 / $$

## FLY SHOPS IN AREA (DUNSMUIR)

**Dunsmuir Fly Fishing Company**, 5839 Main Street, Dunsmuir, CA 96025 / 916-238-0705 / Open during season.

**Ted Fay Fly Shop**, 4310 Dunsmuir Ave., Dunsmuir, CA 96025 / 916-235-2969 / Call for hours

## AIRPORT
See Redding

## HOSPITALS
**Mercy Medical Center**, Mt. Shasta / 916-926-6111 / Many services available / Also see Redding

## AUTO RENTALS
See Redding

## FOR MORE INFORMATION
Mount Shasta Chamber of Commerce
300 Pine Street

Mount Shasta, CA, 96067
916-926-6212

# The Pit River

## By Dick Galland

With the opening of a giant valve inside the Lake Britton dam in July of 1986, the modern era of flyfishing on California's Pit River began. When the dam was completed 60 years earlier, water flow into seven miles of river in the Three Reach was simply stopped. National enthusiasm for rural electrification didn't consider water for fish. Springs in the riverbed and tributaries provided just enough flow for native Pit rainbow to survive. The rewatering of Pit Three was a signal event. It marked the rebirth of the Pit as a wild trout fishery, both in fact and in the imaginations of those who have come to fish here.

The 30 miles of the Pit below Lake Britton are divided by hydro projects into five individual reaches, each defined by a dam at the upper end and a powerhouse and reservoir at the downstream end. Between each dam and powerhouse are seven to 13 miles of fishable water. Controlled releases of 150 cubic feet per second from the dams create tailwater conditions — constant flows, good clarity, and stable temperatures—that produce the tremendous food-rich environments typical of great fisheries. It is in these reaches that the Pit's reputation as a great wild trout fishery has been built. One fisheries biologist has called the Pit the finest naturally-occurring wild trout river in California.

Since that day in 1986, more and more anglers have been exploring the canyon water in the Three, Four and Five reaches. They have discovered that no river in northeastern California has the catch rate of the Pit. In the Three Reach, where the average fish is 14 inches, the catch rate for experienced anglers approaches four fish an hour. Nymphing is the most effective technique, but dry fly anglers do quite well. Evening dry fly fishing can find fish up everywhere, and it is not uncommon to catch 15 or 20 trout in an hour's fishing. New nymphing techniques have made it possible to fish the long pools successfully.

The Pit is a river for gaining all the skills of freestone fishing. It is a river for nymphing, a river for sink tips and full sinking lines, a river for dry flies. Above all, it is the place to develop good wading skills. An angler at home on the Pit will be at home on any freestoner in the world. Most other rivers will seem easy compared to the Pit, particularly in the wading. The Pit has every type of freestone water except pure riffles. It is without gravel and cobbles, and this is where the challenge lies. If the Pit were as easy to wade as the Madison or the Frying Pan, or the Sacramento, it would be beset with anglers every day of the season.

Wading is the limiting factor in the Pit's popularity. It is a river without flat spots. It should be called the Big Boulder River, a name that captures the true nature of the river, evoking an image of a bright cascading freestoner, holding fine populations of native rainbows. It is the Big Boulder River, in fact, if not in name. Those boulders put many anglers off. One or two trips into the canyon, scrambling around, bruising shins, and with mixed fishing results is discouraging. Easier perhaps to drive an

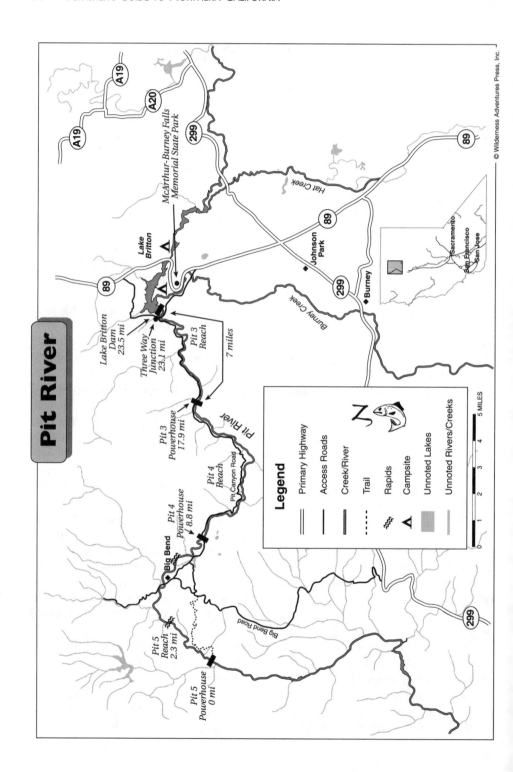

hour to the upper Sacramento or the McCloud, where wading is straightforward, and roads, railroad tracks, and trails afford good access. But like the famous spring creek tributaries of the Pit — Hat Creek and Fall River — the river reveals its secrets to those who are patient, who are willing to put in the days, the seasons, it takes to master the fishery and wading skills.

## Wading

On the face of it, wading the Pit is a fairly simple matter. It requires proper gear, in the form of sturdy, felt-sole wading boots and a wading staff — a good tall, stout one, preferably an old metal ski pole. Leave the fancy, collapsible staffs at home. The Pit will destroy them. Tie a length of strong cord around the ski pole's shaft just below the grip. Tie the other end to the ring on the back of your vest or waders, adjusting the length so that when you reach behind you, engage the cord, and extend your arm, the pole ends up in your hand, ready for use.

The river averages three feet in depth, and its velocities are not particularly high. The key to moving around in the Pit is to go slowly and always have two points of contact. Plant your staff upstream and lean into the current; this will help right you if you lose your balance. Your pole plant should be on the river's bottom, at the intersections of rocks, not on top of a rock. Likewise, when you move your feet, keep them on the bottom. Go around the bigger rocks rather than up and over them. Slide your foot into the intersections of rocks. Keep your body sideways to the current, to reduce the force of water on your legs. Commit yourself to your staff and move as far as that pole plant will allow. Keep your stance wide and don't get cross-legged. Find a secure position, then move your pole again. The pole is your anchor, the vital third point of contact. Keep your center of gravity low. Achieving mastery of wading will leave you free to concentrate on fishing.

## Hatches and Other Food Items

The Pit is a rich soup of a river, with exceptional water quality and profuse hatches. The pH is high and there is an astonishing amount of food. On any day of the season, there will be six or eight or 10 different species of bugs in the air — always the ubiquitous midges, generally dragons and damsels, usually one or more small mayflies and microcaddis, and frequently stoneflies. The Pit is not hatch-driven in the same sense as nearby Fall River and Hat Creek, but there are superhatches on the Pit that provide superb nymph and dry fly opportunities. These begin with the salmonflies and golden stones in April and May. In late May the *Epeorus* mayfly duns and spinners fill the evening air in such profusion that one can only stare in wonder. Late May also sees the beginning of heavy caddis hatches that last much of the summer. The bright hot days of high summer mean afternoon water temperatures can reach 70. Wet wading is pleasant and the bugs are very small: microcaddis, baetis, Tricos, midges. The first storm in mid-September signals the arrival of fall and with it, autumn's first superhatch: the big *Isonychia velma* mayfly. The dark nymph shucks appear on downstream sides of certain rocks along slow margins. The big spinners

*A prime Pit River riffle*
*next to a powerhouse.*
*(Photo: Seth Norman)*

form vast flights over the slower runs. A sparsely-dressed, black AP nymph with a soft hackle collar, dead-drifted in the seams and retrieved with jerky little strips along the slower edges brings slashing strikes.

The *Isonychia* are followed by October caddis. These giant caddis are a uniquely western hatch. We begin to see the big *Dicosmoecus* pupal shucks on rocks at the beginning of October. Adults, with fat, pumpkin-colored bodies, labor upstream in the afternoons, dropping heavily to the surface to lay their eggs, are taken eagerly by the trout. October caddis are the autumn equivalent of spring's stoneflies and they are greeted with the same enthusiasm by the fish. They bring the very biggest fish in the river to the surface. This fine dry fly fishing will last most of October.

For the biggest trout, the piscivorous trout who want more than caddis and mayflies, the Pit is truly a groaning board. There are trout fry, of course, plus the fry and young of Sacramento squawfish, hardheads, and suckers. There are Pit sculpins in astonishing numbers. There are Pit-Klamath brook lamprey, a little eel-like fellow who grows to perhaps five inches. There are remarkable numbers of crayfish enjoyed by the trout and by the many otters who live in the canyon. The Three, Four, and Five Reaches have very large trout. (My guides and I have had our 10-or 12-inch rainbow, hooked while nymphing, seized by much larger over five pounds. I just haven't figured out how to land one of these big fish after it has grabbed my small fish as an appetizer!)

## Tackle

Ideal tackle for the Pit begins with a long rod. A nine-footer provides a long lever for casting BBs, a long reach for line control, and enough backbone to fish sinking lines or tips. The basic line will be a 4, 5, or 6-weight floater in a double taper for ease in rollcasting when stack mending. Leaders will be rod length, tapering to 5X. It is well to carry 6X tippet. You'll catch more fish (and lose more!) than with 5X. A supply of BB shot is essential as well as an indicator material in the form of strike putty and poly yarn. A net and wading staff are helpful. And, of course, lots of flies. The Pit eats flies at an alarming rate. If you become truly enamored of this river, you will want to take up fly tying.

## Shortline Nymphing

The Pit is first and foremost a nymphing river. Three nymphing styles are invaluable, the choice depending on water depth and how close you can wade to the spot you wish to fish. Visibility in the Pit is typically three to four feet and combined with the bouldery nature of the bottom, means an angler can wade very close. This is perfect for shortline nymphing: controlled, drag-free drifts with line entering the water directly beneath the rod tip. A fluorescent 18-inch butt section of Amnesia between the fly line and the leader makes a useful indicator. A bit of strike putty rolled onto the leader, sufficient to just coat the leader for an inch, is equally effective. If two of these little coatings of putty are used, the first about four feet above the fly and the second midway between the first and the end of the fly line, you can see one or the other easily, depending on the depth of the water. Having two, it is also easy to tell when the leader gets downstream of the fly, making strike detection impossible. The actual presentation is a lob, lift, and lead. Wade into position directly across from the lie you intend to fish, shake 10 to 12 feet of line out the rod tip and let it hang below you in the current. Raise the rod tip to 45 degrees, look at your target, and lob the BBs toward it with a high, arching cast so the BBs enter the water as nearly vertical as possible, penetrating the water quickly to get to the fish's level without a long drift. Immediately raise your rod tip to horizontal and lift the extra line off the water surface, reducing the chance for drag and establishing a connection with the BBs. Lead the BBs downstream at the exact rate the current is flowing by holding the rod steady in a horizontal position and rotating your upper body at the waist. Sweep your rod downstream, keeping a tight line to the BBs and fly. This is the critical part. Done properly, you will see and feel the slight hesitation in the drift that signals a take. This is true shortline nymphing.

### Indicator Nymphing

It isn't always possible to wade close enough to make a true shortline presentation. As the distance from the rod tip increases and the angle of the line goes from 90 degrees toward horizontal, it becomes increasingly difficult to get a drag-free presentation. For these longer casts, use a floating indicator, a highly buoyant one that sits up on the water rather than in the surface film. Poly macramé yarn is ideal. Pull a few strands out, enough to make an indicator about the size of a large olive, comb out (yes, combed with a little plastic comb) to increase their volume, thoroughly grease with floatant, and tie into the same tapered leader with an overhand or overhand loop at about one and one half times the depth of the water. In the Pit this generally means about five to six feet. The poly yarn sits so high that drag is minimized. It's superior to the cork and foam styles which guarantee drag. Cast as before and immediately lift as much line off the water as possible, leading the indicator downstream. This large indicator technique is less sensitive than shortlining. It's necessary to be particularly attentive. Takes are not felt; they are purely visual.

### Puffball Nymphing

These two styles of nymphing are fine for water up to about five or six feet deep. Over this depth — and there is plenty of good, deep water in the Pit — effective nymphing relies on still another strategy that we call "puffball nymphing" after the nature of indicator we fashion. Popularized by California anglers Dean Schubert and Dave Hickson (and described in *Fly Fisherman* magazine), it has opened up water to dead-drift nymphing that was once fished with sinking lines and the traditional wet fly swing or with streamer techniques. With puffballs, an angler can drift any sort of nymph, large or small, at whatever depth, in a natural manner. It has dramatically increased catch rates in the fine deep pools and runs on the Pit.

Rig for puffballing with the same rod and double taper line. On the end of a seven-foot leader, tapered to 3X or 4X, tie a poly yarn indicator. This can range in size from a large olive to a ping-pong ball, depending on how much weight you wish to suspend. A Duncan loop or improved cinch knot works well here. Tie a length of 5X tippet around the leader above the puffball using the same knot, then slide the tippet knot down the leader until it stops at the puffball. The tippet will hang at a 90-degree angle to the leader. Set the length of the tippet at just less than the suspected depth of the run you want to fish. Tie your fly (or flies) on and add a BB or two a few inches above the fly, and you're ready to fish. Less weight is needed to penetrate the water column with this setup than with the shortline technique.

There are more than just trout in the Pit. The river holds fine populations of suckers, as well as squawfish and hardheads, two members of the minnow family that grow to very large sizes. Trout and nongame fish seem to have worked out an interesting living arrangement: trout occupy the fastwater and the others the slow water. Concentrate on the fastwater at the heads of pools.

It is in these zones that puffballing excels. Begin by positioning yourself about 30 feet below the cascade at the head of the pool. Feeding the indicator and fly downstream 25 or 30 feet, raise your rod tip smoothly from horizontal to vertical, water loading the rod, and make a high arching cast, with a big open loop. You want your BBs to hit the water vertically and penetrate the water column quickly. Give the BBs a three count to sink. Then raise your rod tip to vertical and make a short, fast roll cast called a stack mend to flip the indicator upstream, thus taking the pressure completely off the tippet and allowing the fly to sink as deeply as possible without drag. As the drift continues, additional stack mends create brief, perfectly neutral "turnover points." Takes are very likely to come at these moments. Pay careful attention to the puffball. Set on any hesitation — a dip, a turn, a tiny sideways movement. As the puffball drifts by, flip the flyline upstream of the indicator and shake line out the tip of the rod to continue the drift until you've gotten into slow, nontrouty water. Then strip in line, raise your rod tip high and recast. Puffballing is deadly, but beware! Keep your casting loops open. A long drop of fine tippet with BBs at one end and a big poly indicator at the other is a tangle waiting to happen. The BBs head in one direction at high speed, and the puffball goes off slowly in another.

Learning this technique can be frustrating, but there is no more deadly way to present a nymph to a fish in a natural manner in deep water. As the inevitable tangles occur, remember the two-minute rule: if it looks like it will take longer than two minutes to untangle, cut the fly and BBs off and rerig with fresh tippet. Perhaps take a break, sit down on a rock, enjoy the water flowing by without an indicator on it!

### Sinking Lines and Streamers

The Pit is admirably suited to sinking line strategies. In runs and pools, enormous numbers of trout and rough fish fry, plus sculpins, eels, and crayfish mean that big trout are always on the lookout for more of a meal than a bug. Wooly buggers in black and brown are fished to great effect with a 10 or 15 foot high speed tip. That same tip works well with soft hackles in the shallower runs fished in the conventional across and down manner. An olive wooly bugger in a size 8 or 10 dead-drifted like a nymph and then crawled back among the boulders is an attractive crawfish presentation when used with the same sinktip. In the big deep pools, a Teeny 200, or the like, cast downstream and then retrieved very slowly with the rod tip underwater and a sculpin pattern on a short stout leader is often highly productive. There are enough very large trout in the Pit to make such prospecting worthwhile. Your catch rate may go down, but your average size will certainly go up!

### High Stick Dry Fly Fishing

A dry fly technique developed by northern California guide Joe Heuseveldt is exceptionally effective on the Pit. Joe calls it high-stick, dry fly fishing and it is truly precision fishing — thoughtful wading, careful casts, complete line control and

*Pit River pocket water makes for tough wading. (Photo: Seth Norman)*

absolutely drag-free drifts. It is the perfect compliment to the Pit style of nymphing. Instead of the LOB, lift, and lead of shortline nymphing, presentation might be described as SWAT, lift and lead. With 10 to 12 feet of line out the rod tip, the rod is loaded with the casting stroke to turn the fly over just above the water's surface. Joe calls it the fly swatter cast — a fast, up-down stroke, the rod coming up to vertical and down about 20 degrees. The fly is placed very precisely on the exact target and the line immediately lifted off the water, without moving the fly. Casts are precise. Every fishy spot is covered. Drifts are rarely more than 6 or 8 feet. The leader is the same length as the rod, tapered to 5X. Joe prefers a Royal Humpy — it's highly visible — in size 12 or 14, tied on with a Duncan loop to allow it to move. His rod choice is a 9' four weight. It's remarkable to watch Joe make his way up the Pit, wading staff in one hand and rod in the other, covering a 10-foot arc of water, placing his fly carefully, and taking fish after fish.

The Pit, then, is a river of many parts, a river demanding time, energy, and skill of those who would do well here. It does not give up its fat rainbows easily. But for the angler willing to make a commitment to walking, to aggressive wading, to forging a long-term relationship with this extraordinary fishery, it is a river of great rewards and deep satisfactions, a river for every season.

**Pit River Access**

The best-known reaches of the Pit begin below the Lake Britton Dam, west of Highway 89, and about 10 miles north of Burney. Pit's Three, Four, and Five make up a total of about 30 miles of river. Pit Three begins at the base of Lake Britton dam and flows for seven miles to the outflow from Powerhouse Three. Three has the easiest access of all the lower reaches. The Pit Canyon road, which runs from Lake Britton Dam to the Pit Five Dam and on to the community of Big Bend, is at river level for the lower three miles upstream of Powerhouse Three. This prime water is essentially catch and release. Fish below Britton Dam or drive down the canyon road on the north side of the river. The road is well above the river, but two ridges force the river into southerly bends and make access possible at these places. The road reaches river level at the bridge over Rock Creek, principal tributary of Pit Three. Between Rock Creek and Powerhouse Three, there are many fine fishing spots visible from the road.

Below Pit Three Powerhouse, the road becomes graveled. Pass Pit Four dam. The Four Reach has no special regulations. All types of tackle are permitted and the take is five fish per day. Nonetheless, the fishing is good. The road is near the river for the first mile and then begins to climb up through the timber to crest a ridge and afford a great view downstream from several hundred feet above the river. The canyon is steep here, and it's a long way to the river on foot. However, as you drive toward Pit Four Powerhouse, there are a number of places where small ridges allow access or the canyon widens enough to make a descent possible. The road passes the Pit Four Powerhouse and the Pit Five reservoir, crosses the dam and leaves the river completely for three miles, arriving at Big Bend, a tiny community on the Pit River. It is possible to fish both below the Pit Four Dam and around the Big Bend area.

The main road to Big Bend runs due south 15 miles to intersect with Highway 299 at the top of Hatchet Mountain. Driving south for two miles, there is a signed turnoff to the west for the Pit Five Powerhouse. This is the principal access for the lower section of the Pit Five Reach. Following this road to the river, there is an old paved area on the right, where anglers park to fish miles of water above the powerhouse and on upstream toward Big Bend, 13 miles away.

**Caveat Piscator!**

When you fish in the more remote sections of Four and Five, you must be self-reliant. Carry water or a filter bottle, food, a butane lighter, a flashlight, and, in the spring or fall, a space blanket. It's hard to get lost, but not inconceivable to be caught out after dark. Let someone know where you are going and when you expect to be back. Be aware of wading hazards — twisted ankles, bruises, and contusions — and environmental hazards. It can get plenty hot in the Pit Canyon in summer. Walking in neoprene waders in summer can dehydrate you. Keep drinking water and rest regularly. There are rattlesnakes in the canyon. They are anxious to get out of your way; watch for them. Poison oak is found throughout this area. It is easily recognized in the late spring, summer and early fall: a low, thin shrub with a distinctive oak-shaped leaf. Without leaves, it's difficult; but with waders on, you are pretty well protected.

*A fastwater rainbow from the Pit. (Photo: Duane Milleman)*

## Super Hatches on the Pit
*Late April to Early June*

>*Pteronarcys californica* — western salmonfly
>Bird's salmonfly or Kaufman's stimulator #6–8 (orange)
>
>*Acroneuria californica* — golden stonefly
>Lawson's Henry Fork Golden Stone #8–10
>
>*Baetis* species
>Light Cahill, olive or tan paradun #16–18

### *June, July, August*

>*Epeorus* species — Little yellow mayfly
>Yellow humpy or White Wulff #14–16
>
>*Tricorythodes minutus*
>Trico spinner #20
>
>*Baetis* species — Blue wing olive
>Olive paradun #18–20
>
>Caddis species
>Tan or brown elk caddis #12-14

### September and October

Isonychia velma
Burgundy Spinner #10

Tricorythodes minutus
Trico spinner #20

Baetis species
Olive paradun #18–20

Dicosmoecus species
Kaufman's stimulator #10–12 (orange)

### November

Baetis species
Olive paradun #18–20

## A Pit River Fly Box

In addition to the dries listed in the hatch chart, carry these patterns as well:

➤ **Dries**
Madame X #6–10
Royal Wulff #12–14
Royal Humpy #12–14
Yellow Wulff #12–14
Yellow Humpy #12–16
Elk Caddis-brown #12–16

➤ **Nymphs (with and without beadheads)**
Birds' Nest #12–16 ( black, tan, gray, brown, olive)
Pheasant Tail #12–18
Black Rubber Legs # 6–10
Prince #10–16
Black AP #10–12
GRHE #8–18
Orange Caddis pupa #10
Red Squirrel #6–10
Z-wing caddis pupa #12–16

➤ **Streamers**
Sculpin pattern #2–6 (brown, black, dark olive)
Crayfish pattern #2–8 (olive, tan)
Woolly Bugger #4–8 (black, olive and brown)
Marabou Leech #6–10 (black, olive and brown)
Trout Fry pattern #2–6

# STREAM FACTS: PIT RIVER

## Seasons
- Last Saturday in April through November 15.
- Below Pit No. 7 dam downstream to Shasta Lake, open all year.

## Special Regulations
- Upper River to Pit No 3 dam, limit 2 fish, no tackle restrictions.
- From Pit No 3 (Britton Dam) downstream to the outlet of Pit Powerhouse No 3 only artificial lures with barbless hooks, minimum size limit 18 inches, 2 fish limit
- Below Pit No. 4 dam downstream to Shasta Lake, limit 5 fish

## Trout
- Varies by reach: generally rainbows averaging 14 inches. Conditions on the Pit make population surveys difficult, but the catch rate for experienced anglers in the Powerhouse #3 reach approaches four fish an hour.

## River Miles
- Described here, the 30 miles of the Pit below Lake Britton, divided by hydroelectic projects into five individual reaches of seven to 13 miles in length.

## River Flows
- Controlled releases of 150 cubic feet per second.

## River Characteristics
- Tailwater conditions — constant flows, good clarity, and stable temperatures — produce tremendously food-rich environments. The Pit has every type of free-stone water except pure riffles, but it is a difficult, even dangerous river to wade, requiring special caution.

## Hub City
- Burney

## PIT RIVER MAJOR HATCHES

| Insect | A | M | J | J | A | S | O | N | Flies |
|---|---|---|---|---|---|---|---|---|---|
| Salmonfly *Pteronarcys californica* | | ● | | | | | | | Black Rubberlegs #6; Improved Sofa Pillow #6 |
| Golden Stone *Acroneuria pacifica* | | ● | | | | | | | Whitlock Red Squirrel Nymph #8; Golden Stimulator #8 |
| Epeorus mayfly | | | ● | | | | | | GRHE and Poxyback Mayfly Nymphs #12–14; Yellow Humpy #12–14 & Hackle Tip Cream Spinner #12–14 |
| Caddis (various heavy hatches) | | | ● | ● | | | | | Birdsnest and Prince Nymphs #14–16; Elk Caddis #14–16 |
| Microcaddis, Baetis Tricos & Midges | | | | | ● | ● | | | Microcaddis Adult #20; Baetis Dun #18–20; Trico Dun and Spinner #18–20; Griffiths Gnat #20 |
| Mayfly *Isonychia velma* | | | | | | | ● | | Black AP Nymph #10; Purple Hackle Tip Spinner #10 |
| October caddis *Dicosmoecus atrips* | | | | | | | | ● | Orange Caddis Pupa #10; Orange Caddis Adult/Orange Stimulator #10 |

# BURNEY

### Elevation – 3,100 • Population – 3,000

Eastern Shasta County is the wild trout center of California. Within a 60-mile radius of Burney are the five finest wild trout rivers in the state, plus several smaller streams and excellent stillwaters. These waters include Hat Creek, Fall River, the Pit River system, the McCloud, the upper and lower Sacramento, Burney Creek, Baum Lake, Manzanita Lake, and Eastman and Big Lake. The best fishing coincides with the general trout season: the last Saturday in April through the 15th of November. Stillwaters are open all year.

Burney is a full service community with several motels, cafes, restaurants, banks, gas stations and garages, grocery stores, fly shops and other major services. The next little community, Johnson Park, two miles east of Burney, also has a fly shop, service stations, and restaurants.

## ACCOMMODATIONS

Clearwater House on Hat Creek, 21568 Cassel Road, Cassel, CA 96016 / 916-335-5500 / A Fly Fisher's Inn on Hat Creek, in Cassel, minutes from Baum Lake and the Wild Trout Water / 7 bedrooms with private baths; excellent meals and service; guides for all area waters; California's only Orvis endorsed lodge / $$–$$$

*Burney motels in order of author's preference:*

Shasta Pines, 37386 Main, Burney, CA 96013 / 916-335-2201
Burney Motel, 37448 Main, Burney, CA 96013 / 916-335-4500
Charm, 37363 Main, Burney, CA 96013 / 916-335-2254
Green Gables, 37385 Main, Burney, CA 96013 / 916-335-2264
Sleepy Hollow Lodge, 36898 Main, Burney, CA 96013 / 916-335-2285

## CAMPGROUNDS

There are four types in the area: US Forest Service, State Parks, PG&E, and private. The most conveniently located for fishing Hat Creek is the **PG&E Cassel Campground** in Cassel. Walk to fishing on the Cassel Flats or Baum Lake. Running water, pit toilets, fee. About 15 campsites set in pines and oaks. Pleasant. Cassel General Store nearby for limited groceries. First come/first served. Fills up in the summer.

**McArthur Burney Falls State Park** is 6 miles north of Hwy 299 on Hwy 89. A wonderful little park. Nice campsites. Little store. Fee. Swimming in Lake Britton. Fishing and sightseeing around the falls of Burney Creek. The creek above the falls is stocked weekly and open to bait fishers. Below the falls is artificials only, 14-inch max. All wild trout. A beautiful place and a must-see in the area: 100' falls with over one million gallons of spring water per day pouring over and out of the side of the cliff. Cool even in August. Nature trail. A five-minute drive to Lake Britton dam on the Pit for good angling. 128 sites, but in summer, you will likely need reservations. McArthur Burney Falls Memorial State Park, 24898 Highway 89, Burney, CA 96013; park telephone: 916-335-2777 . For reservations call 800-444-PARK.

There are numerous **USFS campgrounds** along Hwy 89 south of Hwy 299. They are all sited on upper Hat Creek, a boisterous little freestone stream, heavily stocked.

**The Hat Creek Hereford Ranch** has a campground with Hat Creek running through it. Ponds stocked with trout.

**Unimproved casual camping** possible throughout the USFS lands in this area. You will need a campfire permit, and a map. Make certain you're not on private timberlands, of which there are a great many hereabouts. Campfire permits are easily obtained at the CDF office in Johnson Park, or at USFS Hat Creek Work Center, a few miles south of Hwy 299 on Hwy 89.

## RESTAURANTS

The author recommends for general ambiance and food:

**Art's Outpost**, 37392 Main, Burney, CA 96013 / 916-335-2835 / Food and service are good; ambiance is pleasant; generous portions; no smoking; bar with cable TV; an attractive and comfortable dining room with a measure of privacy

**The Rex Club**, 37143 Main, Burney, CA 96013 / 916-335-4184 / Good food; OK ambiance; smoking allowed in the adjacent bar, which drifts over into the dining area; salad bar; good filet mignon

**BJs Coffee Hut**, 37314 Main, Burney, CA 96013 / 916-335-4909 / The local cafe; open for breakfast, lunch, and dinner; country food; great breakfast; acceptable dinners

**The Bears Den Restaurant**, Burney, CA 96013 / 916-335-5152 / Fast food a la Denny's; good for breakfast and lunch; avoid it at dinner

**Half Time Pizza**, Burney Shopping, Burney, CA 96013 / 916-335-3998 / Salad bar, big screen TV

**Clearwater House on Hat Creek**, 916-335-5500 / Superb entrees and desserts served family-style in the relaxed atmosphere of the author's fishing lodge; reservations a must for those not staying at Clearwater House

*Also in Burney:*

**Alpine Drive In**, 37148 Main, Burney, CA 96013 / 916-335-2211 / $

**Alvarez Mexican Cafe**, 37063 Main, Burney, CA 96013 / 916-335-2998 / $

## FLY SHOPS AND SPORTING GOODS

As you might expect, there are many good fly shops in this area. Their hours vary by seasons, however, and some close in winter.

*In Cassel:*

**Rising River**, 21549 Cassel Road, Cassel CA 96016 / 916-335-2291 / Full service shop

**Clearwater House in Cassel**, 21568 Cassel Road, 96016 / 916-335-5500 / a destination shop at the author's lodge (see Clearwater House description)

*In Burney:*

Trout Country, 38247 299 E Burney, CA 96013 (PO Box 58, Cassel) / 916-335-5304 / Full service shop; closed during winter

### HOSPITALS

Mayers Memorial, Fall River Mills, CA (17 miles east of Burney) / 916-336-5151 / An emergency room and physicians on duty; helicopter ambulance service is available to the regional hospital in Redding

### AIRPORT

Horizon Air / 800-547 9308

United Express / 800-241-6522

Fall River Mills County Airport / 916-336-9948 / Accommodates prop planes and small jets; no commercial flights

Redding Municipal Airport / 916-224-4320 / Anglers can fly commercially into Redding and drive the 1.5 hours to Hat Creek; the Redding airport is served several times a day from the north and south by United Express, Horizon Air and others; major rental car agencies have desks at the airport

An often overlooked option for traveling to the intermountain area is to fly into Reno, Nevada, and rent a car for the 2.45 hour drive to Burney. It's a beautiful passage from desert to mountains. Flight schedules and fares from out-of-state points can be more attractive than those to Redding.

### AUTO RENTALS

It is often possible to arrange to rent a late model car through the airport operator in Fall River Mills (check in advance — not available as of this writing). Auto rentals are available at Redding Airport:

Avis / 916-221-2855

Budget / 916-228 8416

Hertz / 916-221-4620

### AUTO MECHANIC

Al's Engine Rebuilding, Johnson Park / 916-335-4251 / Favorite auto mechanic in the Burney area: Al Vaught

### FOR MORE INFORMATION

Burney Chamber of Commerce
37088 Main Street
Burney, CA, 96013
916-335-2111

### OTHER ACTIVITIES IN THE AREA

Not to be missed sights/activities/etc. in the Hat Creek area:

1. Crystal Lake State Fish Hatchery. See where the greatest portion of your license dollars go. Interesting, particularly at feeding time. Call to find out when that happens. 916-335-4111

2. Lassen Volcanic National Park. Beautiful. Steam vents, boiling mud, great views, etc. Step across Hat Creek. Walk to Hat Lake, its source. Walk up Lassen Peak. See forever. 595-4444

3. McArthur-Burney Falls State Park. A must-see, as noted. Take the two mile nature trail around the falls. 916-335-2777

4. Fort Crook Museum. Pioneer history and native American artifacts, photos. Fall River Mills. 916-336-5110

5. The Fall River Golf Course. Those who play consider this one of the state's great ones. Cheap. 916-336-5555

6. Thousand Lakes Wilderness. A 25-square-mile pocket wilderness halfway between Burney and Lassen Park, west of Hwy 89. Several pretty lakes. Easy to walk into. Good fishing for smallish fish, mostly rainbow and brookies. Some larger ones in Lake Eiler, the closest to the trailheads. Cool in summer. Permits at the USFS office at Hat Creek. 916-335-4103; or in Fall River 916-336-5521

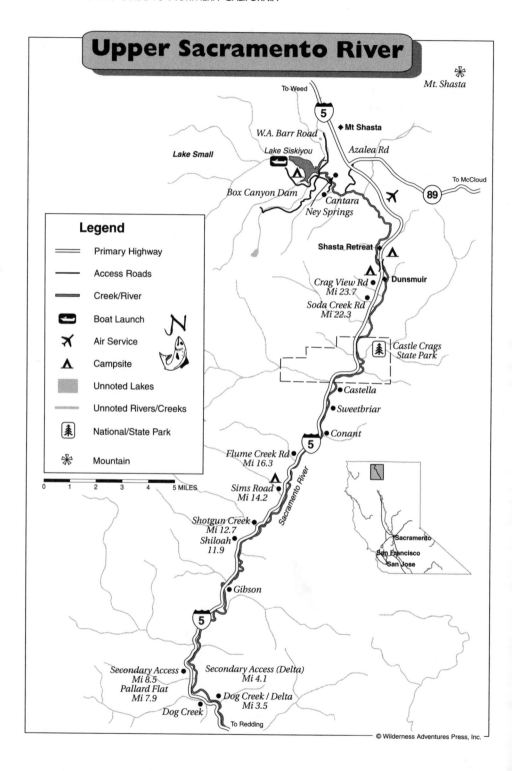

# Upper Sacramento River

To Weed

✳ Mt. Shasta

5

◆ Mt Shasta

W.A. Barr Road

Lake Small

Lake Siskiyou

Azalea Rd

To McCloud

89

Box Canyon Dam

Cantara
Ney Springs

Shasta Retreat

Crag View Rd
Mi 23.7

Dunsmuir

Soda Creek Rd
Mi 22.3

Castle Crags
State Park

### Legend

| | |
|---|---|
| ═══ | Primary Highway |
| ── | Access Roads |
| ═══ | Creek/River |
| 🚤 | Boat Launch |
| ✈ | Air Service |
| ⛺ | Campsite |
| ▨ | Unnoted Lakes |
| ⋯ | Unnoted Rivers/Creeks |
| 🌲 | National/State Park |
| ✳ | Mountain |

N

• Castella

• Sweetbriar

• Conant

Flume Creek Rd •
Mi 16.3

5

Sims Road •
Mi 14.2

Sacramento River

Shotgun Creek •
Mi 12.7
Shiloah •
11.9

0  1  2  3  4  5 MILES

Sacramento

San Francisco
San Jose

• Gibson

5

Secondary Access •
Mi 8.5
Pallard Flat
Mi 7.9

Secondary Access (Delta)
Mi 4.1

• Dog Creek / Delta
Mi 3.5

Dog Creek

To Redding

© Wilderness Adventures Press, Inc.

# Upper Sacramento River: Freestone by the Freeway

*by Duane Milleman*

What begins in rivulets running off the Trinity Divide west of Mount Shasta ends as a behemoth floating oil tankers beneath the Golden Gate Bridge. At the uppermost reaches, tiny trout spawn in clear springs; in the lower skulk sturgeon longer than a man, their ancient bodies dense with the heavy-metal pollutants of a century. Between snowmelt and sea, the Sacramento River offers diverse opportunities to the inquisitive flyfisherman — beauty and bounty and exquisite races of fish. It is the stem into which water flows from much of northeast California via the McCloud, Pit, Feather, Yuba, and American Rivers. Add to these the drainage of the west and east sides of the Sacramento Valley, and this great river's watershed encompasses many thousands of squares miles.

Two sections are presented here, each premier trout fisheries: the Upper Sacramento, from the town of Mt. Shasta down to the vast reservoir of Lake Shasta; and the top end of the tailwater called the "Lower Sacramento," between the cities of Redding and Anderson. In terms of fishing conditions, the two are related only by name.

To those who have spent time on the upper Sacramento River, it would seem trifling to characterize it as a "roadside fishery". This is a majestic freestone stream plunging down a deep canyon beneath peaks like Castle Crags. The fact is, however, that the great majority of the river's 37-mile course now races right along I-5, the main north-south freeway in California. Further indignity — convenient to fishers, when not deadly to all aquatic life — the upper Sac is paralleled for most of those miles by the tracks of the Southern Pacific Railroad. A roadside fishery, in other words—spectacular but accessible. But there is so much river here that solitude, or at least a lot of room, is usually a quick hike down the tracks.

## Fishing the Upper Sacramento

Any overview of fishing this river must begin with the effect of water flow. With as large an area as the upper Sacramento drains, the spring thaw can make of it a brawler best suited for kayaks. Of course the river can be fished then, just as a brawler may be boxed — "knock yourself out," is the proper phrase — by pounding big stonefly nymphs deep into current.

When the Sacramento drops to normal summer flows, usually around early or mid-June, it is not merely more easily waded, but quite a bit warmer, with more intense and predictable hatches.

By mid-June another important cycle has begun, that of fish migrating from the vastness of Shasta Lake. Lake rainbows first make an appearance at the Delta and LaMoine sections, with a run of 15–18 inches. Many will go higher upstream. Soon, these fish, augmented by successive waves and the year-round local residents, will make the upper Sacramento a premier dry fly fishery. Throw terrestrials during warm days, particularly hoppers and beetles — streamside foliage here is sometimes dense with the latter—about jassid-size (a quarter inch) and shape. By evenings, July through September, make sure to take a station on one of the big pools or wide runs — the dry fly fishing doesn't get better than this.

In late August of some years, yet another run of lake fish will enter the river — brown trout spawners. These are comparably rare, however, and seldom get much higher than the Gibson area.

A last general note: the upper Sacramento is considered the homewater of Ted Fay, an innovative, unpretentious guide and tier, whose big, buggy flies are considered classic (and collectible, if wrapped by his hand). They are also deadly, especially when fished on the upstream short- or close-line technique popularized by Fay, and now practiced by Joe Kimsey, of the Ted Fay Fly Shop in Dunsmuir, and by other shrewd nymph fishers on many freestone Western streams.

## Tactics and Tackle

The upper Sac has the right sort of water for your favorite rod and technique, from a two weight to cast a midge at a slick in the dusk, to a seven-weight for hurling streamers to brutes holding deep. Fay's short-line tactic, however, takes particular advantage of the uppers Sac's many miles of riffles, shallow to medium depth runs, and pocket water. Essentially, it is close-range fish-hunting adapted to covering a great deal of water in conditions where an angler's approach to a fish is disguised by turbulence — often to within four or five feet. On this river the system will produce from morning until mid afternoon all season long.( It will produce elsewhere as well.) If you opt for a lesson, contact any of the guides listed or the fly shop that Fay started in Dunsmuir. For the solo artist, a somewhat abbreviated version follows:

First of all, short line fishing generally requires aggressive wading, usually up and across stream in heavy current. In early and late season, that calls for chest-high neoprenes. Lighter waders are fine for summer, and you might even want to wade wet when fishing midday. A wading staff is recommended if you're not used to fronting freestone water — and even if you are experienced but expect to cross the river often. All season long use boots with felt soles. Studs help.

While a floating flyline is the rule with Fay's technique, line type is almost irrelevant, since you will be using so little. Rod weight is also pretty much up to the angler, though the tactic would be rough on a light, split cane heirloom, and a heavy rod will soon prove exhausting. Longer is better, however, to allow for greater coverage. An ideal rod might be a five-weight between 9 and 10 feet.

The leader should be six or seven feet long, ending at 3X or 4X. In his two-fly system, Fay used a double-slip loop and a cinch knot to attach a short, stiff dropper between 18 inches to two feet up from the point fly. The dropper fly might sometimes be a brushy dry that would do double duty as indicator. Usually, however, both flies are wets and heavy.

*Fish on! Prime nymph
run on the upper
Sacramento
(Photo: Ken Morrish)*

The key is to get these down fast, in a cast of no more than 10 feet (or 15 — if you count the length of the rod, plus leader, plus two feet or less of flyline extending from the tiptop). Wading up-or-cross stream, use the weight of the flies to slap casts down along seams, or quarter casts upstream into current-cushions in front of large stones and in the pockets of slower water beside and behind these. No long drifts here; in these tumbles it's a matter of inches. Even so, line control is critical: the rod is held high, extended at about a 45-degree angle, to follow the leader as it pricks the surface of the water. With any apparent motion at this point of entry — a twitch, a jerk backward or forward or to either side — strike. Strike hard. Duck until you've got the technique down. Practice.

While close-lining lacks something of flyfishing's traditional elegance, it is an intense process — easy to try, difficult to master. It's also astonishingly effective in an expert's hands, works well on any stream under similar conditions, and can be easily adapted to fishing with an indicator, even a big one supporting several large split shot.

With indicator or without, there are miles of upper Sac water perfect for Fay's game. What's sometimes overlooked, however, is that the same kind of rough, strongly flowing riffle or run on which his system works deep is also excellent for fishing dry flies. Dapping deer hair humpies or elk hair caddis on a short line can bring up rainbows most of the season. The best bet is to fish quickly, covering likely spots with a few casts; then move on upstream.

Another form of dry fly action on the upper Sacramento is classic. The river has scores of long, slow pools where 15-foot leaders are required, along with a close match to one of the upper Sac's many hatches. This can be 6X or 7X work for the two-to-four weight rod, throwing flies sized 16 to 22.

In deep sections of the same pools, however, you may wish to dredge woolly buggers on a sink tip for the big lurkers that live here...the Sac offers enough opportunities to baffle.

Between extremes, however, is an abundance of shallow to medium depth water perfectly suited for standard techniques and tackle, say a four or five weight rod. Longer rods will allow better line control on a freestone stream like this one and also help you to reach pockets just beyond wading reach — say nine to 10 feet. Rigged with an easy-to-mend floating line and a 10 foot, 4X leader, this setup is fine for dries in fast water, will serve for indicator nymphing, and may be extended with 5X, 6X or 7X tippet to fish dries and emergers in slow pools. It can also be chopped back three feet at the butt in order to make a dedicated close line nymphing rig. Split shot or heavily weighted flies — sometimes both — will suffice to fish the majority of deeper runs and pools.

Hatches on the Sac are surprisingly diverse and pleasingly predictable for a river that has scant weedbeds and a heavy winter flow. The early season (May to early June) usually sees the emerging migrations of the large stoneflies, *Pteronarcys californica* and *Acroneurias*, though stoneflies in general are the insects that have not come back quickly from the spill (see "Upper Sacramento: Poison and Redemption"). As noted earlier, spring is also the brawling season of water, when you may hook fish by working big flies along edges of the river where friction slows the flow.

Early summer (June and July) brings the season of mayflies, particularly *Ephemerella* and *Baetis* species, along with more stoneflies (little yellows) and various caddis. Midday action diminishes with hotter days until nearly all hatches come off in the evening; then it's not unusual to have several species hatching hard at once, filling the air of dusk with wings as trout rise the length of a pool.

Midsummer (late July through early September) is definitely terrestrial time, with hoppers, beetles, and ants the major daytime players. As indicated and now reiterated, beetles frequent streamside foliage on the upper Sac in significant numbers — the fish expect them. Note that there is often a lull in action, however, this time of season, between 2 p.m. to about 5 p.m. Mayflies and caddis still make the evenings, though they are now smaller in size, 18-20.

Late season (late September through October) is an exciting time on the upper Sac. Though the blizzard hatches are long gone, fish are on the feed and nymphing is the best of the year. An added bonus is the enormous October caddis. While rise to big adults are just tremendous — boils, really — it's caddis pupae swimming up through the water column that turn the fish on; they will pound emergers on a swing. Leaves are turning color by this time of autumn, the water runs low and clear, and the crisp air cools. The crowds have all gone home.

## Fly Patterns by Season

### Early Season (May 1 to June 15)

Hartwell stonefly, size 4
Madame X, size 8
Lempke's Salmon Fly, size 4

Black rubberlegs, sizes 6-8
Poxyback Golden Stone, sizes 8-10
Birds nest, size 10

### Early Summer (June 1 to July 15)

Yellow humpy, size 12-16
Light cahill, sizes 14-16
Adams, size 14-16
Silhouette dun, sizes 16
Elk hair caddis, sizes 12-14 Z-
Matthews' X caddis, size 14

A.P. Black Nymph, sizes 12-14
Poxyback Golden Stone, #12
Birds Nest, size 12-14
Poxyback PMD, size 16
Wing Caddis, size 12-14
Prince Nymph, size 12-14

### Late Summer (July 15 to September 15) --Same flies as early summer except one to two sizes smaller

Griffith's gnat, size 20
Ascending midge pupa, size 20
Palomino midge, dark, size 20
Parachute ant, size 16

Burk's Para-Hopper, size 12
Burk's Yellow Jacket, size 10
Evasote Beetle, size 12
Yellow stone nymph, size 16

### Late Season (September 15 to November 15)Same flies as early summer except one or two sizes smaller, plus:

Stimulators, size 8 October
Red fox squirrel, size 10

Caddis Emerger #8
Gold Bead Red Fox Squirrel

## Access on the Upper Sacramento

As already noted, I-5 and the Southern Pacific Railway parallel almost all the upper Sacramento. Not at the very top, however, in the feeder streams, or along the South Fork of the Sacramento, which may be accessed by paved roads above Lake Siskiyou. Small, wild trout abound in these waters — a walking fisher can find a day's solitude catching rainbows as colorful as their name. By the time these tributaries mix together in Lake Siskiyou behind Box Canyon Dam, brown trout, stockers and bass have joined the natives.

From Box Canyon Dam to the city of Dunsmuir, the upper Sacramento flows through a beautiful canyon with limited access. The upstream edge of this stretch is "Box Canyon" of the dam's name; the walls are shear rock. With some difficulty an angler can wade up about two miles from Ney Springs fisherman's access. This is exciting water — springs bubble out everywhere, often in tiny waterfalls — with some big fish. Downstream from the access point, it's much the same: excellent. Ney Springs Access can by reached by crossing Box Canyon Dam and turning left onto the Castle Lake Road. Take the first gravel road to the left, then follow signs to the parking area.

The second access into this canyon stretch is called Cantera. Take the Old Stage Road south from Mt. Shasta to Cantera Street, then turn right. The road quickly turns to gravel and drops down 1.3 miles into the canyon to an area called Cantera Loop. Note that the railroad tracks that follow the river from Shasta Lake to Mt. Shasta climb out of the canyon at this point in a series of switchbacks. Note also that it is here that the toxic spill took place, killing all aquatic life downstream to Shasta Lake, some 35 miles. (see sidebar). Fish above this point were not affected, so from these natives the fisheries biologists took brood stock to repopulate the dead river below.

From Cantera Loop, a fisher can either walk or wade upstream toward Ney Springs Access above, or travel down the railroad tracks for several miles. A popular way to fish this water is to hike down the tracks, then fish back to your vehicle. This section of river is still relatively small water and can be easily crossed. The fish are not always small — 20-inchers have been hooked.

Last access to the canyon is in the city of Dunsmuir. Take the road to Shasta Retreat at the north end of town, cross the bridge and park, then hike up the tracks into the canyon. Here the routine is just the opposite as described above: anglers fish upstream all day, then "take the tracks" back to their cars.

Once again, small waterfalls and springs make this portion of the canyon particularly beautiful. So many springs, too — the authors know of no river where may be found as many springs as in this part of the Sacramento's canyon. One testimonial to their chilly prevalence is the presence of brook trout up to 12 inches; another is a swelling volume of water that makes crossing back and forth more difficult than in the Cantera section upstream.

Exit the canyon with this in mind: California Trout, a nonprofit conservation organization noted elsewhere in this book, has purchased property at both ends of the canyon and now is pushing to make the entire stretch a designated catch-and-release fishery. Cal Trout's long-term plans include building a trail the entire length of the canyon to keep anglers from having to hike the rails.

As of this writing, the five-mile stretch of river from Dunsmuir to Soda Creek is planted with hatchery trout by the State Department of Fish and Game. It is easily accessed from both sides of the river by paved roads. Though much of the bank is lined by houses, the river is easily wadable — and a joy to fish. There is, however, a marked increase in flow, with still fewer places to cross.

*The upper Sacramento under Mt. Shasta's watchful eye. (Photo: Chip O'Brien)*

Five trout a day may be killed in this planted area. That regulation and the stocking program make this a much-used baitfishing section, with fairly intense pressure during summer months. While these are not necessarily reasons to avoid the area, keep the put-and-take prerogative in mind.

From Soda Creek downstream to the small community at Sweetbriar, some 4.5 miles in all, much of the river bank is colonized by vacation homes and cabins. There are fish here, but the proximity of people is more conspicuous than elsewhere on the river, except in the section contained by Castle Crags State Park, with a picnic area at Castella. This is a nice lunch spot, and a well maintained trail follows the river for several hundred yards.

For a less traveled piece of water, consider instead the Conant Access, one mile south of Sweetbriar. Here you can drive up or downriver for short distances after exiting I-5, or park next to the tracks within a few yards of the freeway. The water is quite similar up or downstream, and though the volume of flow is visibly greater, the river may still be crossed in many places. In fact, much of this stretch has made-to-order wading. With the railroad tracks so close, you can quickly hike to more remote pockets.

Just one mile downriver of Conant is the Flume Creek area. There is a Flume exit off the freeway, but a better choice is a wide pullout just below that. If the gate is open, you can drive right down to the river; if it's locked, make sure to park well off

*Beautiful falls on the Upper Sacramento. (Photo: Ken Morrish)*

the freeway. Now you have the choice of fishing up toward the Conant area or going downriver. Down is probably a better bet, as it will put you onto a rare two-mile section of the river away from I-5. This is bigger water, however, and crossing must be attempted with caution. Pick your spot, go slowly, use a wading staff. If you proceed sensibly you can fish as you wade upstream, so once again it's a good bet to walk down the tracks for a mile or so and then fish your way back.

The next exit going south on I-5 is Sims road. This leads to Sims Campground and a slew of water, both upstream and down, that can only be accessed by hiking the tracks. The same rules apply here: walk downstream until you feel you have enough water to fish and start working back to the car, or fish upstream and then walk back. If you do head upstream, hike past the first half mile of water to get beyond some very heavy water. Soon after, you'll come to one of the prettiest stretches of the river.

There are accesses before Shotgun Creek, but they are secondary, with no exit signs on I-5. If you want to try one of these, look sharp for a dirt road heading toward the river 1.3 miles south of Sims on I-5 (it's nothing more than a wide pulloff from the northbound lane). Shotgun Creek does have a well-marked exit. The creek flows under the freeway. After parking well off the road, you may look down and see a train trestle. Cross this to the railroad track on the opposite side, follow the rails downstream a mile, then fish your way back to the trestle.

The Gibson exit is next on your trek down I-5. Once you get down to the tracks you'll have a lot of water to fish in either direction. It's almost two miles upstream to the trestle by the last access described. There is a tunnel on the way, however, that is best to fish or hike around. This is water that is still manageable, but you will find few places to cross. As you proceed south on I-5 from the Gibson area, you will see the truck stop at Pollard Flat. There is no easy access to the river here, but the restaurant is fun, the food edible.

LaMoine Exit is 1.4 miles south of Pollard Flat and will get you down to the tracks. From here it is the same story as always hike up or down to water that best suits your fishing style.

Three miles south of LaMoine is the Delta exit. You can drive right down to the small community of Delta and park by the tracks. Don't let the presence of houses dissuade you. There is some terrific water upriver of Delta that is well worth your attention.

There is a secondary access between Delta and LaMoine at a road approximately .5 miles north of the Delta exit. It's tricky to find but leads to the tracks, where you can actually drive up or down for a ways to some wonderful water. Big water and heavy going — only very strong waders should even attempt to cross.

When you exit the freeway at Delta you can also drive downstream to Dog Creek. There is a bridge there that will permit you to cross the river. The tracks, as always, will let you access that mysterious water just out of sight around the next bend.

The last exit of note on our trek along the river is at Lakeshore. After taking the exit, follow Lakeshore for 1.5 miles to a dirt road that will lead you down to the river.

If it sounds like a lot of water, and a great deal of opportunity…then you do have the idea.

# Stream Facts: Upper Sacramento

### River Characteristics
- From below the dam it flows through a canyon where it is fed by many springs and tributaries, gaining size until it becomes a major river marked by deep pools and runs. Lots of riffle water in the upper and middle reaches...Any and everything an angler might want in a freestone stream.

### Seasons
- Last Saturday in April to November 15.

### Special Regulations
- Box Canyon Dam below Lake Siskiyou to Shasta Lake—Catch and release, artificial lures with barbless hooks only, except for six mile section between Scarlett Way Bridge (in Dunsmuir) and the confluence of Soda Creek, where there is 5-kill limit, artificial lures with barbless hooks only.

### Trout
- Rainbows both wild and stocked (most of the latter in the 5-kill limit section between Scarlett Way Bridge and the confluence of Soda Creek.) Trout to 22 inches have been taken since the spill, but the average—at the moment—is something less than a foot. Total fish is now at about 2500 per mile, with catchables closer to 1500. A few migrating browns from Lake Shasta may enter the lower end of river.

### River Miles
- Just over 37 miles

### River Flows
- Typically very high the first 4 to 6 weeks of the season. Levels drop dramatically in June, when the river is much easier to wade. Call a local shop or guide to inquire about river conditions.

### Boat Ramps
- None

### Maps
- Delorme pages 36 and 46

### Hub Cities
- Dunsmuir, Mount Shasta (see McCloud River), Redding (see Lower Sacramento)

## UPPER SACRAMENTO RIVER MAJOR HATCHES

| Insect | A | M | J | J | A | S | O | N | Flies |
|---|---|---|---|---|---|---|---|---|---|
| Salmonfly *Pteronarcys californica* | ■ | | | | | | | | Nymphs: Black Rubber Legs #6–8; Kaufman's Stone #4–6 Dries: Sofa Pillow #6 |
| Golden Stone *Hesperoperla pacifica* | | ■ | ■ | | | | | | Hare's Ear #8–18; Poxyback Golden Stone #8–10; Burlap Golden Stone #8–10; Madame X #8; Stimulator (Gold) #6–8 |
| Little Yellow Stone *Isoperla* | | | ■ | ■ | ■ | ■ | ■ | | Nymphs: Poxyback Yellow Stone #14–16 Dries: CDC Yellow Stone #16; Yellow Humpy #16; Pale Yellow Elk Hair Caddis #16 |
| Midges | | | ■ | ■ | ■ | ■ | ■ | ■ | Palamino Midge #20; Ascending Midge Pupa #20; Griffiths Gnat #20 |
| October Caddis *Dicosmoecus* | | | | | | ■ | ■ | ■ | October Caddis Emerger #8; Gold Beadhead; Red Fox Squirrel #10; Stimulator #8 |
| Sedges *Hydropsychid Rhyacophila* | | | ■ | ■ | ■ | ■ | | | Nymphs: Mercer's Z-Wing Caddis; Bird's Nest; LaFontaine Sparkle Caddis #14-18 Dries: Elk Hair Caddis #14-18 |
| Pale Morning Dun *Ephemerella infrequens* | | | ■ | ■ | ■ | ■ | ■ | ■ | Poxyback PMD #16; Burk's Hunchback Infrequens #14–18; Pheasant Tail Nymph #14–16; Quigley's Cripple #16–18; Rusty Spinner #16–18; Paradun #18–20 |
| Blue Winged Olive *Baetis* | | ■ | ■ | ■ | ■ | ■ | ■ | ■ | Pheasant Tail; Burk's Legged Nymphs; Mercer's Poxyback Baetis; Olive Paradun #18–20; Parachute Adams #18–22 |
| Grasshoppers | | | | ■ | ■ | ■ | | | Dave's Hopper #12; Spent Hopper #12 |
| Beetles | | | ■ | ■ | | | | | Evasote Beetle #12 |
| Carpenter Ants | | | ■ | ■ | | | | | Parachute Ant #16 |

# Upper Sacramento: Poison and Redemption

*by Seth Norman*

It may well be true that the Sacramento River is northern California's fortune and its future. Without Sacramento water — or that now included in its drainage — much of the valley that produces valuable crops would be barren; and the metropolitan areas that depend on its waters would be in serious trouble, as would those fisheries still nurtured in the Delta and Bay.

Given this value, cavalier treatment of the river is at least peculiar, maybe deadly. Vast quantities of water are diverted to grow rice in a desert and cotton, which demands even more water than rice. From Anderson down — a distance of more than 150 miles — no resident fish may be safely eaten, due to the PCBs, dioxins, heavy metals, and other toxins found in their flesh. (Most are too tainted to be legally used as fertilizer.) Of course, anadromous stocks are seriously depleted, and some salmon and steelhead runs are endangered.

Unhappily, that's all old news on the Sacramento. It took a massive chemical spill to bring the upper river into the public eye: on July 14, 1991, a Southern Pacific railroad tanker spilled from the Cantera Bridge Loop — a section of track known for mishaps — dumping its load of metam sodium pesticide, a soil fumigant, into the water. Within days a solution never deemed "toxic" — remember that — had annihilated virtually all aquatic life downstream to Lake Shasta, leaving it dead as a septic tank...35 plus miles, at a density of 6700 to 8800 fish pe r —those figures based on a carcass count.

Five years and $32,000,000 of reparation later the river begins to recover. Wild rainbow stock captured from above the spill site were captured and spawned, their young transplanted. Their population now rises to perhaps 30 percent of what it was. Some insect species have returned in abundance, notably the various may and caddis fly families. Other bugs, particularly the *Pteronarcys californica*, or salmon flies, have not yet made much of a comeback.

In the meantime a variety of battles were fought and are still in the offing. Perhaps the most acrimonious of these conflicts pits people who hope to develop the upper Sacramento as a wild fish river against folks who want to augment the natives with Department of Fish and Game stockers, "like it's always been" for the last half century.

An uneasy compromise exists at this writing, as reflected by the regulations: a six-mile stretch receives stockings of fish that anglers may kill at the rate of five, but zero limits apply above and below this section, artificials only, with barbless hooks required.

In the case of the upper Sacramento, there's a beneficial task that visiting flyfishers can perform rather simply: when you buy gas here, stay in a motel or eat in a restaurant — whenever you put money down and into this economy — make it clear that you came for good flyfishing. Consider yourself feathering a nest: later decisions will certainly consider locals' vision of their best interest, as well as the health of the river. If you're a particularly subtle sort, you might also sidle around to asking about the Southern Pacific. Given that conditions at Cantera Loop Bridge have been little improved...just when do the railroad's neighbors expect the next big spill? and their next bout with economic and environmental devastation?

"Never" would have been the answer you got on July 13, 1991.

For more information see "The Return of the Upper Sacramento," by Chip O'Brien in *California Fly Fisher*, Volume 2 Number 5.

*Nymphing a pool on the upper Sacramento. (Photo: Ken Morrish)*

# Dunsmuir

### Elevation – 2,301 • Population – 2,170

Dunsmuir, population 3780, is located along the river, 44 miles north of Redding. While not as large as Redding, nor as upscale as Mount Shasta has become, Dunsmuir makes a good hub, with all the services and accommodations most anglers will need.

From the town of Mount Shasta, near the northern end of the river, you can reach most of the better water in 10 minutes to an hour. In Mount Shasta, the author recommends the Mount Shasta Ranch, a Bed and Breakfast which will please anybody; and the new Mount Shasta Resort. The Strawberry Inn, Mount Aire Motel and The Tree House are also good bets. (See Mount Shasta in McCloud River chapter.)

You can also easily reach the Upper Sacramento from Redding to the south, in 40 minutes to an hour. In Redding, the Red Lion, LaQuinta Inn, and Oxford Suites are very comfortable, and the Palisades Paradise, a bed and breakfast overlooking the city and river, is especially nice. The number of eating places in Redding is enormous. (See Lower Sacramento chapter.)

## ACCOMMODATIONS

**Cave Springs Motel Resort**, 4727 Dunsmuir Ave., Dunsmuir, CA 96025 / 530-235-2721 / $$

**Cedar Lodge Motel**, 4201 Dunsmuir Ave., Dunsmuir, CA 96025-1723 / 530-235-4331 / $$

**Acorn Inn,** 4310 Dunsmuir Ave., Dunsmuir, CA 96025-1707 / 530-235-4805 / $

**Nutglade Station B&B**, 5829 Sacramento Ave., Dunsmuir, CA 96025-2321 / 530-235-0532 / $$

**Oak Tree Inn**, 6604 Dunsmuir Ave., Dunsmuir, CA 96025-2626 / 530-235-2884 / $$

**River Walk Inn B&B**, 4300 Stagecoach Rd., Dunsmuir, CA 96025 / 530-235-4300 / $$

**Private Cabins**, available through Bill Tate, Dunsmuir Fly Fishing Company, 5839 Dunsmuir Ave., Dunsmuir, CA 96025 / 916-238-0705 / $45 for a one bedroom to $100 for three bedrooms for up to six people; both are right on the water.

**Eagle's Nest**, 1.5 miles south of Dunsmuir at the Railroad Avenue offramp / 800-300-2850 / This is a private home with eight fenced acres on the river, two bedrooms, two baths, a deck overlooking the river, views of Mount Shasta, and a professional kennel with a 30-foot run. The river in this section is a mix of flatwater, riffles, and runs — a good place for tubing and kids. Two night minimum, $150 per night. There is also a separate studio with kitchenette and bath, available with house rental, for $35 a night.

Other cabin rentals and lodging are available by calling 800-235-2028

## CAMPGROUNDS

**Lake Siskiyou,** Mount Shasta National Forest / 530-235-2684 / Above the river on the Lake, east of the town of Mount Shasta

**Sims Flat Campground,** right on the river at the Sims Flat exit, Mount Shasta National Forest / 530-235-2684

**Castle Crags State Park,** opposite side of the freeway from the river / 530-235-2684

## RESTAURANTS

**Micki's Better Burgers,** 4905 Dunsmuir Ave., Dunsmuir, CA 96025-1807 / 530-235-2220 / $

**Maddalena Cafe,** 5801 Sacramento Ave., Dunsmuir, CA 96025-2321 / 530-235-2725 / $$ / Excellent food, dinners only, Thursday – Sunday

**Mandos Restaurant** 412 N Mnt Shasta Boulavard / 530-918-9158

**River Cafe,** Dunsmuir, CA / 530-235-4702

## FLY SHOPS AND SPORTING GOODS (see also Lower Sacramento chapter)

Dunsmuir Fly Fishing Company, 5839 Dunsmuir CA 96025 / 530-235-0705

Ted Fay Fly Shop, 4310 Dunsmuir Ave. Dunsmuir, CA 96025 / 530-235-2969

## AUTOMOTIVE REPAIRS

**Advanced Automotive,** 5756 Westside Rd., Unit F, Redding, CA 96001 / 530-244-4423 / Good mechanics, reasonable prices

## AIRPORT

**Redding Municipal Airport** / 916/224-4320 / Served by Horizon Air 800-547-9308 and United Airlines / 800-241-6522.

## HOSPITALS

**Mercy Medical Center,** 2175 Rosaline Ave., Redding, CA 96001 / 530-225-6000

**Redding Medical Center,** 1100 Butte St., Redding, CA 96001 / 530-244-5400

**Redding Specialty Hospital,** 2801 Eureka Way, Redding, CA 96001 / 530-246-9000

## AUTO RENTALS

The following have offices at the airport:

**Avis** / 530-221-2855

**Budget** / 530-228 8416

**Hertz** / 530-221-4620

## FOR MORE INFORMATION

Dunsmuir Chamber of Commerce
4841 Dunsmuir Avenue
Dunsmuir, CA, 96025
530-235-2177

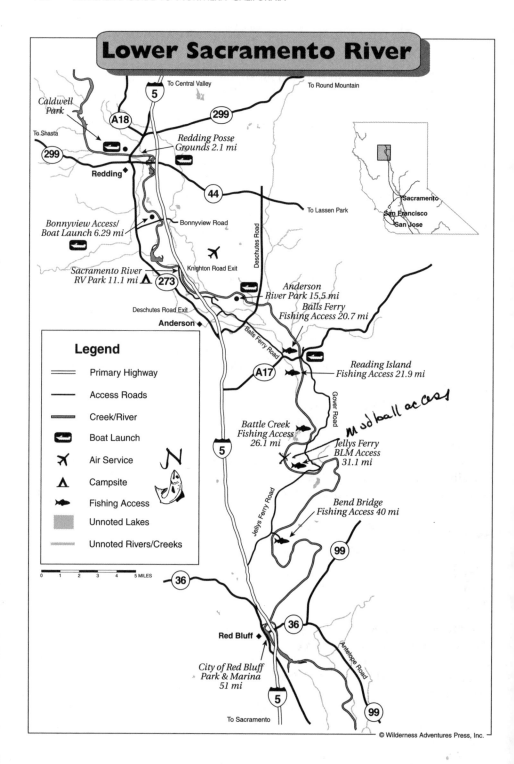

# Lower Sacramento River

To Central Valley
5
To Round Mountain

Caldwell
Park
A18
299

To Shasta
299

Redding Posse
Grounds 2.1 mi

Redding

44
To Lassen Park

Bonnyview Access/
Boat Launch 6.29 mi
Bonnyview Road

Deschutes Road

Knighton Road Exit

Sacramento River
RV Park 11.1 mi
273

Deschutes Road Exit
Anderson

Anderson
River Park 15.5 mi
Balls Ferry
Fishing Access 20.7 mi

Balls Ferry Road

A17
Reading Island
Fishing Access 21.9 mi

Gover Road

Mudball access

Battle Creek
Fishing Access
26.1 mi

Jellys Ferry
BLM Access
31.1 mi

Bend Bridge
Fishing Access 40 mi

5

Jellys Ferry Road

99

36

36

Red Bluff

City of Red Bluff
Park & Marina
51 mi

Antelope Road

5

99

To Sacramento

## Legend

| | |
|---|---|
| ═══ | Primary Highway |
| ── | Access Roads |
| ── | Creek/River |
| 🚤 | Boat Launch |
| ✈ | Air Service |
| ▲ | Campsite |
| 🐟 | Fishing Access |
| | Unnoted Lakes |
| | Unnoted Rivers/Creeks |

N

0  1  2  3  4  5 MILES

Sacramento
San Francisco
San Jose

© Wilderness Adventures Press, Inc.

# Lower Sacramento River: Bright Water, Big Fish

### by Chip O'Brien

If a small stream feels as intimate as a familiar old writing desk then the lower Sacramento might suggest the vastness and complexity of a modular furniture warehouse. Often 100 hundred yards wide in the 25-mile section of most interest to flyfishers, running 4,000–15,000 cubic feet per second in fishing condition — to 79,000 cubic feet per second at peak flow — this section of river will likely convince an angler that, "You've Reached the Big Time" and anything can happen on water so bright, wide open and beautiful.

What's certain is the chance to land some very large trout.

## Overview

The lower Sacramento flows out from beneath Keswick Dam just above Redding, a town of 72,000 straddling Interstate 5, 200 miles north-northeast of San Francisco. The river sweeps through sections heavily wooded with oaks and cottonwoods and along steep cliffs studded with modern office buildings. It glides through quaint city parks and bird sanctuaries, under bustling city streets, past river front homes ranging from humble to palatial. It is the lower Sac that provides Redding with its unique character — few urban areas anywhere can claim such terrific opportunities for anglers. Since much of the best fishing water is within or just below the city limits, Redding residents are happily accustomed to gazing from their back porches or windows at determined guides rowing drift boats against heavy current, watching as anglers cast, mend and cast again. It's a familiar ritual to these viewers, but you may be sure that if somebody hooks a better fish, the event will be described in detail around water coolers, kitchen tables, and coffee shop counters.

In Redding you can always find someone who wants to talk fishing, as well as every accommodation for the fisher. "River City" Redding has numerous modern hotels, campgrounds, restaurants, services and hospitals.

## The Fishery

Rainbow trout are the primary focus of most anglers on this section of the Sacramento. If you've ever played a big fish in a big river, you understand why. Because of the strength of these trout ( what they can do to tackle), experienced fishers invest in a quality fly reel rather than risk that wrenching pop as a spool spins out to the backing knot. Powerful and lovely, these 'bows are also a bit mysterious. Little is known about their specific origins and classification.

It's also difficult to sort them out. In a "normal" Western river that runs to the ocean, the lunkers would be steelhead. In the lower Sac, however, rainbows routinely live six to eight years — lots of time to grow. The range in their coloration is also unusual. You might first catch a fish with an olive back, big black spots, and a white belly underneath a lateral of rusty maroon. Then, from the same spot, you'll land another with a gray back, a few tiny spots and just the slightest hint of pink down the side. The third specimen will confuse things again, having all the features of a rainbow trout and a bright orange slash under its head like a cutthroat.

Theories abound as to how such variety came about. The current consensus — if there is one — opines that the olive-backed fish with big spots are probably native, resident rainbows of the area. The gray-backed fish with tiny spots are either steelhead, or a steelhead strain that, for reasons unknown, didn't swim to the sea. (Scientists differ on exactly why certain rainbow trout with access to the ocean make the trek to salt water and others do not.) Then there's the real steelhead in the system, still anadromous .

Some locals claim the talent to distinguish resident rainbows from stay-at-home steelhead and the sea-run variety, but the only sure way is to check scales under a microscope. And nobody's saying too much about the cutthroat-marked rainbows. for while the species will cross-breed, there's no record of cutts ever entering the Sacramento River system...Suffice it to assert that these are fine-looking fish, bulldog fighters — that once you've had one on the end of your line you'll likely declare them a mystery you enjoyed hooking into.

The lower Sacramento also hosts an astonishing array of other fish species besides trout, including largemouth and smallmouth bass, several kinds of sunfish, four distinct runs of Chinook salmon, Sacramento suckers, hardheads, squawfish, carp and others. A few people will quietly insist that the river still contains centuries-old sturgeon in the deepest sections, but few facts are available (except that the editor has seen and hooked them). One day while trout fishing, the author nearly walked on water after spotting what looked like a three-foot snake wrapped around a rock next to his wading boot, presumably some kind of eel or lamprey, that ran up from the ocean to spawn. Let's hope it went back.

### Flows: The Ups and Downs

The lower Sac is subject to seasonal high and low flows that contradict the cycles of nature. Releases from massive Shasta Dam blast water through Redding during the summer "dry season" to generate hydroelectric power and satisfy water contracts for agriculture downstream. During the winter, however, even as the drainage area receives virtually all its rain for the year, flows are kept to a minimum in order to re-fill Shasta Lake for the next summer. Knowing the river's "cfs" (cubic feet per second ) is crucial for anglers and makes all the difference in what to expect.

In brief, "normal" flows during summer high-water (mid-May through mid-September) range from 12,000 to 15,000 cfs. At this time the river is best accessed from a drift boat. Some anglers use these primarily as transport between riffles where wading is possible; others split the day between fishing from the drift boat and wading.

When the river drops around mid-September, wading opportunities become more numerous, and a drift boat is not necessary to access the best water. Winter

*Drift boats offer the best access to the Sacramento. (Photo: Chip O'Brien)*

flows between 4,000 to 5,000 cfs favor the angler who enjoys thoroughly covering an area on foot, while anglers who prefer drifting during this season have the chance of fishing many places in a day.

The two best months of the year to fish the lower Sac are April and October. Each is excellent for a distinctly different reason: April is the peak of the *Brachycentrus caddis* hatch, an emergence so abundant that it may cover the water, and therefore is known as the "Blanket Caddis." October, on the other hand, offers great fishing partly because there's so little insect activity, which works to the advantage of a fisher who understands a prime mover in the system: salmon.

During fall and winter the river supports spawning runs of Chinook coming in from the ocean. These kings dig round, bowl-shaped depressions in the gravel bottom of shallow riffles, "redds" where they deposit eggs for the next generation of salmon to emerge. As a kind of housekeeping ritual, the hen salmon fans accumulated debris from the redd. Inevitably, a few eggs are washed away.

They won't survive — not on the lower Sac, where salmon "omelets" are the season's favorite trout food. This is when, and why, a well-presented single-egg pattern, dropped deftly below a redd, will yield aggressive strikes. The run of a fish fat with such protein will warm your heart.

However, the same spawning process that creates angling opportunities creates a need for extreme caution while wading in order to avoid stamping redds and disturbing spawning salmon. One misplaced boot by an oblivious angler can inadvertently destroy thousands of eggs. Even places without obvious redds may contain fertilized eggs, especially those where the bottom looks like an old washboard. Fish below these areas, but stay out of them

## Hatches and Feed

The benthic environment of the lower Sac is rich beyond belief. Entomologists have identified approximately 2,500 insects per square foot of river bottom here. Oddly enough, studies show the most common thing found in trout stomachs on the lower Sac is moss. This puzzles scientists somewhat, but one theory suggests the vegetation probably contains numerous organisms — snails, scuds, Baetis and midge pupa. Second and third to moss on the trout's diet are caddis nymphs and salmon eggs, respectively. Compared to some other streams, this makes imitating the naturals with fly patterns a relatively straightforward proposition.

During the warmer months, mainly March through September, caddis patterns reign. To match the early spring *Brachycentrus* caddis hatch, pick patterns like Mercer's Z-wing caddis, LaFontaine sparkle pupa, peeking caddis, Bird's nest or bead Head nymphs in #12–14. For emergers try the LaFontaine emergent caddis or Mathew's X-caddis, in #14 and #16. Note that emergers will often out-produce dry flies even at the height of the hatch. For dry flies it's hard to beat Al Troth's elk hair caddis in #14–16. Because the *Brachycentrus* is an olive-colored bug, all these early season flies should be tied or bought with that in mind.

During May, the larger, brownish-colored *Hydropsychid* caddis flies replace the *Brachycentrus*. An angler can easily adjust by using the same patterns noted above, using a fly one hook size larger, tied from materials with a brownish cast.

In the cooler months those single-egg patterns in a #6 will do nicely. Try several different colors, from milky orange to bright pink. However, salmon eggs aren't the only food available to the trout during winter. Some of the best fishing of the year can be had by imitating the tiny blue wing olives. Also known as *Baetis* mayflies, these smaller insects seem to thrive in the nastiest weather. The height of their hatch occurs in December and January, but conditions have to be just right — cool, drizzly afternoons with no wind can produce truly memorable dry fly fishing. The naturals have a body about the size of a #16 hook, but the wing should be a size larger than normal. Almost any paradun or haystack mayfly pattern in the right size will catch fish. Presentation is more important than imitation.

In hard rain or high winds the trout have a hard time seeing these little duns on the water. An angler can still score very well fishing #14 or #16 PT nymphs under an indicator.

Summer air temperatures in Redding often exceed 100 degrees, while the water remains in the mid-50s. It's an odd sensation: Even with the insulation of neoprene waders, your feet get cold at the same time as your face and arms soak up enough solar radiation to run a small power plant. Bring plenty of sunscreen and liquids. Polarized sunglasses and a hat with a brim are strongly recommended.

*Nymph fishers will consistently take large Sacramento rainbows.*
*(Photo: Chip O'Brien)*

Fall weather on the lower Sac is usually favorable, with warm temperatures and ample sunshine. Winters often bring almost constant rain, but the wet season usually doesn't begin until some time in November. December through February is wet, but with air temperatures often in a comfortable range of 50–60 degrees.

### Tackle and Techniques

Creel census data from the lower Sac indicates catch rates of only .5 fish an hour. But, the average trout is over sixteen inches long — a big payoff. Sacramento River rainbows are sturdy, wild fish that never fell off a hatchery truck. Catching them consistently demands competent handling of equipment and sound techniques. Anglers with intermediate to advanced skill levels can expect to greatly improve on the average catch rate cited. Of course, once you've experienced one of those "glory days," catching large fish one after the other, slower times will seem to matter less.

Unlike trout in other parts of the country, Sacramento rainbows are reluctant to rise vigorously except under hatch conditions described above. In other words, when there are no rising trout visible it would be unusual to catch many fish using a searching dry fly — you're much better off fishing a nymph. The three most productive methods here are strike indicator nymphing, swinging nymphs on a floating line, and swinging nymphs on a sinking line.

Most experienced river guides prefer using a hank of polypropylene yarn for a strike indicator to tell when a fish has taken the submerged nymph. This material is more buoyant than other floats and can be used in just the right amount to cast well while maintaining maximum visibility.

The setup looks like this: start with a leader 9–12 feet long, tapered to 4X. Fasten the fly to your tippet, then connect 2-3 medium-size split shot 12–14 inches above your fly. Cut two pieces of yarn about 1.5 inches long — the author prefers contrasting colors, such as bright yellow and fire orange. Using an overhand or slip knot, fasten the yarn to the thick section of your tapered leader, seven to eight feet above your fly. Pick out the yarn with a comb to make it fuzzy. Now fold together the two yarn "wings" created by the knot, and trim both at once to a length about three-fourths inch long. Then dress the yarn with paste fly floatant.

By fine-tuning the size of the yarn indicator and the number of split shots used to sink the fly, you can create a system that's highly visible, casts well, and sinks your fly to the fish's level.

While fishing this rig, keep in mind that this is big water. Longer casts will show the fish your fly for longer periods. Quartering casts upstream, mending as necessary to keep a natural drift, is an effective method for covering shallow riffle sections. If, however, you've learned to present a fly with a downstream "dead drift," so much the better.

The latter technique was popularized in eastern Shasta County as an effective way to present flies downstream to spooky fish. Named the "Fall River Twitch," it has an important role on the Sacramento as well. Cast slightly upstream and throw a big upstream mend in the line as the floating strike indicator passes in front of you. With the indicator below you, point the rod at the water and start flipping your rod tip up and down while feeding line out through the guides. This method actually relies on the surface tension of the water and gravity to extend your drift for long distances.

Observe that you will jerk your indicator on that first big mend — that's all right. If the initial mend puts the fly line upstream from the indicator, the rest of the drift should be natural, as long as you can feed line out fast enough. Then it's just a matter of feeding line out until either a fish grabs your bug or the line goes tight. This is a maneuver worth learning.

Swinging nymphs on either a floating or sinking line is an easier technique to learn than perfecting indicator nymphing on big water, but once again, long casts will make the most of each presentation. The method for swinging a nymph with a floating or sinking line is the same. The only difference is in how deeply you present your nymph.

Cast as far as you can across or slightly downstream. As soon as your cast hits the water place a big upstream mend in the line, allowing your fly to sink to the appropriate level. Now let the current tighten your line — picture your fly slowly "swimming" in the current, enticing hungry fish. Continue putting small upstream mends in the line every few seconds to insure that it doesn't rip through the water too quickly. Since this is a tight line technique, you will normally feel the grab rather than see it.

At the end of the swing, let the line straighten out below you and hang in the current for a moment before you strip back in for the next cast.

Of course, fishing a dry fly on the lower Sac can produce memorable thrills when done properly and at the right time. You will notice a relationship between tippet size and the number of grabs you get. The author has experimented with this — 5X draws more strikes than 4X. Don't go any farther, however. While 6X will increase the number of strikes yet again, it is difficult for most anglers to avoid break-offs with tippet this light, fish this big, and in current so strong. Stick to 5X tippet.

Anglers fish this river with 8 to 10 foot rods, throwing anywhere from 4-to 8-weight lines. They may or may not do a good job of it. Recognizing how personal this subject may be, the author will only suggest that if pressed to pick a single, all-purpose rod, he would take 9.5 foot rod for a 6-weight line. Once again, this is big water, where casting wind-resistant strike indicators and a moderate amount of lead is often the best tactic. You may need to cast such rigs a long way. True, most anglers prefer a lighter rod for casting dries…until a stiff breeze kicks up, or one of the big fish is difficult to turn. Better to have the right tool for the job.

As noted, those same fish make demands on a reel. A good one with a quality disc drag is in order. Putting aside the chance of hooking a large steelhead, remember that river trout exceed 25 inches, and they will run. Equipment adequate for smaller fish and venues may lose the rainbow of a lifetime here.

## Regulations

Though the river is open all year, most of the water in this section carries so-called "special regulations" to help maintain the trophy nature of the trout fishery.

From Keswick Dam just above Redding down to Deschutes Road Bridge just below Anderson there is a one trout limit. Flies, lures or bait may be used, but all hooks must be barbless. It is illegal to fish for salmon in this section.

From Deschutes Road Bridge downstream to Bend Bridge, there is a three-trout limit, and barbless hooks are not required. August through January 14, two salmon may also be kept.

## Access: Catch My Drift

The most efficient way to fish the lower Sacramento day-in and day-out is from a drift boat; something about experiencing a big river this way just seems "right." For those with craft, there are six launch ramps in the upper 25 miles to choose from.

The first launch site is a few miles below Keswick Dam at Caldwell Park, the top of venue for our purposes (with each successive launch ramp downstream). Located off Quartz Hill Road just above the Market Street Bridge in north Redding, this water gets less attention than drifts down below and is the only stretch where a motorized water craft is really necessary. Most of the section is more like a long, deep spring creek, with glassy smooth flows — below Keswick Dam, the water is close to 45 feet deep. Nevertheless, there are a few shallow riffle sections where wading is productive, and you will usually have the place to yourself.

Caldwell Park proper is just about the lowest fishable part of this uppermost section, which means you must motor up and drift back down to the launch. Do not attempt to go further downstream because a board structure called the ACID Dam blocks the way to Redding throughout winter.

The Posse Grounds may be one of the most popular starting points for half and full-day floats through some of Redding's best trout water. Just downstream from Caldwell Park, it may be reached by taking the Central Redding exit off I-5, marked for Highway 299 west. From there go 1.6 miles to the Park Marina-Auditorium exit. You can launch a boat here, do a comfortable half-day trip, and take out at the Bonnyview ramp. Or, for a longer run, take out at Anderson River Park about 14 river-miles downstream.

Bonnyview boat launch ramp is Redding's newest facility, located right off of I-5. Toward the south end of Redding, look for the Bonnyview/Churn Creek exit, turn west over the river, and then left into the parking lot. Bonnyview is a good choice for beginning floats down to ramps at Anderson River Park or Balls Ferry.

Although opinions vary, most people generally float down as far as Anderson River Park during the summer season, and no farther. Call it rumor or superstition, but the water below Anderson River Park is generally held to fish better during the cooler months. This author, however, believes it's all good water, winter and summer.

Anderson is a small town located about ten miles south of Redding. Take the Central Anderson exit from I-5 and turn right on Balls Ferry Rd. Go .5 miles and turn left on Stingy Lane. After another .3 miles turn right on Rupert Road. Rupert dead-ends at Anderson River Park.

This is an interesting takeout spot for several reasons. For one thing, any time of the year you can drift under the Airport Road Bridge, beach your boat on river right there, and have dinner. Amigos Mexican Restaurant is a great place to eat and watch the fish rise (sorry, no waders allowed). During low winter flows you can drift down a little farther and anchor across from the tall stadium lights you see above the trees on the right. Be careful not to drop anchor on spawning redds. Fish below this area to egg-sucking trout.

Though there is still some productive water downstream, Balls Ferry launch ramp is the southern-most take-out spot popular with drifting trout anglers. Below here the water starts getting warmer and more cloudy, and thus supports fewer trout. Since salmon fishing is legal below the Deschutes Bridge, you might be sharing parking, if not the same water, with salmon anglers.

### Access: Wade a Minute

While October through April includes some of the wettest months of the year, there is still plenty of pleasant weather, a number of good places to do it. Here is a brief description of some favorite wading spots.

The first area is called the "Posse Grounds" and is located just behind the Redding Civic Auditorium, just below the popular boat launch ramp. There is a park-

*The Sacramento is big water — bring chest waders and a powerful rod. (Photo: Chip O'Brien)*

ing area in back of the auditorium a few feet from the river. Wade out and fish off the gravel bar. Next to the Civic Auditorium you will also notice construction on the new Turtle Bay Park and Museum complex. Hike a short distance behind these structures and fish the faster runs and riffles between the islands. Just park at the museum itself and follow any number of paths through the thick blackberry vines to the river. Note that this area is also a bird sanctuary.

The next area heading downstream is known as East Turtle Bay. Exit I-5 on Cypress Avenue and turn left under the freeway. Go .2 miles and turn right on Bechelli Lane. Take Bechelli one mile to the parking lot at the end. Fish around the island and the long runs just below.

Cascade Community Park is right on the river, just above the inflow of Clear Creek. There are numerous islands to hike around, with good fishing in every direction. Fish the faster water here, since the long flats in this area contain primarily nongame fish species like Sacramento sucker, hardhead and squawfish. To get to Cascade, take the Bechelli Lane-Churn Creek Road exit from I-5. Go left over the freeway and 1.8 miles to the stop sign at Eastside Road. Turn left on Eastside and go 1.2 miles until it runs into Girvan Road. Make a left on Girvan and go .7 miles. Park on the right side of the road.

The sewer treatment plant access is the next one downstream, not far below Clear Creek. Take the same route as to Cascade Community Park, but instead of turning left on Girvan, go right, then make a quick left onto Hwy. 273 heading south. Drive 1.2 miles and turn left at the sign for River Ranch Road. Cross the railroad tracks, make the quick left on Eastside Road. The very next road to the right will take you to the "Fisherman's Access" sign and parking area. This water is just below Clear Creek with abundant riffles and flats to probe. You will have to hike past the so-called "brown trout ponds" at the sewer plant to access the river.

The nearby "Kutras Property" is city-owned public land providing access to the lower end of a long island. Be content to fish up and down the shore as the water here is usually too deep and fast to get to the island. Once again, take the route toward Cascade Park, turning right on Eastside Road. Go .9 miles and turn left at River Ranch Road. After .6 miles River Ranch will dead end into River Crest. Turn right on River Crest, continue .2 miles to the parking area. There is a short hike past some ponds containing lots of small bass and bluegills. Why not make a cast or two?

The so-called "Knighton Road" wading access is actually on Riverland Road. As you drive north on I-5, exit at Knighton Road and turn left over the freeway. There are several turnouts for parking close to the river. During low water months most of this area is very wadable and contains some good fish. Be careful, however — you might be tempted to try wading out to the long island you will see in this section — not a good idea. This is big water, with currents that can be dangerous. In this river, underestimating the speed and force of water can cause serious problems: treat with extreme caution.

Anderson River Park offers numerous good wading opportunities in the park and below. There is a lot of water to work, but the riffles offer the best chance at success. You might also check out the lower end of the park, where there is a long levee from which you can fish some very productive water. Below this, the river makes a jog to the right, with several riffles and dropoffs well worth prospecting. Winter or summer, keep an eye on the slower eddies in this section where you can often find rising fish. The drifts can be tricky but the fish are often large.

Obviously, the lower Sacramento is the kind of river you could spend considerable time getting to know, with enough mysteries to explore over the course of a lifetime. But therein lies the joy of it all.

# Stream Facts: Lower Sacramento

## River Characteristics
- Big water — as much as 100 yards wide, with deep runs and long, wide riffles. Wadable in a few places when cfs is 13,000–15,000, more when water level drops to 4,000-5,000 cfs. Fishable by driftboat most months of the year.

## Getting There
- From San Francisco it's a 3.5–4 hour drive on freeways. Take I-80 out of the city toward Sacramento. Just past Vacaville veer north on I-505, which runs right into I-5 north. Stay on I-5 until you hit Redding.

## Season
- All year.

## Special Regulations
- From 650 feet below Keswick Dam to the Deschutes Road Bridge below Anderson, one-fish limit, any method of take, barbless hooks required.
- From Deschutes Road Bridge downstream to Bend Bridge, there is a three-trout limit, any method of take, barbless hooks not required. August 1 through January 14, two salmon may also be kept.

## Fish
- Rainbows of several apparent origins, along with resident and anadromous steelhead. The rainbows average over 16 inches; trout over 20 inches are common, and are caught up to 27 inches. The river also has several runs of Chinook salmon, shad, stripers, and sturgeon, along with resident populations of squawfish, smallmouth and largemouth bass.

## River Miles
- From Keswick Dam to the Balls Ferry boat launch ramp is about 25 river miles.

## Flows
- Summer season: 13,000–15,000 cfs. Winter season: 4,000–5,000 cfs . Call Bureau of Reclamation for recorded updates: 916-246-7594

## Boat Ramps
- Caldwell Park – Redding
- Posse Grounds – Redding
- Bonnyview – Redding
- Anderson River Park – Anderson
- Balls Ferry – Anderson

## Hub City
- Redding

# LOWER SACRAMENTO RIVER MAJOR HATCHES

| Insect | J | F | M | A | M | J | J | A | S | O | N | D | Flies |
|---|---|---|---|---|---|---|---|---|---|---|---|---|---|
| Caddis *Brachycentrus* | | | | ■ | | | | | | | | | Mercer's Z-Wing Caddis, LaFontaine Sparkle Pupa, Peeking Caddis, Bird's Nest, Beadhead Nymph (all #12–14); LaFontaine Emergent Caddis & Matthew's X-Caddis (#14–16) |
| Caddis *Hydropsychid* | | | | | | | | ■ | ■ | ■ | | | Use same flies as *Brachycentrus*, except one size larger and brownish cast |
| Blue Winged Olive *Baetis* | | ■ | | | | | | | | | ■ | | PT Nymphs #14–16 Paradun or Haystack #16 with oversize wing |
| Tubafex Worms | | ■ | | | | | | ■ | | | | | San Juan Worm |
| Salmon Eggs | | ■ | | | | | | | ■ | | | | Single-egg Pattern #6, colors from milky orange to bright pink |

# Redding

## Elevation – 400 ft. • Population – 78,000

### ACCOMMODATIONS

Redding has scores of places to stay.

River Inn Motor Lodge, 1835 Park Marina Dr., Redding, CA 96001 / 916-241-9500 / $$
Best Western Hilltop, 2300 Hilltop Dr., Redding, CA 96002 / 916/221-6100 / $$$
Super 8, 5175 Churn Creek Rd., Redding, CA 96002 / 916-221-8881 / $$
Oxford Suites, 1967 Hilltop Dr., Redding, CA 96002 / 916-221-0100 / $$
Red Lion Hotel, 1830 Hilltop Dr. Redding, CA 96002 / 916-221-8700 / $$$
Holiday Inn Express, 1080 Twin View Blvd., Redding, CA 96003 / 916-241-5500 / $$$
Comfort Inn, 2059 Hilltop Dr., Redding, CA 96002 / 916/221-6530 / $$

### CAMPGROUNDS

Woodson Bridge State Recreation Area, 5 miles east of Corning / 916-839-2112
Bidwell Sacramento River State Park, 6 miles west of Chico

### RESTAURANTS

Redding has hundreds. Recommendations:

"Tacos," next to McDonald's on East Cypress, Redding, CA / Better-than-average Mexican fare / $
Pietros, 995 Hilltop Dr. Redding, CA 96002 / 916-223-1392/ Darned good Italian food and pizza just north of the Mt. Shasta Mall / $$
Hometown Buffet, 1380 Churn Creek Rd., Redding, CA 96002 / 916-224-1711 / Good for a buffet; popular with big eaters / $$
Amigos on the River, 1542 Cluad Lane, Anderson, CA 96007 / 916-365-6142 / Great views of the river / $$
C.R. Gibbs, 2300 Hilltop Dr., Redding, CA 96002 / Central location (part of the Best Western Hilltop complex) / $$
Marie Callender's, 1987 Hilltop Dr., Redding, CA 96002 / 916-223-4310 / Great salad bar. / $$
Demercurios, 1790 Market St., Redding, CA 96001 / 916-246-3922 / Unusually good food in a formal, yet relaxed atmosphere / $$$
Maxwell's, 1344 Market St., Redding, CA 96001 / 916-246-4373 / Elegant atmosphere / $$$
Jack's Grill, 1743 California St., Redding, CA 96001 / 916-241-9705 / Nationally acclaimed steak house, bring an appetite / $$$

### SPORTING GOODS AND FLY SHOPS

The Fly Shop, 4140 Churn Creek Rd., Redding, CA 96002 / 916-222-3555 / Full service

**Camps Sporting Emporium**, 3048 S. Market St., Redding, CA 96001 / 916-241-4530 / General sporting goods shop with fly fishing section.

## AUTOMOTIVE REPAIRS
**Advanced Automotive**, 5756 Westside Rd., Unit F, Redding, CA 96001 / 916-244-4423 / Good mechanics, reasonable prices

## AIRPORT
**Redding Municipal Airport** / 530-224-4320 / Served by Horizon Air 800-547-9308 and United Airlines -800-241-6522.

## HOSPITALS
**Mercy Medical Center**, 2175 Rosaline Ave., Redding, CA 96001 / 916-225-6000
**Redding Medical Center**, 1100 Butte St., Redding, CA 96001 / 916-244-5400
**Redding Specialty Hospital**, 2801 Eureka Way, Redding, CA 96001 / 916-246-9000

## AUTO RENTALS
The following have offices at the airport:

**Avis** / 916-221-2855
**Budget** / 916-228 8416
**Hertz** / 916-221-4620

## FOR MORE INFORMATION
Redding Chamber of Commerce
747 Auditorium Drive
Redding, CA, 96001
916-225-4433

# Sidebar: A Scourge of Squawfish

### by Seth Norman

"One of my favorite summer pastimes is fishing for massive squawfish with dry flies in the lower Sac. Even with so much terrific trout fishing available right in the center of Redding, a few anglers have learned the valuable lesson that fish don't have to have adipose fins to be fun." —Chip O'Brien

Sacramento squawfish will take a dry. They will also take an egg pattern or a streamer. The big ones will take a mature trout or half pounder steelhead —

— and they do, untold thousands of times every year, so it's no wonder that on another river, the Columbia, the Washington and Oregon fish and game departments administer a program that pays such handsome bounties for squawfish that folks make a living hunting them down, at $3 per, for every fish over 11 inches.

Natives to the Sacramento system, squawfish — also known as "Sacramento pike," and for good reason — have always preyed on the eggs and spawn of salmon, trout, and steelhead. Thirty years ago they were a relatively innocuous species, just another interesting piece in the macro-puzzle.

"They're more of a problem now," says Don Wideline, fisheries biologist at the Department of Fish and Game's Redding office, "because of manmade changes to the river, like the conditions created at the Red Bluff Diversion Dam," where the squaws lay in wait for juvenile salmon, savaging these as they are disoriented by vertical eddies. "In fact," says Wideline, "we attribute most of the losses at the Diversion not to mechanical damage, but to squawfish depredation."

Unhappily, it's not just by establishing ambush stations that human efforts have assisted squawfish. The dams on the Sacramento may seem to benefit them, possibly by altering water temperature or flows. It's ironic that, in one regard, the 1991 toxic spill on the Upper Sacramento River was a blessing -- it helped to curtail a squawfish invasion which threatened trout populations. The year before, DFG was so concerned about a decline in catch rates that they sent down divers near Simms pool, who turned up squawfish in the 10-pound range, eager and able to eat trout to 13 inches.

Worse yet, some Lower river guides and oldtimers believe that the most significant damage done by squawfish isn't to the young of anadromous fish, but to their eggs. "They 'marry' the hens," reported Bud Moore in a 1991 California Game and Fish article. "That's what we call it when the squawfish pick out a Chinook salmon and follow her upriver. You can see 'em on your fish finder, 20 or 30 sometimes. I think they follow her for miles, to get a peck at those eggs."

Various management methods have been tried and, for the most part, discarded, though recent efforts to reduce the amount of time smolts are subject to strong flows (at the Red Bluff Diversion Dam) may help. An annual "Squawfish Fish-Out, held by DFG at Red Bluff Diversion below the dam in the section of water usually closed to fishing was canceled after an accident; other fishouts take 100 or 2000 fish from the 20,000 that show at the dam. Another plan, a contract with a commercial fisher who wanted to sell squawfish to Bay Area markets, was derailed when the fish were found to have concentrations of pollutants that rendered them too contaminated for use even as fertilizers.

And they will take dry flies, and streamers...

Many flyfishers don't deliberately kill a fish all season. Many more have come to respect the various players in any larger environmental picture — all things have their place — and in some drainages, species of squawfish are even endangered. But man has changed the odds for these "pike" of the Sacramento and may well have produced a situation in which a priest is in order, if not to pray for the river, then to bludgeon a threat.

It's an ugly experience for some. But at least one other guide on the lower river would take a squawfish program even farther, suggesting that everybody who takes a salmon (or steelhead, or trout) should catch and kill a squawfish in turn.

Perhaps it's better to start now than to wait for this river to find itself in dire straits — say those of the Columbia.

# A Tour of Feather River Country

## by Ralph Wood

The first white men on record to explore the Feather River and its canyon were the Spanish explorer Luis Arguello and his band of soldiers in the year 1817. In 1848, a gold strike at Bidwells Bar on the Middle Fork brought miners streaming into the territory, eventually leaving behind such colorful camp names as Hottentot Bar, Poverty Flat, and Minerva Bar. Later came the lumber interests and the cattle ranchers. Though still of limited importance, their activities have declined, and the area now belongs to the tourist and and angler.

The Feather River is treated here as an area — Feather River Country — rather than as a single venue. The watershed is vast, draining thousands of miles, from icy streams funneling down the slopes of Mount Lassen to form the North Fork of the Feather, to spring-fed creeks collecting in Sierra Valley to make the Middle Fork — all the way to the outflow of Lake Oroville and down the Central Valley to the Sacramento. It spans counties — it's the size of some eastern states; the change of elevations is many thousands of feet; and dams fragment the various branches, isolating species of fish and insects. The major branches offer tremendous opportunities: steelhead, smallmouth, stripers, and salmon below Oroville, runs of browns in the main stem above the lake, rainbows in all the forks. The many tributaries present California anglers the chance for that rare combination of solitude and good fishing.

In other words, a whole lot of water coming down.

### Fishing Feather River Country

This chapter examines several distinct sections of the Feather river and its tributaries, from the piney creeks above Lake Almanor to the broader flows of the Middle Fork, descending through mixed oak and conifer forest. Such different venues suggest different types of tackle: for the small freestone tributaries, fishers may prefer a 6.5 to 7 foot 3-weight rod, and a 7.5 foot leader ending with 5x. On both the North and Middle Fork of the Feather, 4- to 5- weight rods, 8.5 to 9 feet long, will serve best; lengthen the leader to nine feet, ending in 5X tippet. On either rig, double taper lines will allow for better mending and roll casts.

As for wading — as on all of our freestone streams, the water is usually cold enough to wear neoprenes, and felted soles are almost always a must.

### Upper North Fork of the Feather

Like all tributaries to Lake Almanor, the season on the North Fork above the lake opens late — Saturday preceding Memorial Day — in order to protect spawning rainbows. This section is best accessed not far from the mouth, from the town of Chester, 13 miles east of the junction of Highways 36 and 89.

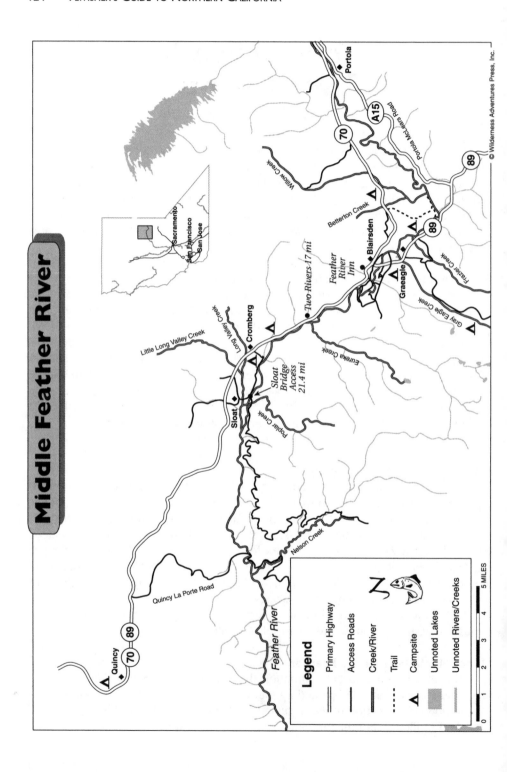

Middle Feather River

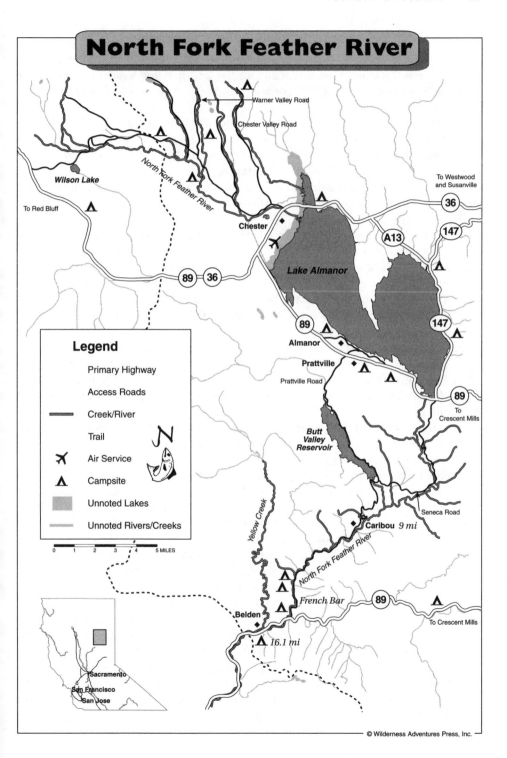

# North Fork Feather River

Warner Valley Road

Chester Valley Road

North Fork Feather River

Wilson Lake

To Red Bluff

Chester

To Westwood
and Susanville

36

147

A13

Lake Almanor

89   36

89

147

147

Almanor

Prattville

Prattville Road

89

To
Crescent Mills

Butt
Valley
Reservoir

## Legend

Primary Highway

Access Roads

Creek/River

Trail

✈  Air Service

△  Campsite

Unnoted Lakes

Unnoted Rivers/Creeks

0   1   2   3   4   5 MILES

Yellow Creek

Seneca Road

Caribou  *9 mi*

North Fork Feather River

*French Bar*

89

To Crescent Mills

Belden

△ *16.1 mi*

Sacramento

San Francisco

San Jose

© Wilderness Adventures Press, Inc.

Feather River Drive intersects Highway 36 from the left just across the bridge. Within a mile it forks and bears left onto Warner Valley Road. Soon you will see the first of a series of unmarked dirt roads on the left (heading south) that reach the north side of the river. Most of these are passable by two-wheel drive vehicles, but take it slow.

Just under 5.5 miles from the turn at Highway 36, Warner Valley Road reaches the High Bridge Campground. Shortly thereafter, it divides, with the main access road continuing right toward Warner Valley, and the secondary access to the left, veering toward Domingo Springs Campground. Stay left.

After passing the campground at Domingo Springs (approximately three miles from High Bridge, or eight miles from Highway 36), the road divides again, this time into three. So do a fisher's options.

First, the right hand road: this cuts away from the North Fork. Approximately five miles on, it reaches one of the nicest tributaries to the upper section, the north arm of Rice Creek, a lava rock stream with deep holes and riffles interspersed by larger boulders. You can walk either up or downstream. As will be typical everywhere, the further you go from easy access, the better the fishing.

The average trout in Rice Creek will be a rainbow between 7 and 12 inches. Attractor dry fly fishing is extremely productive: use elk hair caddis in sizes 14–18 both olive and tan, Adams parachutes 12–16, and Royal Coachman parachutes 14–16.

Second, the middle track (just beyond Domingo Springs): continuing straight on along the main access road for four miles will lead to the North Fork of the Feather, just below the property line of the Feather River Rod & Gun Club. (Sideroads heading south along the way hit the North Fork.) Downstream, there are many miles of fishing: the river through this section is composed of larger lava rock pools leading into riffles. Depending on the runoff conditions, there can be some excellent golden stone hatches here in early June.

Other tributaries to check out in this general area (nearer to Chester) are Warner Creek (via Warner Valley Road); Benner Creek, (via Juniper Lake Road); and Last Chance Creek, reached by taking a right off Juniper Lake Road (Walker Forest Road). All three streams have campgrounds, and all provide rainbows in the 7- to 12-inch range. The same patterns that succeed on Rice Creek will serve on any one of these.

The lower section of the Upper North Fork, below the Highway 36 bridge, flows through a meadow to empty into Lake Almanor (a great fishery in its own right). You'll find plenty of parking places around the bridge.

This is an unusual section of river. While fish rarely hold here for long periods of time, they do come in for "special occasions." In early spring, spawning rainbows move up; mid-June through early July, a few fish will rise to hatches of *Callibaetis* and *Hexagenia* (though the lake itself has better hatches along its western shore, near Prattville, especially around 4th of July). During November, brown trout enter the stream as they begin their spawning migration from Lake Almanor. Generally speaking, in spring and fall the best fishing is with woolly buggers in sizes 6 and 8, muddler minnows, and assorted streamer patterns.

The Feather River exits Almanor at the southeast end of the lake, near Camp Almanor, reached from Chester by heading south/southwest on Highway 36, then south/southeast on Highway 89. Six miles from that juncture, and before the Feather River outlet, 89 meets Humbolt/Humbug Road, the turnoff to Yellow Creek.

Turn right on Humbolt/Humbug from 89. Stay on Humbug when Humbolt Road splits off to the right.

A concrete bridge crosses Butte Creek. Just beyond, Humbug appears to branch into three forks (lumbering in this area has created a jumble of tracks). Take the middle one — the main road and most traveled — and continue on to Humbug Valley, where you should see a sign for a Pacific Gas & Electric (PG&E) campground. A gorgeous mile or so beyond is one of the prettiest meadow streams in California.

Yellow Creek rushes full force from out of a huge spring near the head of the valley. A habitat restoration project completed in the mid-eighties restored the stream from damage sustained through years of overgrazing. Special regulations now apply to the meadow section — a maximum size limit of 10 inches, artificial lures with single barbless hooks only — and end where the creek dives into a canyon toward its eventual meeting with the North Fork of the Feather, below Beldon.

Hatches in the protected water are prolific: green drakes, *Baetis*, orange stones, PMDs, and numerous caddis species. The size of some of the browns suggests this rich diet, but the big ones do not come easy or often. (*Editor's note:* Yellow Creek is usually one of California's more difficult fisheries, routinely humbling the proud and disappointing the hopeful. It's fair to say that often, the stream is alive with the sound of whining.)

Below Lake Almanor, the North Fork of the Feather flows on through an area with poor access but excellent fishing. The best way to reach this stretch — "best" is a relative word — is from Seneca Road, which heads south from Highway 89, nine miles south of the junction of 89 and Highway 36. After driving 5.6 miles, you will reach the river at Seneca Bridge; from there you can hike up or downstream. The river here is typical pool and riffle water, holding fish in the 8- to 12-inch range. By hiking a mile or more from the access point, however, an angler will find less pressured water, with wild trout and the opportunity of hooking a brown in the 19- to over 20-inch bracket.

By continuing on across Seneca bridge another 1.8 miles, you will come across a deadend road to the left. This is a 4-wheel drive track only. From there Seneca Road veers away from the river, northwest toward Butt Valley Reservoir. Just before it reaches the lake it doubles back, somewhat tortuously, toward the town of Caribou.

Near town you will note an access road on the left. From there you can walk half a mile to the powerhouse and past it. Along a trail that leads upstream — 16 to 18 miles — you can access all the way up to the Seneca bridge. (*Editor's note:* eight miles up this trail — a long, long way — there may still be a mining claim. Avoid it.)

At the town of Caribou, what was Seneca Road turns to pavement and becomes Caribou Road, which edges along the forebay (called Beldon Forebay on some maps, Caribou Forebay on others). Downstream from the dam — the roughly seven miles to Highway 7 — is a popular piece of river, where three campgrounds are located.

This water is both heavily stocked and fished. Except for the three-quarters of a mile below the Forebay Dam, access is readily available at numerous turnouts and campgrounds. Even with all the traffic, some good-sized browns can be found here, as well as resident rainbows and holdovers. Wading is not a problem, although there is a great deal of streamside brush to contend with. Exercise caution, however, as dredging takes place during the summer months, and the holes left behind can leave your hat floating.

Water types include both pool and riffle. During May and June there are excellent stonefly hatches. Throughout the season there are hatches of caddis. Downstream, below the junction of the North Fork and the East Branch just above Belden, fishing becomes inconsistent due to the manipulation of water levels by PG&E.

### Middle Fork of the Feather

Another part of Feather River country that merits a fisher's attention is the Middle Fork of the Feather, where it can be reached by Highway 70/89, beginning from the town of Quincy. This fork of the river is accessible in its upper stretches, before it plunges into a canyon area below the old logging community of Sloat; then access becomes very difficult.

Starting from Quincy, anglers will reach the lower section first. This canyon section of the Middle Fork can be approached by taking the Quincy/Laporte Road off 70/89, then using one of several forest service access roads to reach the canyon rim. (This exploration should be planned with the help of a Forest Service ranger, since conditions vary from year to year. It's wise to purchase a Forest Service map of the area.)

Numerous trails lead down from the roads on the rim to the canyon floor. Many of these were hacked out by miners in their feverish search for gold. They are steep — it might take only an hour to get down, but plan on at least twice that time to get back out.

On the stream itself, sections of cliffs and boulders can make mobility a problem, especially during spring runoff. But once you reach the water, you will find a high quality, wild rainbow trout fishery, along with some trophy browns. The river in this area is composed of deep pools interspersed with long riffles. Patterns for this section include black woolly buggers #8–12, black and olive leech patterns, and heavily weighted nymphs like the black A. P., hare's ear, rubberlegs, and olive Bird's nests in sizes 12–16. During October there are excellent hatches of BWOs beginning in the early afternoon and extending into the evening. Olive parachute patterns in sizes 18–22 will do the trick.

By following the Quincy/Laporte road west for six miles from where it leaves Highway 70/89, you will come to a bridge over Nelson Creek, a major tributary of the Middle Fork. Nelson Creek is a typical freestone stream with excellent attractor dry fly fishing. You may work upstream or down; by heading downstream for approximately a mile, you will hit the Middle Fork. Typical patterns to use in this area are Adams parachute #14–16, royal Wulff #12–16, elk hair caddis #12–16 and the red or yellow humpies #12–16.

*The North Fork Feather racing through beautiful, densely-forested banks.*

Back to Highway 70/89: Above the town of Sloat, the Middle Fork is more accessible than it is in the lower section. Railroad tracks parallel most of the river; you can gain access at the various road crossings. Once again, you will find the freestone pool and riffle combinations so common to California.

Sloat is the site of a closed lumber mill — what's left of a logging community that has given way to the environmental wave in California. It is an excellent point of access to this part of Middle Fork. From the Sloat Bridge, you can hike up or downstream. As happens so often, the vast majority of anglers will stay within 100 feet of their car. A little bit of walking will put you into lightly fished water and provide a sense of isolation.

The water here can be deceiving. A cursory once-over will give the impression that it is flat and featureless. Closer observation reveals that thigh-deep and deeper runs create lies for fish. Cuts along the banks shelter rainbows averaging 8 to 12 inches.

A wise approach here is to fish nymphs in the morning and dries in the evening. For the former, a strike indicator will prove extremely useful. It should be positioned at about twice the depth of the water you are fishing and adjusted whenever it changes. In the higher water of spring, apply a microshot six to eight inches above the fly.

Short, accurate casts are best for this fishing. Keep as much line as possible off the water, ideally less than two feet lying on the surface. Suggested standard patterns include hare's ear nymphs #10–16; golden stone nymphs #6–10; A.P.s in black and olive #10–18; and Bird's nest in olive and tan #10–16.

Some of the best dry flies will vary with the season. During late May and early June, there is a good golden stone (*Acroneuria*) hatch along the upper section of the Middle Fork, and a golden stone stimulator in sizes 8–10 works well. Little yellow stones (*Isoperla*) will hatch during the latter part of June and throughout July. These are best imitated by a partridge and yellow soft hackle with a fur thorax in sizes 10–12, and yellow elk hair caddis in sizes 10–14.

Throughout the year there are numerous caddis present as nymphs or adults. These include *Rhyacophila* (green rock worm), *Hydropsyche* (spotted sedge), *Glossosoma* (turtle caddis), and *Brachycentrus* (grannom). Suggested patterns again include the elk hair caddis in olive and tan #10–18; LaFontaine's deep and emergent pupa in brown and bright green #10–16; green rock worm #10–16; and the Z-wing caddis in tan and green #10–16.

Above Sloat, the Middle Fork of the Feather enters a canyon. Access can be gained by almost any of the many roads heading west of Highway 70/89 (as you head south to Graeagle) or by hiking along the railroad tracks that parallel the river. The same patterns already suggested work in this section, as do the same techniques — short line nymphing in the morning, and dry fly fishing in the evening when the light begins to disappear in the canyon.

As you approach the resort community of Graeagle, the Middle Fork begins to change from a riffle-and-pool river to a slower, more sedate flow. The gradient is not so steep, and the river is beginning to accumulate water from the numerous springs pouring out of the Sierra valley. The same types of flies work in this area as did further down in the canyon section. One of the more successful techniques used in the slower flow is to use a dry fly such as an Adams Parachute in size 14 as an indicator, with a small nymph on a 5- or 6X dropper, 12 to 18 inches long, tied to the bend of the hook.

By the time you have reached the town of Clio, about half a mile from Graeagle, the river is a meadow stream. You can approach this stretch from the bridge near the northern edge of Graeagle. It's a particularly beautiful area, especially in the spring, when it is alive with wildflowers.

Taken altogether — and this has just been a tasty sampler — Feather River country is a great region of California to explore. Everywhere are opportunities for wild trout flyfishing in semi-wilderness surroundings. And after you've spent time on more famous — and more crowded — venues, remember that here are many stretches of water that probably see less than a score of anglers a year.

# Stream Facts: Feather River Country

## Seasons
- North Fork of the Feather above Lake Almanor: All tributaries to Lake Almanor are open from the Sunday preceding Memorial Day to November 15.
- North Fork below Lake Almanor, Yellow Creek, Middle Fork of the Feather River: Last Saturday in April to November 15.

## Special Regulations
- Yellow Creek: From Big Springs to the marker at the lower end of Humbug Meadow: 2 fish, maximum size limit, 10 inches total length, artificial lures with barbless hooks only.

## River Characteristics
- Above Lake Almanor, the (Upper) North Fork is a river of modest size and gradient, composed of riffles and lava rock pools.
- The Wild Trout section of Yellow Creek is a meadow stream, with smooth flows, many hatches, and wary fish—including some large browns.
- Below Lake Almanor the North Fork is a tailwater with freestone characteristics.
- Nelson Creek is a small freestone tributary to the Middle Fork.
- The lower part of the Middle Fork runs through a steep canyon, with difficult access to deep pools and long riffles. The upper part of the Middle Fork described in the text is a flatter section of river, with runs and undercut banks.

## Trout
- Most of the wild fish caught from these streams are rainbows in the 7 to 12 inch range. The rarer browns will run to 20 inches.

## Hub Cities
- Chester
- Quincy

## FEATHER RIVER MAJOR HATCHES

| Insect | J | F | M | A | M | J | J | A | S | O | N | D | Flies |
|---|---|---|---|---|---|---|---|---|---|---|---|---|---|
| Giant Orange Stone *Pteronarcys californica* | | | ■ | ■ | ■ | ■ | | | | | | | Kaufman's Blackstone #6; Orange Stimulator #6 |
| Golden Stone *Acroneuria californica* | | | ■ | ■ | ■ | ■ | | | | | | | Kaufman's Golden Stone #18; Gold Stimulator #8 |
| Little Yellow Stone *Isoperla* | | | | | | ■ | ■ | | | | | | Mercer's Little Yellow Stone #14-16; Yellow Elk Hair Caddis #14-16 |
| Blue-winged Olive *Baetis* | | | | | | | | | | ■ | ■ | | Pheasant Tails #18-22; Paradun #18-22 |
| Speckle-winged Quills *Callibaetis* | | | | ■ | ■ | ■ | | | ■ | ■ | ■ | | Herb Burton's Bug Lite #12-16; Burk's Hunch Back; Parachute Adams #12-16 |
| Pale Morning Dun *Ephemerella* | | | | | | ■ | | | | | | | Burk's Hunchback Infrequens #14-16; PMD Paradun #14-16 |
| Western Green Drake *Ephemerella* | | | | | | ■ | | | | | | | Lawson's Emerger #10-12; Paradun Lawson's Extended Body #4-8 |
| Big Yellow May *Hexagenia* | | | | | | | ■ | | | | | | Andy Burk's Hexagenia Nymph #4-8; Extended Body Paradun #4-8 |

# Feather River Country

This area contains scores of campgrounds, resorts, motel, restaurants, et al. Two hub cites are included here: Chester, close to the upper part of the North Fork above Lake Almanor; and Quincy, the largest town near to the section of the Middle Fork described in the text. Also included are accommodations available in smaller towns along both parts of the river and on Yellow Creek.

A valuable resource for anglers interested in Feather River country is the Plumas County Visitor's Bureau, 1-800 326-2247. Ask for their Visitor's Guide.

## Chester

### Elevation – 4,525 • Population – 2,500

The town of Chester sits at the northern edge of Lake Almanor. where the Upper North Fork of the Feather River enters the lake (there are many more resorts on the lake itself). Below is a partial list of motels and B&Bs.

## ACCOMMODATIONS

**Antlers Motel**, 268 Main St., Box 538, Chester, CA 96020 / 916-258-2722 / 12 units, kings and doubles; one apartment; color cable TV, coffee in room, picnic area and restaurant next door, phones; weekly and monthly rates negotiable; commercial rates; no pets / $-$$

**Chester Manor Motel**, 306 Main St., Box 1163, Chester, CA 96020 / 916-258-2441 / 18 units, king beds, refrigerators, phone, cable TV, HBO / $-$$

**Motel De Las Plumas**, 29615 Hwy. 89, PO. Box 249, Canyon Dam, CA 95923 / 916-284-7994 / $

**Sierra Motel**, 229 Main St., Box 532, Chester, CA 96020 / 916-258-2500 / $$ / 10 units, 2 with kitchens, restaurant next door, HBO, pets allowed

**Timber House**, 1st & Main St., Box 1010, Chester, CA 96020 / 916-258-2729 / $$ / 16 units, 2 with kitchens, restaurant, lounge, cable TV, pets allowed

### Bed and Breakfasts:

**Bidwell House**, #I Main St., Box 1790, Chester, CA 96020 / 916-258-3338 / $$$ / Restored ranch house built in 1901, 14 units, 2 with shared bath, full breakfast

**Cinnamon Teal**, 227 Feather River Dr., Chester, CA 96020 / 916/258-3993 / $$-$$$

**Lake Almanor Inn**, 3965 Hwy. A-13 (at junction of Hwy. 47), Lake Almanor, CA 96137 / $$-$$$ / 916-596-3910 / 5 rooms, 4 with shared bath; lounge, pool tables, fireplace, deck; restaurant on site; on Hamilton Branch of Feather River; seasonal; no pets/smoking

## CAMPING

*Upper North Fork of the Feather, above Lake Almanor:*

There are many rough camping spots near or along the North Fork, as well as some more developed United States Forest Service campgrounds, Almanor Ranger District / 916-258-2141. Some of these are:

**High Bridge Campground**, 5+ miles west of Chester off Warner Road, has 12 sites, some okay for RVs, and piped water

**Rice Creek Campground,** about a mile beyond High Bridge Campground, less developed (no RVs)

**Warner Creek Campground** (on Warner Creek) is 8 miles out of Chester, also off Warner Valley Road, 15 sites, RVs, and pets okay

**Domingo Springs** is 8 miles out of Chester, Warner Road to County Road 211, RVs okay, piped water, pets okay

**Last Chance Creek**, Pacific Gas and Electric Campground (Last Chance Creek is a tributary to the North Fork), off Juniper Road, north of Chester, where RVs and pets are okay, call 1-800-743-5000 for information

*Yellow Creek:*

PG & E maintains the campground at Yellow Creek, 8. 8 miles off Highway 89 on Humbolt/Humbug Road. Piped water, RVs and pets okay.

*North Fork below Lake Almanor, above Caribou:*

Rough camping is possible at the Seneca Bridge, 5.6 miles from the Highway 89 turnoff onto Seneca Road.

*North Fork below Lake Almanor, Caribou to Beldon:*

Seneca Road joins the Caribou Road at the forebay (which can also be reached via Highway 70 out of Oroville). There are three campgrounds along this section of the River: **Ganser Bar**, **North Fork Campground**, and **Queen Lily Compound**. All can accommodate RVs and have piped water. (North Fork has an RV dump station.)

**North Fork of Feather River at Beldon** (off Highway 70, across the Red Bridge) / Beldon Town / 916-283-2906 / $-$$$ / This is a private resort, campground and lodge with cabins, lodge, restaurant, store and bar.

## RESTAURANTS

**Ming's Dynasty**, 605 Main Street, Chester, CA 96020 / 916-258-2420 / $-$$ / Closed Tuesday, beer and wine

**BJ's BBQ and Deli**, 3881 ZA-13, Hamilton Branch / 916-596-4210 / $

**Corner Pocket**, 118 Watson, Chester, CA 96020 / 916-258-3969 / $ / Deli, pizza, wine, billiards

**Timber House**, 1st and Main, Chester, CA 96020 / 916-258-2729 / $$-$$$ / Steaks, seafood, early bird specials, bar

**Knotbumper**, 274 Main St., Chester, CA 96020 / 916-258-2301 / $ / Steaks, seafood, Mexican, beer and wine

**Copper Kettle**, Main St. and Myrtle, Chester, CA 96020 / $ / Coffee shop

**Bidwell House**, #1 Main St., Chester, CA 96020 / 916-258-3338 / $$ / Country breakfasts, reserve a day in advance

**Moon's**, 497 Lawrence Street, Chester, CA 96020 / 916-283-0765 / $$-$$$ / Italian and American, fine dining, patio

### Sporting Goods and Fly Shops

**Ayoob's Sports**, 201 Main St., Chester, CA 96020 / 916-258-2611 / Some flyfishing tackle can be found here; no other dedicated fly shops

### Airport

**Chester Airport** / 916-258-3616 / No commercial flights but capable of handling larger private craft

### Auto Rental

**Chester Auto Sales**, 640 Main St., Chester, CA 96020 / 916-258-2277 / Free airport pick up and delivery

### Hospitals

**Seneca District Hospital**, 130 Brentwood Drive, Chester, CA 96020 / 916-258-2151

### For More Information

Chester Chamber of Commerce
529 Main, Box 1198
Chester, CA
916-258-2426 or 800-3504838

# Quincy

## Elevation – 3,500 • Population – 5,000

Quincy is a large town near the Middle Fork of the Feather (above Sloat) on Highway 70.

## ACCOMMODATIONS

**Gold Pan Motel**, 200 Crescent, Quincy, CA 95971 / 916-283-3686 / $-$$
**Lariat Lodge**, 2370 E. Main St., Quincy, CA 95971 / 916-283-1000 / $$
**Pine Hill Motel**, Highway 70 West, Quincy, CA 95971 / 916-283-1670 / $
**Spanish Creek Motel**, 233 Crescent, Quincy, CA 95971 / 916-283-1200 / $$
**Ranchito Motel**, 2020 E. Main St., Quincy, CA 95971 / 916-283-2265 / $$

*Bed & Breakfasts:*

**Feather Bed**, 542 Jackson St., Quincy, CA 95971 / 916-283-0102 / $$-$$$$
**New England Ranch**, 3 miles out of Quincy on Quincy Junction Rd., Quincy, CA 95971 / 916-283-2223 / $$-$$

## RESTAURANTS

**Bobs Fine Foods**, 525 Main St., Quincy, CA 95971-9377 / 916-283-3344 / $
**El Torito Loco**, 2200 E Main St., Quincy, CA 95971-9660 / 916/283-0139 / $
**Express Coffee Shop**, 2061 E Main St., Quincy, CA 95971-9658 / 916-283-1949 / $
**Mi Casita Mexican Restaurant**, 875 E Main St., Quincy, CA 95971-9799 / 916-283-4755 / $
**Moons Restaurant**, 497 Lawrence, Quincy, CA 95971 / 916-283-0765 / $-$$
**Morning Thunder Cafe**, 557 Lawrence, Quincy, CA 95971 / 916-283-1310 / $
**Pizza Factory**, 490 Main St., Quincy, CA 95971-9376 / 916-283-4545 / $
**Polka Dot**, 2043 E Main St., Quincy, CA 95971-9658 / 916-283-2660 / $
**Main Street Pub**, 461 W Main, Quincy, CA 95971 / $ / Beer, good Mexican food
**Stoney's Country Burgers**, 11 Lindan Ave., Quincy, CA 95971-9367 / 916-283-3911 / $
**Ten-Two Dinner House &Bar** (on way to Bucks Lake, 10 miles out of town) / 916-283 1366 / Full bar, outdoor patio on the creek

## SPORTING GOODS AND FLY SHOPS

*General tackle stores where some fly fishing tackle can be found:*

**Sportsman Den**, 1580 E. Main Street, E. Quincy, CA / 916-283-2733
**Sierra Mountain Sports**, 501 Main Street, Quincy (across from the Court House / 916-283-2323

## HOSPITALS/MEDICAL

**Plumas District Hospital** (24-hour emergency), 1065 Bucks Lake Road, Quincy, CA 95971 / 916-283-0650
**Plumas Community Clinic** (open all week and Saturdays for medical and dental care), 112 Buchanan St., Quincy, CA 95971 / 916-283-3915

**AIRPORT**

Quincy Airport / 916-283-2600 / No commercial flights

**CAMPING**

There are a number of public and private campgrounds in and around Quincy. For private, contact the Quincy Chamber of Commerce. For USFS, call 916-283-0555

*Nelson Creek:*

There is an undeveloped site at Red Bridge, about 11 miles south of Quincy on the Quincy / LaPorte Road.

*Cromberg is on the Middle Fork, 18 miles east of Quincy. Two resorts in the area:*

**Long Valley Resort**, 5932 Highway 70 / 916-836 0754 / $$ / Motel and cottages

**20 Mile House** (end of Old Cromberg Road of Highway 70) / 916-836-0375 / $$- $$$ / Caters to fly fishers, and offers a fishing program with shared lodging, and access to a mile of private water on the river; choice of breakfast or "afternoon refreshment"

*Camping on Middle Fork between Sloat and Graeagle:*

There is no public campground on this stretch of river, though it is nearly all National forest; with fire permits, visitors may rough camp almost anywhere. For information, call the Quincy office of the USFS / 916-283-0555

*Graeagle is a small resort community:*

Gray Eagle Lodge, PO Box 467, Quincy, CA / 800-635-8778 / $$-$$$ / Lodging and dining, cabins and log lodge, breakfast and dinner included, half-mile from Graeagle on Gold Lake Road.

*Clio (the town is about as big as the resort below):*

White Sulfur Springs Ranch, 42 miles north of Truckee on Highway 89 North, 7 miles off Highway 70 (89 south) / $$-$$$ / The "Big House" is the oldest continuously utilized inn in California (same family since 1867); a B&B with cottages (up to seven people); large breakfasts; two miles from river; Olympic swimming pool; will set up fishing packages

**FOR MORE INFORMATION**

Quincy Chamber of Commerce
Quincy, CA, 95971
916-283-6345

# Yellow Creek and CalTrout

## by Seth Norman

The restoration project at Yellow Creek is one of many in which CalTrout has participated, lead, organized, aided, implemented, or managed. Among these are some of the state's major triumphs for fisheries:

- The California Wild Trout Program;

- The California Wild and Scenic Rivers Act;

- Granting of Wild and Scenic status to the Tuolume River;

- Preventing diversion of water at Hat Creek, and at rivers Eel, Pit, Kern, North Fork of the Feather;

- The campaign for Fall River regulation (and buying property to create the only public access);

- Conceiving the plan that made Martis Creek Lake California's first no-kill lake;

- Design of effective steelhead policy, including monitoring and funds provided by the punch card program;

- A 320 tons-of-trash clean-up of the Upper Sacramento, and the purchase of property there;

- The Hat Creek Wild Trout Program;

- Reform of timber harvest and grazing practices (i.e., the land management plan of Sequoia National Forest, now applied also to Six River, Mendocino, Shasta/Trinity and Klamath National Forests;

- and, recently, suing for — and winning — protection for Rush Creek (which incidentally saves Mono Lake) and the Owens River.

In the case of Yellow Creek, CalTrout's involvement began in 1971, when the organization urged into existence California's wild trout program, intended to help manage the state's best trout waters on a "quality" basis. A key section of Yellow Creek was submitted for that designation,

That effort failed. "Disappointed but undaunted, the organization's leaders conceived a play to bring the coveted meadow under special protection and management, to restore a natural, pristine, vibrant trout population like the pioneers were the first and last to see." *

What that meant was habitat repair and enhancement — and, ultimately, to regulations adjusting limits and the fishing techniques allowed. Before any of that could begin, however, it was necessary to solicit and win cooperation from the private parties and public agencies that held influence over the property: Department of Fish and Game, Pacific Gas & Electric, Dye Creek Cattle Company, Plumas County Fish and Game Commission, and the US Forest Service. With a consensus among these — add money, time, and a great deal of hard work — came results, fishable today on mornings when the light edges up on a meadow run where you have one more cast to a great golden riser who will sink with the sun.

CalTrout represents the interests of the "citizen angler." Anyone with a passion for California's wild trout, and for the wild places they live, likely fits that description.

For more information about the organization, contact the headquarters. Of course, those who have already caught and released the benefits of what Cal Trout has provided — may want to pay their dues.

**How to Contact:**     CalTrout State Headquarters
870 Market Street, #859
San Francisco, CA 94102
415-392-8887

* From the CalTrout brochure "Yellow Creek: For California, A Rare Spring Creek Angling Experience."

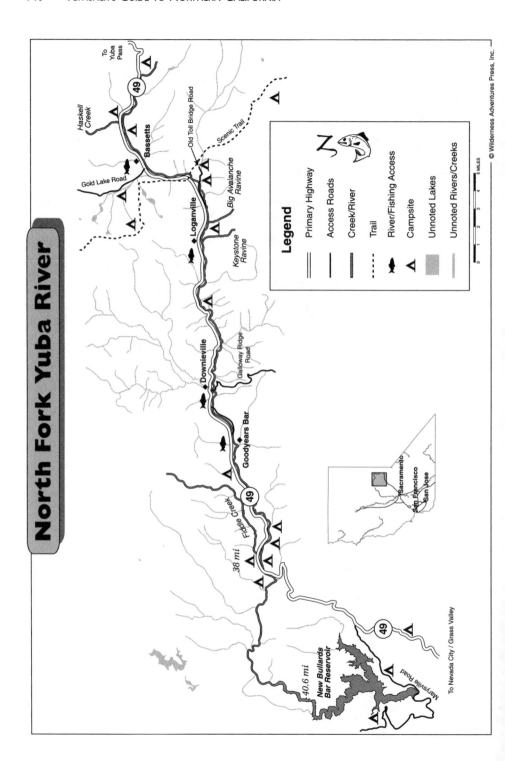

North Fork Yuba River

# Recovering Gold:
# The North Fork of the Yuba

*by Ralph Wood*

Gold miners rushed to the Yuba Valley in the 1850s, transforming hillsides into torrents of mud and gravel as they hosed away earth with high-pressure jets and diverted rivers to access bedrock beneath them. Strikes caused towns to appear overnight. In their lighted moment, men starved for the company of women turned out in mass to escort a fair arrival down the inevitable "Main Street."

Towns vanished when veins tapped out. Miners moved on to rude settlements of tent camps and shacks, there to survive on hardtack, hard liquor, and gleaming dreams while grubbing in the earth, struggling against claim-jumping and murder, asserting law with lynch ropes. A celebrated few struck it rich, the rest exhausted themselves in 16-hour days of hard labor for little or no return. Then they left, leaving scars and place names.

That was life nearly a 150 years ago on the Yuba River and its tributaries. The few towns that did endure — settled, as it were — are now quiet communities of working families or colonies of retirees. Hobbyists still pan for "color" in the area's streams, but most of those who now walk the banks seek another fortune altogether. What glitters gold in the Yuba today are wild brown trout, what flashes silver, rainbows.

Angling for these presents a variety of challenges and diverse opportunities. As elsewhere in California, history, geography, and dams have made several distinct fisheries of this system. Two are of importance to flyfishers: 40 miles of the North Fork of the Yuba, and the lower Yuba River, a 15-mile tailwater fishery. Sierra County contains the former, and the North Fork is a classic Western freestone stream, with stem and tributaries characterized by deep pools, pocket water, riffles, and runs — canyon-country water, coursing down the west slope, often within view of towering peaks.

## Overview — Fishing the North Fork of the Yuba

Pretty, easy to access and wade, with surprising numbers of willing fish, the North Fork is one of the most approachable of freestone streams. Although mostly paralleled by Highway 49 from the time it's a trickle off the Pacific side of the Sierra, the Yuba here is usually uncrowded, and the more adventurous fisher can always detour onto one of the rocky tributaries that feed the North Fork so often and well.

Those feeder creeks are mostly clamber and cast venues; on the main stem, however, hiking is in order. Plan to park at unmarked highway pullouts, walk down, then fish up; or fish down and hump home. Opportunities are greater when the river can be crossed in many places, usually after the spring melt. Perhaps because it's often a shadowed stream, the North Fork has an intimate, smaller water feel. Live oak, elephant ear, and conifers shade pockets much of the day, so browns will sometimes rise at noon, even in August. So will rainbows and brookies near the headwater.

This is a comfortable and exciting river, but don't abandon caution or care. Water temperatures on the North Fork run cold throughout the summer months; neoprenes are in order. So are felt-soled boots and a wading staff if you're unfamiliar with fast and sometimes heavy currents. Always be careful crossing the river, since flow and depth can be deceiving. Remember that in the broad, shallow runs often found here, the bottom will be helter skelter with small boulders. In these areas small crests of whitewater represent obstructions in current, so may be safer to wade than smooth, swift tongues of water coursing without break. Beware of dredger holes that are often deep. And a note about climbing: while the North Fork isn't considered a dangerous stream, the soil along the Yuba and its tributaries is often crumbly and crummy. Slag heaps left by miners look solid, but they're not. On slopes take it slow, plan a route, then an alternate.

(Editor's Note: On a trip up one of the feeder stream gorges, I decided not to backtrack 40 feet to a safe crossing, choosing instead to hup up around a cliff and traverse a game trail along a 20-foot drop. Around a corner the trail disappeared beneath scree of an avalanche. Afraid to retrace my tracks, I was forced up 200 feet, clinging to scrub and stones. Not amused, I did at the moment remember several prayers from childhood. Eventually I even climbed back down on a better trail, to raise a sleek rainbow with crimson cheek plates and a crisp white edge on his fins — 14 inches long, king of his own dark run.)

The fish get much bigger than that, especially when browns migrate up from Bullard's Bar Reservoir in the autumn. As good or better are the numbers of fish, roughly broken down to 60 percent brown trout and 40 percent rainbows, along with the willingness of both species to come up for dries.

Beyond that, there is again the feel of the Yuba. Wild enough in stretches, the North Fork is mostly a bright, dappled place, of a size that will not intimidate beginning anglers, with enough safe wading to make room for backcasts. Intermediates may well get a sense of command here, and experts still find significant challenges.

### Tackle and Tactics

For the majority of North Fork fishing 8.5- to 9-foot rods, 5- or 6-weight, will suffice. These should be rigged with weight-forward floating lines. Some anglers carry a sinktip for deeper holes. Leaders on the former should range from nine to 12 feet in length, with 4X to 6X tippets, depending upon fly size, water conditions, and the size of fish expected. On the sinktip, a four-foot leader should suffice. If an angler prefers, shortline techniques will work well here, with five- or six-foot long leaders on the rod of choice.

Standard tacticians should be keenly aware that drifts in complex currents must be kept close enough to control. Dry flyfishers coming off larger or smoother rivers and spring creeks should shorten casts to play a delicate balance: throwing enough slack to prevent drag, while keeping a tight line for quick strikes that come once.

Since this is difficult when not impossible, practice both casting and stoicism, or fish with a partner who will tolerate spontaneous outbursts.

Another critical point to keep in mind: in water as clear as the North Fork's, shadow and turbulence are the angler's allies wherever they are found. Pay particular attention to eddies along the bank; these are prime lies. Look for browns along slower seams, rainbows any place where there's a cushion or a small break in current.

## Hatches

Although most of the patterns you'll need will be noted below, an overview will suggest the nature of the North Fork's many hatches and indicate representations that have a place in a Yuba expedition box.

Expect good stonefly hatches in June and July, so bring weighted golden stone nymph patterns in sizes #4 through #8, and black rubber legs in sizes #4 through #6. Productive caddis imitations include green or brown LaFontaine larval and emergent patterns in sizes #10 through #16, green caddis larva sized #10 through #14, bead-head caddis pupa in sizes #10 through #16, and olive z-wing caddis in sizes #12 through #14. Other useful nymph patterns include Prince nymphs, Bird's nest nymphs, the A.P. (Andy Puyans) nymph series in olive, black and rust, and pheasant tails. The most productive sizes in these are #10 through #18.

Dry flies should include both golden and yellow stonefly patterns in sizes #4 through #10 and little yellow stones in sizes #12 through #16. Baetis parachute or sparkle dun patterns in size #18 work well when these mayflies are on the water. Orange Stimulators in sizes #6 through #10 will match the October caddis. General purpose dries for the North Fork and its tributary creeks should include the red-bellied Humpy, parachute Adams, parachute hare's ear, and the elk hair caddis in olive or tan — all in sizes #12 through #18.

## Access on the North Fork

Between its headwaters below Yuba Pass and the resort of Bassetts five miles north of Sierra City on Highway 49, the North Fork is little more than a shallow and brush-choked creek. Angling here is typical of most small moving waters of the Sierra: fish are wary and easily spooked. If you prefer a section of unobstructed casting room, seek out the beaver ponds near the Yuba Summit, located at about 6,500 feet, in an open area visible from the highway. Walk-in access is more difficult than it first appears because of boggy ground conditions, downed trees, and beaver holes.

The next six miles are not easily approached and generally require stealth, careful roll casts, and dapping. Those who enjoy such venues will have a stream made lively by beautifully-colored rainbow, brook, and brown trout, from seven to 10 inches in length. Attractor dries and caddis patterns in sizes #14 through #16 work well throughout this section.

Below Bassetts the North Fork is joined by Salmon Creek. This tributary drains the Lakes Basin north and west of Yuba Pass, and its pools and riffles extend up the slope like ladder steps. Rainbows in the six- to 10-inch range predominate in the creek, but it also holds a few browns and can be accessed from Highway 49 where the road crosses the stream about one mile south of Bassetts. The hike upstream is difficult and rewarding. Thanks to the water Salmon Creek provides, the North Fork comes into its own here, tumbling through a steep canyon toward the town of Sierra City. This is pocket water and fishes well with attractor dries such as humpies, Wulffs, and renegades, as well as with nymphs. Interesting fishing is complemented by spectacular scenery — 8,000-foot-high Sierra Buttes dominate the skyline, and in spring, wildflower blooms will delight the eye. Access is available from numerous turnouts along Highway 49.

Haypress Creek, the North Fork's last major tributary before Downieville, joins the river at the eastern edge of Sierra City. It offers small rainbows and, in its upper stretches, small brook trout. Both Haypress and a section of the North Fork are accessible from Wild Plum Road. The Department of Fish and Game plants hatchery-raised trout at Wild Plum Campground, but wild fish and the upper reaches of Haypress can be gained by a four-mile hike up Haypress Creek Trail. The trailhead is located on the north side of the bridge at Wild Plum Campground.

The next section of the North Fork, from its confluence with Haypress 12 miles downstream to the town of Downieville, is probably the premier area of this river for flyfishers. As it happens, this is also the stretch with a four-mile section of special regulation water, from the western edge of Sierra City to Ladies Canyon Creek, where only artificials with single barbless hooks are allowed. But don't neglect other areas — its all classic freestone water here, with fast runs, riffles, and pockets interspersed with long, slow pools. You can wade almost anywhere once the spring runoff has subsided, and you should, since much of the river is situated away from the road. Though the Department of Fish and Game plants trout near the campgrounds, excluding the special regulations stretch, by hiking you will encounter the best fishing opportunities — wild rainbows and browns of up to 16 inches, with larger fish not uncommon.

Important hatches along this section of the North Fork include golden stoneflies (*Calineuria*) during June, little yellow stones (*Isoperla*) during June and July, and Baetis sporadically late in the year on the slower sections of the river. Caddis are present from May through the end of the season in mid-November. The best caddis hatch occurs in October when the appropriately named October caddis (*Dicosmoecus*) emerges. Both fish and flyfishers look forward to this hatch. LaFontaine caddis emergers and orange stimulators in sizes #6 through #10 will often take large trout during the October caddis hatch. Consider your tippet rigging — the autumn often produces 22-inch browns with a #8 orange Stimulator.

If hatches aren't happening, try nymphing the pocket water, heads of runs, and pools. Productive patterns include the hare's ear nymph, A.P. black nymph, Bird's nest nymph and caddis emergers in sizes #10 through #16. Early in the season, try golden stone nymphs in sizes #4 to #8.

At Downieville, the Downie River joins the North Fork of the Yuba, and from it you can gain access to two other favorite creeks, Lavazzola and Pauley. By taking

*Working the North Fork Yuba.  (Photo: Ralph Wood)*

Main Street through Downieville and crossing the second bridge, you will come to Lavazzola Ranch Road. As you cross the bridge you can see the mouth of Pauley Creek on your right; access is available directly across the bridge. Lavazzola Creek is about five miles up Lavazzola Ranch Road, where a wooden bridge crosses it near an unimproved campground. Both creeks are loaded with beautifully colored small rainbows that really hit attractor dries in sizes #14 to #16. This is more canyon country. For the climb in and out, you should be in good physical condition.

The Downie River has productive fishing in its upper reaches for both rainbows and browns. The fish are all wild and respond well to attractor dries in sizes #14 to #16. Access is from Sailor Ravine Road, which is reached off Main Street in Downieville.

From Downieville west to the Highway 49 bridge, a distance of 22 miles, the North Fork widens and parallels Highway 49. Access points along the road are numerous, and hatches are similar to those upstream. Two creeks join the North Fork about five miles west of Downieville: Goodyears Creek on the north and Brush Creek on the south. Both offer good fishing for small rainbows. Access to Goodyears Creek is off Goodyears Creek Road and access to Brush Creek is off Mountain House Road.

You'll encounter planted fish around the various campgrounds situated on this part of the North Fork. To find wild trout, try fishing sections of river away from the road. A good rule-of-rod is that the farther you get from the campgrounds, the better the fishing will be.

During October and November, the section of the North Fork below Goodyears Bar contains a run of spawning brown trout coming up from Bullards Bar Reservoir. Some of these fish will hold over until spring, providing a chance to hook a trophy during the opening weeks of the season. For example, late in the 1992 season, the author hooked and released a large brown just above Indian Valley Campground — a muscular fish that took a #6 black woolly bugger at the head of a run and taped out at a 24.5 inches. Then, the author's friend Gary Smith landed a 25-incher at a location he has not yet revealed, though he will if he knows what's good for him.

Downstream from the Highway 49 bridge the only access to the river is by hiking. A gated road (closed to cars) at the north side of the bridge provides the easiest walk-in route, leading approximately one mile to Shenanigan Flat. This stretch of the river is productive during the autumn when fished with attractor dries and nymphs.

# Stream Facts: North Fork of the Yuba

### Location
• Interstate 80 to Highway 49, up 49 to Downieville (in roughly the middle of fishable water)

### River Characteristics
• A small stream rapidly gathering water from fishable tributaries; soon a river of medium size, mostly wadable, with many fish holding in pockets and shallow runs.

### Seasons
• Last Saturday in April thru November 15.

### Special Regulations
• Four miles of special regulation between the western boundary of Sierra City and the confluence of Ladies Canyon Creek: only artificial lures with single barbless hooks, limit of two fish over 10 inches.

### Trout
• The brown to rainbow ration is about 60:40, with average size fish 10-12 inches, larger fish to 25 inches (or better); small brookies at the extreme upper reaches.

### River Miles
• 40, of which four are wild trout, artificial fly, with single, barbless hooks, two-fish, 10-inch minimum

### River Flows
• No listed cfs for this freestone stream. Snowmelt is usually over by the end of June — the river may be fishable early in the month, if you're careful. For info, call Mike Fisher at Nevada City Anglers, 916-478-9301.

### Boat Ramps
• None

### Hub Cities
• Sierra City, Downieville, Bassetts

## NORTH FORK YUBA RIVER MAJOR HATCHES

| Insect | J | F | M | A | M | J | J | A | S | O | N | D | Flies |
|---|---|---|---|---|---|---|---|---|---|---|---|---|---|
| Golden Stones *Acroneuria californica* | | | | | | ▮ | | | | | | | Yellow Stimulator #6–10; Golden Stone Nymph #6–10 |
| Pale Morning Dun *Ephemerella infrequens* | | | | | | | ▮ | | | | | | Nymph: Hunchback Infrequens; Dries: PMD Paradun; PMD Emerger |
| Hydropsyche | | | | | ▮ | ▮ | ▮ | ▮ | ▮ | | | | LaFontaine's Deep Pupa Green #12–14; LaFontaine Emerging Pupa Green #12–14; Olive Z-Wing #12–14; Olive Elk Hair Caddis |
| Green Rock Worm *Rhyacophila* | | | | ▮ | ▮ | ▮ | ▮ | ▮ | ▮ | | | | Olive Elk Hair; Olive Z-Wing; Green Caddis Larva |
| Glossosoma | | | | | ▮ | ▮ | ▮ | | | | | | Cream Soft Hackle #16–20; Elk Hair Caddis Tan #16–18 |
| October Caddis *Dicosmoecus* | | | | | | | | | | ▮ | | | La Fontaine Caddis Emerger (Orange & Brown) #6–10; Orange Stimulator #6–10 |

Also: Woolly Buggers (Black & Brown) #6; Marabou Muddler Multicolored #4–6; Marabou Muddler (Yellow & White); Little Brown, Little Rainbows #8–12

# Sierra City

## Elevation – 4,200 • Population – 250

### ACCOMMODATIONS

Bed-and-breakfast inns and motels are located in both Downieville and Sierra City.

**Herrington's Resort,** 101 Main Street, Sierra City, CA 96125 / 916-862-1151 / AAA, Good accommodations, housekeeping or motel units, a good restaurant on site, and is located at the eastern edge of the special regulation section of the river, author recommends / $$-$$$

**Yuba River Inn,** on Highway 49 in Sierra City, CA 96125 / 916-862-1122 / Both new and log cabins, with and without kitchens, for 2 to 6 persons, on river / $-$$$

**Kokanee Kabins,** Housekeeping cabins in Tahoe Forest / 916-862 1287 / low end of $$

**The Buttes Resort,** Highway 49 in Sierra City, CA 91625 / 800-991-1170 / A variety of housekeeping cabins and rooms from simple to complete with wet bar and whirlpool / $-$$$

**Near Bassetts (*upper end of river*):**

**Bassetts Station,** Highway 49 and Gold Lake Road, Bassetts, CA 96125 / 916-862-1297 / Small, quiet, year-round motel a rest stop for 125 years. "We gladly accept children." Fishing close by and a small store that doesn't gouge / $$

**High Country Inn,** Bed and Breakfast, Highway 49 and Gold Lake Road, Bassetts,CA 96125 / 800-862-1530 / 15 miles above Sierraville at the top end of the river near Bassetts, large rooms, fireplaces, country breakfasts, own trout pond, river frontage / $$$

*In Downieville:*

**Saundra Dyer's Resort,** off Highway 49, on the river. Downieville,CA 95936 / 800-696-3308 / Walking distance from Downieville shops, rooms with or without kitchens; pool, picnic areas, breakfast available / $$

**Sierra Shangri-La,** off Highway 49, Downieville, CA 95936 / 916-289-3455 / B&B rooms, housekeeping cottages, some on or near river, with patios, meeting room, breakfast plans daily and weekly rates, weekday discounts / $-$$$

### RESTAURANTS
**Coyoteville Cafe,** before Downieville in Coyoteville / Good diner
**Herrington's Restaurant** (see Herrington's Resort under Accommodations) / $$$

### FLY SHOPS AND SPORTING GOODS
*The closest dedicated fly shop is in Nevada City*
**Nevada City Anglers** / 916-478-9301
**Bassetts Station,** Highway 49 and Gold Lake Road, Bassetts, CA 96125 / 916-862-1297 / Some tackle is available

**Will's Wild Sports**, 231 East Main Street, Grass Valley, CA 95945 / 530-272-8324 / Some fly tackle is available

**Sierra Hardware**, 305 Main Street, Downieville, CA95936 / 916-289-3582 Downieville, downtown next to post office, small selection of tackle

## AIRPORT

Commercial air service in Sacramento and Reno, both about two hours away.

## AUTO RENTALS

Also in Sacramento and Reno

## CAMPING

The North Fork of the Yuba runs through the **Tahoe National Forest**, 916-265-4531, and there are many public campgrounds along the river just off Highway 49. At the lower end of the river, the campground of choice is **Indian Valley**. **Loganville Campground** is on Wild Trout section.; you may ask also about **Union Valley**, **Carlton** (tents only), and **Wild Plum**.

## OTHER ATTRACTIONS IN AREA

Highway 49 runs through an area rich in the history of gold: there are many old mines, museums and Indian sites located here. Information about these, as well as a map and brochure "49 Miles Along Highway 49" is available through USDA Forest Service Office, 631 Coyote St., PO Box 6003, Nevada City CA 95959,

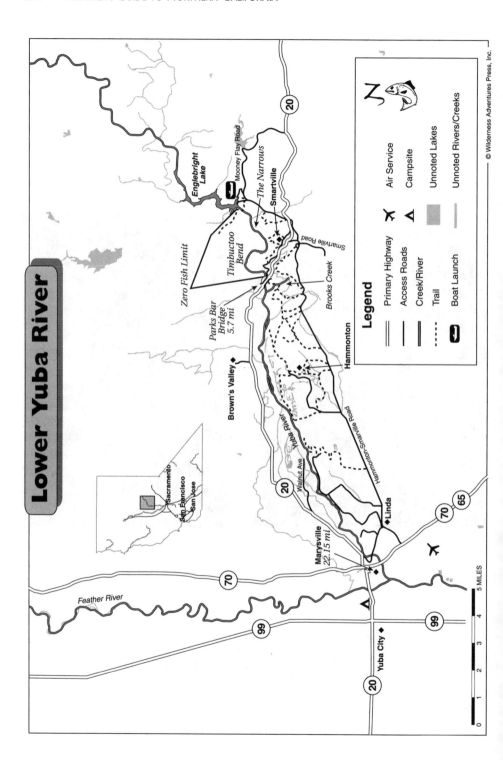

Lower Yuba River

© Wilderness Adventures Press, Inc.

**Legend**

Primary Highway
Access Roads
Creek/River
Trail
Boat Launch

Air Service
Campsite
Unnoted Lakes
Unnoted Rivers/Creeks

Englebright Lake
Mooney Flay Road
The Narrows
Smartville
Timbuctoo Bend
Zero Fish Limit
Parks Bar Bridge 5.7 mi
Brooks Creek
Smartville Road
Hammonton
Brown's Valley
Yuba River
Walnut Ave
Hammonton/Smartville Road
Linda
Marysville 22.15 mi
Feather River
Yuba City
Sacramento
San Francisco
San Jose

70
20
65
70
99
99
20
20

0 1 2 3 4 5 MILES

# Lower Yuba River: Just Don't Call Them Steelhead

## *by Ralph Wood*

Although this is not a book about steelhead fishing in California, the Lower Yuba - broad and stony, winding through lowlands so hot in summer the riverbed gleams white-drains into the Feather River, which enters the Sacramento, which spills into the Bay and on to the sea ... thus California Fish and Game considers any rainbow trout caught here a steelhead when it measures 18 inches or longer.

Some of these big Yuba fish certainly make that saltwater migration. Others, the author is certain, do not; and so this river appears here as a trout venue until such time as each of those gleaming fish contributes a scale to science. In the meantime, buy the steelhead punch card with your license and call the fish whatever you like.

If you can get to them. Angling access along the main stem of the lower Yuba is limited at best. The first 8 miles of the river below Englebright Dam can be reached by hiking upstream from the Highway 20 Bridge (also known as the Parks Bar Bridge), which crosses the river about 16 miles west of Grass Valley. The water below the bridge is accessible either by hiking downstream or by paying a parking fee at Sycamore Ranch Resort, located off Highway 20, 4 miles west of the bridge on the way to Marysville.

Many of the special regulations on the Yuba are tied to Parks Bar Bridge. Above it, tackle is restricted to artificial lures with single barbless hooks, and a zero-fish limit. Steelhead season (and so rainbows) on the upper section runs from December 1 to September 30, with a closure imposed to protect migrating salmon. Downstream from the bridge, the river is a year- round fishery (check regulations for limits, as they are constantly changing).

### Overview

The Lower Yuba is a tailwater fishery composed of long runs, deep pools, and broad riffles. During early spring the upper section runs cool, with temperatures of 45 to 50 degrees. These will rise to between 50 and 60 degrees during summer and autumn.

Fishing conditions are dependent on water releases from Englebright Dam, which are dictated by run-off and demands for irrigation. Spring flows can range from 700 cubic feet per second (cfs) in drought years to 30,000 cfs at flood. During normal summer months, when farms are needy, flows may rise to 1,400 cfs or more. The river is typically fishable at less than 3,000 cfs. Any angler headed here should first call for river conditions. One source for information is Nevada City Anglers, 916-478-9301.

### Hatches, Flies, Techniques

In December, January and February, most fishing is done with nymphs under indicators or with standard steelhead tactics — traditional patterns swung on sink-

*Working the Yuba's flatwater. (Photo: Seth Norman)*

ing lines and shooting heads through holding water. Trout tactics and flies are preferable because Yuba fish will feed at the surface in winter, during the Skwala stonefly hatches in January and February, and when overcast conditions generate hatches of blue wing olives (*Baetis*).

March and April bring out Western March browns (*Rhithrogena*), gray drakes (*Siphlonurus*), pale morning duns (*infrequens*), and caddis, both *Hydropsyche* and *Brachycentrus*. Little yellow stones (*Isoperla*) begin to make their appearance in April. Morning fishing can be very productive using #14 to #18 nymphs under an indicator. As the day warms, dry fly fishing comes on.

Golden stones (*Calineuria*) emerge during June, but caddis will predominate for the balance of the season. As summer progresses the best angling occurs in the morning and the evening. If you intend to fish mid day, carry water and sunscreen, and be prepared for heat. The river is near sea level here, and temperatures often rise to over 100 degrees.

### Fishing the Lower Yuba

The trout are not difficult to find. During the morning hours they tend to feed over midstream gravel bars, and in the faster sections near deeper water. Look for convergent flows, the edges of fast and slow water, and deep water near shore. If flows are high the fish will hold along the edge of the river where the current is slow-

*A big, colorful Yuba
river rainbow .
(Photo: Ken Morrish)*

est. In the evening, search for fish in smoother water, such as runs and tailouts. In these sections the river bed is composed of gravel and rubble: fish hold in depressions, often in surprisingly shallow water.

The average temperature of the river rises as it flows toward Marysville, and as summer days warm the river. Around Memorial Day, when the water below Daguerra Point Dam reaches 60 degrees or more, the shad migration hits its peak. Of course, no trout fiend would ever bother with these spunky fighters, remarkably like a tarpon, but if they did, good access could be found at the Hallwood Avenue run, and at Walnut Avenue off Highway 20, just west of Marysville. Standard shad patterns would work, in red and white, yellow and white, and chartreuse, sizes #4 to #8.

(For more information on the Yuba River shad fishery, refer to "Yuba River Shad" in the March-April '94 issue of *California Fly Fisher*.)

*Working channels on the lower Yuba.*

**Tackle**

For the majority of fishing on the North Fork and the lower Yuba, 8.5 to 9.5 foot rods are recommended. A six-weight rod and reel, ready with spools of both weight-forward floating lines and sinktips, is a good choice. Leaders should range from nine to 12 feet in length, with 4X to 6X tippets, depending upon fly size, water conditions, and size of fish encountered. During the lower Yuba's early season, a 7- or 8-weight rod would do better (especially for those who might hook a shad) with corresponding Type IV sinktips and shooting heads. Appropriate leaders for these sinkers range from 6 feet to 7.5 feet, tapering to 3X or 4X tippets.

As noted, the water here runs cold, even through summer, so consider neoprene waders with felt-soled boots. Use a wading staff if you're uncomfortable in fast and sometimes heavy flows. Be sure to wade cautiously, especially when crossing the river. Current and depth can be deceiving.

Although some anglers will already have favorite patterns for insects, this review might enhance fly boxes for a Yuba River excursion.

Bring weighted golden stone nymph patterns in sizes #4 through #8, and black rubber-legs in sizes #4 through #6. Productive caddis imitations include green or brown LaFontaine larval and emergent patterns in sizes #10 through #16, green caddis larva in sizes #10 through #14, beadhead caddis pupa in sizes #10 through #16, and olive Z-wing caddis in sizes #12 through #14. Other useful nymph patterns include Prince nymphs, Bird's nest nymphs, the A.P. nymph series in olive, black and rust, and pheasant tails. The most productive sizes are #10 through #18.

Dry flies should include both golden and yellow stonefly patterns in sizes #4 through #10, and little yellow stones in sizes #12 through #16. Baetis parachute or sparkle dun patterns in size #18 work well when blue winged olives are on the water. Try using a yellowish #8 stimulator when the skwala stones are hatching,

Steelhead flies appropriate for the lower river — for trout, of course — include such traditional patterns as the skunk, boss, comet, silver Hilton and popsicle in sizes #4 through #8. Glo bugs in sizes #6 through #10 are useful during fall and winter, when fish lie in wait for errant eggs from salmon redds below Parks Bar Bridge.

# Stream Facts: Lower Yuba

## Seasons
- Above Parks Bar Bridge: open December 1 to September 30, closed from October 1 to December 1 to protect migrating salmon.
- Downstream from the bridge: open all year

## Special Regulations
- Above the Parks Bar Bridge (aka Highway 20 Bridge), restricted to artificial lures with single barbless hooks, zero-fish limit. For limits below the bridge check current regulations, as these are subject to change.

## River Characteristics
- The Lower Yuba is a big, broad and stony, low-elevation tailwater, with wide- ranging flows and runs of anadromous fish, including shad, steelhead, and salmon.
- Trout (rainbows — or are they steelhead?) average 13 to 14 inches, some up to 25 inches. Sea-run browns have been reported.

## River Miles
- Approximately 15

## Flows
- From 700 cfs to 30,000. Fishable at 3,000 cfs or below, better at half that.

## Shops
- Nevada City Anglers (916-478-9301) is a full-service fly shop in Nevada City. Call them for up-to-date information on both the North Fork and lower Yuba including flow information on the lower river.
- See also transit city shops, Sacramento shops.

## Boat Ramps
None.

## Hub City
Grass Valley/Nevada City

## LOWER YUBA RIVER MAJOR HATCHES

| Insect | J | F | M | A | M | J | J | A | S | O | N | D | Flies |
|---|---|---|---|---|---|---|---|---|---|---|---|---|---|
| Pale Morning Dun *Ephemerella infrequens* | | | | | █ | █ | █ | | | | | | Nymph: Hunchback Infrequens Dry: PMD Paradun; PMD Emerger |
| Little Yellow Stone *Isoperla* | | | | | | █ | █ | | | | | | Yellow Elk Hair Caddis Mercer's Little Yellow Stone |
| Sedge *Hydropsyche* | | | | | | | | █ | █ | | | | LaFontaine's Deep Pupa Green #12–18; LaFontaines Emerging Green #10–14; Green; Olive Z-Wing #12–14; Olive Elk Hair Caddis |
| Green Rock Worm *Rhyacophila* | | | | | | | | █ | █ | | | | Olive Elk Hair; Olive Z-Wing; Green Caddis Larva |
| Caddis *Brachycentrus* | | | █ | █ | | | | | | | | | LaFontaines Tan & Brown #12–16; LaFontaines Deep Pupa Brown; LaFontaines Emerging Pupa Brown |
| Golden Stonefly *Callineuria pacifica* | | | | | | █ | | | | | | | Golden Stone Nymph #6–10 Yellow Stimulator #6–10 |
| Gray Drake *Siphlonurus occidentalis* | | | | | | | | █ | █ | | | | Stalcup Gilled Nymph (Gray); Adam's Parachute #10–12; Grey Wulff #10–12 |
| Skwala Stones *Perlodidae* | | █ | | | | | | | | | | | Yellow Stimulator #8–10 |
| Blue Winged Olive *Baetis parvis* | | █ | | | | | | | | | █ | | Baetis Paradun Light & Dark Olive #16–22; Baetis Emerger Olive #16–22; Hunchback Infrequens Olive & Brown #16–22; Olive Sparkle Dun #16–20 |
| W. March Brown *Rhithrogena* | | | █ | | | | | | | | | | March Brown Paradun #12–16; March Brown Comparadun #12–16; Hare's Ear #12–16; March Brown Soft Hackle #12–16 |

# Grass Valley / Nevada City

### Elevation – 2,400 ft. • Population – 2,900

The lower Yuba is easily accessed from either Marysville or Grass Valley/Nevada City, and these communities provide a full-range of services and lodging. The author lives in Grass Valley/Nevada City, and recommends it as the hub.

## Accommodations

**Downie House B&B**, 517 W. Broad Street, Nevada City, CA 95959 / 800-258-2815 / $$$

**Deer Creek Inn**, 116 NEvada St. Nevada City / 530-265-0363

**Northern Queen Inn**, 4000 Railroad Avenue, Nevada City, CA 95959 / 530-265-0896 / AAA approved, clean rooms, hot tub, restaurant in nice location / $$

**Best Western (Gold Country Inn)**, 11972 Sutton Way, Grass Valley, CA 95945 or 95949 / 916-273-1393 or 800-528-1234 / $$

## Restaurants

**PJ's of Nevada City**, call for directions, Nevada City, CA 95959 / 530-265-9091 / A great Deli, with homemade sausages and smoked meats

**Lyons Restaurant**, 12075 Nevada City Hwy, Grass Valley, CA 95945 or 95949 / 916-272-8414 / $

**Mountain Mike's Pizza**, Grass Valley Shopping Center, Grass Valley, CA 95945 or 95949 / 916-272-9066 / $$

**Peter Selaya's**, 320 Broad Street, Nevada City, CA 95959 / 916-265-5697 / Truly innovative cuisine; make reservations / $$$

**Cafe Mekka**, 237 Commercial St. Nevada City / 530-478-1517

**Country Rose Cafe**, 300 Commercial St. / 530-265-6248

**Silk Road**, 316 Commercial St. Nevada City / 530-470-0298

## Fly Shops and Sporting Goods

**Nevada City Anglers**, 417 Broad Street, Nevada City, CA 95959 / 916-478-9301 / A full-service fly shop; call them for up-to-date information

**Bob's Fly-Shack**, 488 W. Onstott Road, Yuba City, CA 95991 / 916-671-9628

## Hospitals

**Sierra Nevada Memorial**, Grass Valley, CA 95945 or 95949 / 916-274-6000

## Airport

**Nevada County Airport** / 916-273-3374 / Private planes, no services / See Sacramento for commercial services

## Auto Rentals

**Enterprise**, 797 S. Auburn, Grass Valley, CA 95945 or 95949 / 916-274-400 / Available in Sacramento

**Gold Country A&A Auto Rental**, 745 S. Auburn, Nevada City, CA 95959 /
916-273-6516

## For More Information
Nevada City Chamber of Commerce
132 Main Street
Nevada City, CA
916-265-2692

## Other Activities
Grass Valley is the home of the Empire Mine, the oldest and richest hard rock
gold mine in California. Nevada City was once known as the "Queen City of the
Northern Mines" and is the most complete Gold Rush town left in California.
Northeast of Nevada City is Malakoff Diggings State Historic Park, site of the
last working hydraulic mine in the state. The Nevada City area makes a great
family destination, with restaurants and accommodations ranging from motels
to Victorian bed-and-breakfast inns and historic hotels.

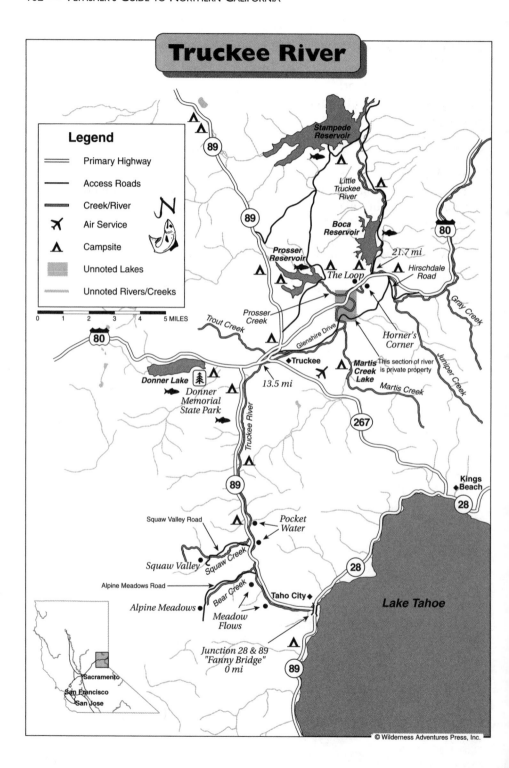

# Truckee River

### Legend

| | |
|---|---|
| ═══ | Primary Highway |
| ─── | Access Roads |
| ━━━ | Creek/River |
| ✈ | Air Service |
| ▲ | Campsite |
| ▨ | Unnoted Lakes |
| ┈┈┈ | Unnoted Rivers/Creeks |

0  1  2  3  4  5 MILES

Stampede Reservoir

Little Truckee River

Boca Reservoir

21.7 mi

Prosser Reservoir

The Loop

Hirschdale Road

Prosser Creek

Glenshire Drive

Horner's Corner

This section of river is private property

Gray Creek

Juniper Creek

Trout Creek

Truckee

Martis Creek Lake

Martis Creek

Donner Lake

Donner Memorial State Park

13.5 mi

Truckee River

267

Squaw Valley Road

Pocket Water

Squaw Valley

Squaw Creek

Kings Beach

28

28

Alpine Meadows Road

Bear Creek

Taho City

Alpine Meadows

Meadow Flows

Lake Tahoe

Junction 28 & 89 "Fanny Bridge" 0 mi

Sacramento

San Francisco
San Jose

© Wilderness Adventures Press, Inc.

# Truckee River:
# An Angler's Edge

*by Frank Pisciotta*

Early this century anglers fished the Truckee River for the largest cutthroat trout in the world: the Lahontan strain spawned in the Truckee, tens of thousands surging up from Pyramid Lake, the vast remains of a freshwater sea. Imagine casting to 20-pound trout in a lovely mountain stream!

By 1938 dams and commercial fishing had completely exterminated the ancient cutthroat run. Doubtless, the process was of benefit to some.

Now imagine this: The US. Fish & Wildlife Service, in cooperation with the Pyramid Lake Paiute Tribe, as well as the California and Nevada Fish and Game departments, began a program to reintroduce Lahontans using stock from Pyramid Lake. Perhaps cutthroat as long as a man's leg will hold once again in a High Sierra water.

## Overview

Truckee River is a lovely stretch of water coursing a canyon along one of the world's great edges, the Sierra Nevada, through a part of the state with an interesting history. The Truckee is not a good choice for beginners — it can befuddle the competent, and while days of several dozen fish occur, they are rare. Make no mistake, however, the fish are here, up to 3,600 per mile, 55 percent browns running to 22 inches, the rest rainbows to 19 inches, with a median for both just under a foot. Trophy trout are available throughout the river system, but nowhere are they easily duped. Truckee is demanding, a place where the patient and attentive hone streamcraft. To succeed here bodes well for excursions on other moving waters. Just as skiers who triumph easily on mountains around Tahoe return to Squaw Valley for a "humbling run," so may anglers receive an "adjustment" on the Truckee.

Like the runs at Squaw, those on this river may prove exhilarating and addictive.

Truckee River is also Lake Tahoe's only outlet, leaving the great blue water at 6,229 feet. A famous landmark spans the river just below the small dam near the junction of state highways 28 and 89. Near a metal sculpture of three 6-foot long trout doing a skyward pirouette, "Fanny Bridge" earns its name, routinely mounting displays of derrieres as tourists lean over to view and feed the large rainbows and browns finning in the placid pool below the dam. If the fish look at ease, perhaps it's because no angling is allowed within 1,000 feet of the 12 federally regulated gates.

From its source, the Truckee heads north, sidling along Highway 89 while slowly descending through a narrow, volcanic-ridged valley, bordered by thick evergreen forest. On its route, the river skirts Squaw Valley, site of the 1960 Winter Olympics. At the end of the corridor, where Highway 89 bisects Interstate 80, river and road reach the

*Working a broad riffle on the Truckee. (Photo: Frank Pisciotta)*

lively ski town of Truckee (6,051 feet). Due west is the infamous Donner Summit, where a winter-bound pioneer party turned cannibal in one of the more alarming experiments in California cuisine. Beyond, down the Sierra's western slope, lie San Francisco and the Pacific Ocean, 200 miles away. The river does not take that course. From the town of Truckee, near the confluence of Donner Creek, the Truckee flows east.

The pool at Donner Creek is the last point on the Truckee where the Department of Fish and Game stocks hatchery trout. From that point downstream the trout are wild and the river accessible, paralleling Interstate 80 and intercontinental railroad tracks for 20 miles until it crosses into Nevada. At last, 88 miles from the dam of derrieres, the Truckee ends what will be a lake-to-lake journey, spilling into vast, alkaline Pyramid Lake, still home to those Lahontan cutts that the Truckee may soon support again.

## Fishing the Truckee: Access

For angling purposes, the Truckee River can be divided into three sections, with the 12-mile long middle section of special interest to the fly-rodder. A special, state-mandated "Wild Trout" sanctuary, it has convoluted regulations (see *Stream Facts*) intended to develop and sustain self-perpetuating natural trout populations distinct from hatchery stock. Current restrictions are always posted, and the area is heavily patrolled against poachers. Meat fishers should stick to the upper and lower sections of the river, where there are now five-trout limits and no gear restrictions.

Although the upper Truckee along Highway 89 receives the greatest angling pressure, it still has plenty of fish, partly because the California Department of Fish & Game seeds this entire stretch with hatchery rainbows to augment a population of streambred browns. In this stretch, the river has formed a long valley; angler access is available via roadside turnouts that are visible as you drive throughout this stretch. Fair warning, however, that during the hot summer months, commercial rafting companies send flotillas down from the lake to the rustic River Ranch Lodge, which sits at the junction of Bear Creek and the spur road leading to Alpine Meadows Ski Area.

This three-mile stretch, from 1,000 feet below Fanny Bridge to the lodge, features smooth meadow flows that occasionally compress into runs like the one rushing into a deep pool just in front of the lodge's deck. In the meadows it's best to fish early or, better yet, late, during the evening hatches.

Between Alpine Meadows and Squaw Valley is a workable mile of pocket water, once again easily accessed by turnouts along the road. One-half mile before the entry road to Squaw Valley, the Truckee crosses beneath the pavement. It will remain on the east side of Highway 89 throughout the gorge.

Also, beginning at this point, the river is frequently bordered by streamside homes, sometimes with their own private, one-lane bridges. It's necessary to secure permission to cross these these private bridges. After the spring thaw, however, an angler can ford the stream in places. Remember, you may fish all of the river below the high-water mark.

As the Truckee proceeds through the canyon, it picks up considerable volume. Seven creeks feed snowmelt into the main stem during spring runoff, with Bear and Squaw Creeks providing the greatest share.

There is little broken water below the entry of Squaw Creek, mostly long, shallow riffles and glides. Fishing is often best at the heads of runs. Bridge supports also provide excellent opportunities, creating deep troughs where wild browns of 16 to 18 inches feed in currents deflecting off the abutments. Work carefully under streamside brush, especially where you find it on the outside of bends.

For those who prefer camping, the Highway 89 corridor is centrally located. Three streamside campgrounds provide 117 tent and RV sites. Included among those are 19 tent and 16 wheelchair-accessible sites with vault toilets. Outdoor accommodations are also available outside the valley, with Donner Memorial State Park the largest and most scenic of these. But Donner does accommodate groups and usually fills up well in advance of major holidays.

At the end of the valley is the confluence with Donner Creek. To reach this juncture, turn right off Highway 89 (if you're proceeding downstream, roughly north) onto West River Street, then drive a quarter mile. As you come to the inflow of Donner Creek at the culvert bridge, you will see a pool at the juncture of the streams. As noted, this is the end of the stocked section of Truckee, and from this point on the trout are usually naturals. Note also that a short walk up the truckee will bring an angler to an area with active beaver. During evening hatches it's quickly obvious that these mammal builders have fishy neighbors.

You may continue on West River Street beyond the culvert bridge. After about 1.5 miles the road will intersect Highway 267. A left turn will take you into town, the district known as Commercial Row, with refurbished turn-of-the-century stores and restaurants. Going straight across 267, you will find that West River has turned into East River at the intersection; then it's about a mile drive to Trout Creek. And finally, a right turn on 267 begins a 10-mile drive to King's Beach on the north shore of Lake Tahoe. This last route passes an economical Best Western Motel, a small-craft airport, and Martis Lake — California's first wild trout lake (this venue is zero kill only, allowing only artificials with barbless hooks). Ultimately, you will find a panoramic vista of Lake Tahoe while descending Brockway Summit.

Back at Truckee: Both East and West River Streets closely parallel the river. While flyfishing this piece of water, one is essentially angling along the back side of town. There are homes, businesses, and some light industrial sites here. Exercise caution on this north side of the river — not all the mountain dogs encountered in the streamside backyards are charmers.

To avoid canine confrontations, it's a better move to cross the Highway 267 bridge in order to fish the south side of the river. South River Street hugs the water for a quarter mile downstream, then deadends at homesites where no vehicles may proceed. Nor do many anglers, as the river's path cuts almost a straight line to Trout Creek in a stretch of deep runs with sparse cover and few current breaks or obstructions.

South River Street also heads upriver, although the pavement ends after 50 yards. From there it's rutted dirt road all the way to Donner Creek. All that distance, 1.5 miles, you will find productive pocket water, and micropools formed behind boulders. Willows shade the water in many places. While this stretch rarely produces outsized trout, it has the potential for quick action. In the early '70s, a fraternity brother and the author once cumulatively (guesstimated) took more than 50 browns in 3 hours, with the biggest about 14 inches.

The premier middle section of the Truckee begins just below the town of Truckee. From Commercial Row's turn-of-the-century landmark, the Truckee Hotel, go one-half mile on Highway 267, heading roughly north northeast, and turn right at Glenshire Road.

Glenshire provides access to the most familiar points of departure for exploration of the Truckee's trophy waters. Trout Creek is the upstream boundary of this designation and can be seen trickling under the tiny railroad trestle. Below this point, both railroad track and Interstate 80 will run near the river all the way into Nevada.

From the Glenshire Road turnoff at Highway 267, it's 3.8 miles to the Glenshire Bridge. On the way you will see many dirt turnoffs where you may park. Cross the tracks — beyond, the river beckons. There's also plenty of parking on the far side of the bridge overpass.

*Working the Truckee's boulder pockets. (Photo: Seth Norman)*

This area is a favorite for visiting fly enthusiasts partly because of its easy access and proximity to town. It's also a pleasant place to wet a line. Wading here is non-threatening, and there are long glides, gentle riffles, and short stretches of pocket water. The chaparral terrain is open and level, with scattered stands of evergreens. You'll also find a spectacular vista — a layered silhouette of Sierra peaks in the western sky. Never mind that those who named the spots you're fishing seemed oblivious to esthetics: enjoy "Cat House Hole" (called Polaris on some maps), "Toilet Bowl" and — euphemistically — "Fornicating Rock Run."

The river courses an east/west axis here, making light and shadow important factors, notably in the evenings. When working upstream, the setting sun can blind you. Mitigate this effect with polaroid glasses and a billed cap, adjust your approach, and stalk. It is critical to do so, because dusk is magic time for dry-fly addicts. Often the hatches come on suddenly — a quiet run will suddenly erupt with a crescendo of splashes, swirls, and kerplunks. Anglers unprepared for this onslaught of opportunity may find themselves a little stunned — body poised to cast, head rotating back and forth like an owl overwhelmed by a lemming run.

Usually, this activity is prompted by emerging caddis or by little yellow stones agitating the surface film. Stiff-hackled, palmered, downwing profile dries and emerger patterns will draw the most takes. When floating dries in the slicks, twitch or skate your offering. This technique may provoke the heart-stopping chase-bulge-attack of a caddis-hunting brown.

Characteristically, the rainbows in the Truckee locate in fast-water seams, sometimes in whitewater lies. Browns hold to smoother flows, creases in the slower currents, and updwellings from subsurface obstructions. Uncharacteristically, however, these browns are jumpers. Between the two species an angler has a chance for double-digit hookups during evenings from mid-June into early August.

The Glenshire Bridge structure also forms the upstream boundary of an exclusive private flyfishing lodge that controls 1.5 miles of the river, both sides, to 100 yards upstream of the Union Mills Bridge at Highway 80 (see regulation sidebar). To approach the stretch of public wild trout water below their property, you have several options, and several choices within each of these.

The first option at this point is to continue driving east from Boca Bridge on the paved road through the community of Glenshire. At 4.2 miles you will reach the junction at Hirschdale Road. From here, proceed to the left under the Interstate 80 overpass, then on a quarter mile to Boca Bridge, an antique trestle preserved for historical reasons. Cross the river via the modern bridge next to the old one; on the opposite side you will find plenty of parking.

(Note: The Glenshire Bridge area became the ingress point for three rafting companies. Thirty raft permits have been issued, allowing drifts from 10:00 a.m. to 5:00 p.m. Rafters are not allowed to disembark their boats until the egress at Floriston. The impact of rafting on the river — on fish and fishers — is yet to be determined. Also, further along Hirschdale Road and over the railroad tracks are Boca, Stampede and Prosser Reservoirs. Decent flyfishing is available at the inlets of these impoundments in spring and autumn.)

Another option is to merge right at the juncture of Hirschdale and Glenshire roads and head toward the hamlet of Hirschdale. A half-mile along the road you will cross the river on a bridge — park on the left side. Upstream are huge, placid, pools; downstream is the top end of the Grand Canyon of the Truckee.

The canyon is a special place, a reach known for heavy flows most of the season, thanks to feed from storage impoundments upriver responding to agribusiness and power demands from Nevada. Nevertheless, local consensus also recognizes this stretch as home to the Truckee system's largest trout.

To reach these brutes, a fisher must walk the railroad tracks. It's a little more than four miles downstream to Gray Creek, the bottom marker of the wild trout area. Along the way you may drop to the river down steep, loose-graveled slopes. Note: this is canyon water and treacherous. However, after a mile and a half it levels out considerably, although by then the better holding water is more spread out.

All things considered, the Grand Canyon is best fished in fall, when the flows are not so turbulent and deep. Fishing pressure is scant relative to other sections of special management. Some bait anglers avoid this stretch because of the two-trout creel limit. As that combination suggests, the adventurous angler has a chance to tangle with trophy browns in the five-plus pound range — it happens.

*Glenshire Bridge during low water. (Photo: Frank Pisciotta)*

Another option for accessing the river below the private water is to head back toward Truckee via Glenshire road. Turn right on Highway 267 for a quarter mile to Interstate 80 east. Take the first exit of I-80, 5 miles down, past the Union Mills overpass. Cross the next bridge about .7 miles down the road at "West Bridge" of "The Loop," a sweeping horseshoe bend in the river. Immediately turn right onto the dirt road. Park under the tree where you will find fishing regulations posted, courtesy of Lisa and Ralph Cutter's California School of Fly Fishing.

From here you have several choices. First, you may cross under the river overpass, to make a mile-long walk along the railroad tracks — keeping a safe distance (the broken metal bands on cargo cars can cut you to bits) — past the controlled inflow of Prosser Creek to the Union Mills Bridge. As mentioned, the latter is the downstream limit of the private club property. Fish the river down Union Mill using large streamers. Or — a variation on this theme — from where you parked at the west bridge, fish upstream to Prosser Creek. Heavy nymphs are generally most effective in this stretch, which is characterized by deep runs.

Second, start at West Bridge (as the bridge name suggests, you stand at the western side of "The Loop" bend). Here, the river is bordered by steep, forested terrain on the far bank, and the water is mostly shallow water with relatively few fish. The limited holding lies are on the edges, under overhanging willows, or in deep pockets immediately below the bridge. But farther downriver, at the apex of the bow (about

*A wade staff aids footing in the Truckee. (Photo: Seth Norman)*

a quarter mile), you will find a couple of productive pools. The one below the high, vertical cliff is known as "Horner's Corner," named after Jack Horner, creator of "Horner's Deer Hair," ancestor of the Humpy and Goofus Bug, among others. Horner was a devotee of the Truckee River and spent many hours fishing and perfecting his designs on its waters. (Note: another Truckee River luminary is the tier Cal Bird, designer of the famous Bird's nest and Bird's stone.)

Third, make a 300-meter beeline across country to the East Bridge, at the return side of the deep river bend. Here, probe the broken water and deep riffles, working upstream up to Horner's Corner.

A last option takes an angler under the interstate — climb the bank to the tracks, and follow them for almost a mile to where the Little Truckee River comes in just above the Boca Bridge (upstream border for the no-gear, no-minimum-size, two-kill sector of the wild trout water). Fish back from here, upstream. You'll find good pocket water and shallow runs.

The lower section of the Truckee, beyond Gray Creek, follows Interstate 80 to the town of Farad (4,000 feet). Downriver three miles, the river enters the arid flatlands of Nevada. Access is limited to a road coming in at Floriston — walk up to Bronco and Grays Creek. Below Floriston, water is mostly diverted into flues. There are no regulations protecting fish here, and no stocking.

The hard fact is that to fish the Truckee effectively, an angler must adeptly select the right times and places. Aside from the normal fly-angling considerations, other variables enter the equation: snowpack and its percentile of water content, weather-related runoff, and human-induced water releases from Lake Tahoe and other downstream impoundments. An understanding of how these factors affect the fishery is what separates the successful fly angler from others.

## Tackle

A 9-foot, 4-weight, medium-action rod is perfect on the Truckee until the wind whips up in the afternoon. Then you want a fast 6-weight with enough body to punch out line. A 5-weight is a good compromise. The 9-foot length is useful for mending, reaching, and "high-stick" nymphing.

A 9-foot, 5X leader is another all-purpose selection — adjust length and diameter as the situation demands. It's rare to fish 7X here, or even 6X, and a .006 diameter tippet is usually the smallest advisable, even when knotting on minute, late-summer/fall patterns of Baetis, *Tricorythodes* and *Pseudocloeon*. For these, tie on a 5X tippet 36–40 inches long, making a total leader length of 12 feet. Tippets of this strength allow for proper presentation — always critical. Strong tippet also helps avoid breakoffs at the hookup and serves well for landing and releasing strong fish in survivable condition.

As implied by the discussion of water flows, felt soles — ideally with studs — and wading staffs are strongly recommended. The river's substrate of cobbles and boulders are algae-laden, and can be slippery. A thermometer is also an essential tool. Temperatures from 57–68 degrees prompt feeding.

## Bugs, Patterns and Techniques

Aquatic fauna on the Truckee is quite diverse. In a nearby creek presumed indicative of the region, a University of California study documents 80 species of caddis, 40 species of mayflies, and 30 species of stonefly.

In angling terms also, caddis predominate. Emerging or ovipositing, spotted and green sedges (*Hydropsyche* and *Rhyacophila*, respectively) are important to the surface/film addict throughout the entire system, especially from early July into August. Keep in mind that while in their net-spinning (*Hydropsyche*) and nude larval forms, "free-living" caddis are seductive to opportunistic drift feeders, and readily available from the start of the season. Fish your imitations in the natural's preferred habitat: rock and gravel-strewn riffles, and deeper runs. One terrific combination is a beadhead green rock-worm pattern paired with Foster's turkey beadhead, sizes 16 and 10, respectively. On a dead-drift this duo can be dynamite.

Don't forget emergers and keep them simple. Try fishing partridge and green or grouse and peacock soft hackles, sizes 14–16, down and across is the preferred method for apparent "surface feeders" reluctant to take dries. Use stout tippet — the thumping grabs occur mostly on the swing. In addition to the colors above, your fly box should contain partridge and orange, or partridge and yellow, sizes 12–16. Last in this category, the most finicky feeder may fall for a LaFontaine emergent sparkle pupae drifted in the film.

One pattern, the Quigley's cripple, deserves a special place in a Truckee angler's fly box — in the box of any California angler, for that matter. Quigley's cripple was originally developed by Bob Quigley as a mayfly emerger for Fall River. Whatever its origin and intent, with careful adjustments for size, coloration and float, this fly also works as a "crossover" imitation for midges or caddis. Throughout the Truckee watershed it has proven effective for representing the Western green drake (Drunella grandis and doddsi), #8–12, pale morning duns (Ephemerella inermis and infrequens) #14–18, and blue-wing olives (Baetis) #14–22. In quick currents, grease both the canted deer-hair forewing and hackle. For the early-season March browns (Rhithrogena) #12–14, apply flotation to the top notch only. The March brown cripple works best in back eddies, foam lines and slow tailouts where trout key on easy pickings.

Several years ago, a brown taped at 22 inches took a #16 Quigley cripple from the film at the tailout of a riffle-fed pool. That's a fine trout on a fine fly. What amazed the angler, however, was that when this fish rushed toward a fallen sweeper during the battle, it flushed from that lie a much larger "torpedo."

Along with free-living caddis, little yellow stones (Isoperla and Isogenus) create the greatest concentrated rise activity. They usually make their initial appearance in late June, when ovipositing females congregate over swift riffles and glides. Fighting mishaps make them available to fish, who often ambush the hapless where fast water spills into the heads of pools. Given that emerging caddis pupae and/or egg-layers are also often present, it can be difficult to discern what bug and/or life-stage the trout are keying on. Attempt to read the rise forms. Generally, Glickman's yellow stone or a yellow-parachute-humpy, both in #14s, are good choices. The latter is a superb floater, highly visible, an efficient attractor pattern; it also rests low in the meniscus, which seems to lead to more solid hookups. Note again: if fish you think are surface feeders consistently refuse your offering, then switching to soft hackles may preserve your sanity.

The previous scenario is one time when you will find Truckee fish difficult. Another period of "technical" angling occurs in the fall, during the last brood, midday Baetis (#18–22) emergence. This is a special time for anglers venturing into the Grand Canyon. Fish take this hatch in the pools, where upstream riffles and pocket-water splash in, and where currents flow tight against steep rock outcroppings to create slow deep eddies and foam lines. Some of the feeding lanes are narrow indeed, especially places where funnels line up trapped emergers, cripples, or stillborns. Here, delicate, drag-free presentation of floating nymphs or cripples catch fish. Flies should be greased, tied with tufts of CDC, or have polypro-balled wing cases . Beware, however — spinner falls and the presence of midges can confuse this game!

One effective way to approach perplexing masking hatches, and selective feeders generally, is by using a two-fly cast, with a soft hackle on the tail and a dry on the dropper. The latter acts as indicator and also as attractor or hatch-matcher.

*The Truckee's medium size makes it ideal for wade fishers. (Photo: Seth Norman)*

Pick a lone fish or a showing pod. Quarter the cast upstream and begin a dead-drift down. At an appropriate moment, twitch the fly with a minute mend of line, using the "induced rise" technique created by the "sudden inch." As the flies proceed downstream and the line straightens out, check your rod occasionally. The stop skates the stiff-hackled dry fly, mimicking an ovipositing female, and simultaneously imitates an emerger by swinging and raising the wet fly just below the film.

Two flies, several techniques — let the fish tell you what works and how. When you're confident that a particular pattern and tactic fit the trout's ticket…enjoy your good fortune.

A last comment on approaching Truckee fish: those anglers who commit to being observant, patient, and flexible relative to techniques employed have the highest probability of hooking (not necessarily landing!) sophisticated, mature fish. With the Truckee's mix of riffles, runs, pools, and pocket-water, all basic techniques will have a place and may produce. Sometimes there are special prizes for innovators at the vise or at streamside. Most of the time, attractor dries, suggestive nymphs, simple emergers, standard streamers, and bucktails will work — sometimes not.

Golden stones (Calineuria) are present in good numbers. Throughout the system, the nymphal form, which takes 2 to 3 years to mature, is always available. Use a Black rubber-legs or a gray ugly, #4–10, bouncing the bottom. In 1987, a reliable source informed me that an 8-pound brown was caught with a large stonefly nymph at Horner's Corner. Again, a two-fly cast can work for you, plumbing different levels of the water-column. Try rigging one of these big guys on point, and a #14, gold bead-head, green sparkle pupae on the dropper. If needed, use lead on the leader or weighted patterns. To use an indicator or not is your preference. Dredge the pockets and deep runs.

Two species rarely seen on the water still play an important part in a flyfisher's opportunities — golden stone adults, and the Western green drake. These bugs often appear at about the same time in late spring/early summer. Both are large, tasty morsels, and trout key to them. Late evening is a good time for both diving golden stone egg-layers and sporadic drakes. At midday, searching can be murderously effective with either a Kaufman stimulator (#6–8) or with Lawson paradrakes (#10). Twitch these in fast riffles, flick them side-armed under the streamside brush; the explosive takes may shock you. In late fall, the exact same scenario applies to fishing the October caddis (*Dicosmoecus*).

### Other Fauna

As in most venues, Truckee lunkers prefer maximum caloric intake when they can find it. Paiute sculpin (*Cottus beldingi*) provide a feast. Data provided courtesy of the California Wild Trout Project shocking survey indicates that the numbers of sculpin — 97.5% of the populations — far outweigh other resident forage fish like the Lahonton redside (*Richardsonius egreius*) and speckled dace (*Rhinichthys osculus*). No other imitation is needed.

Your favorite sculpin imitation, #2–6, may be spurted over the stream bed with staccato strips mimicking injured prey, or worked slowly on the bottom. The latter technique also serves to imitate crayfish, which have experienced an exploding population in recent years.

Terrestrials are also important. August heat dries the grasses found in several open meadows, providing ideal habitat for grasshoppers. For those keen to match color, the wing color of the largest hopper species is teal. Hoppers, however, pale in significance compared to winged, black carpenter ants, which generally make about a two-week appearance in mid-June. When this "hatch" occurs, a #8–10 Milton monstrosity will prove productive. These two terrestrials have saved the day many times throughout the Truckee area.

By the way, do not be caught at Milton Lake — a good side trip about 45 minutes northwest of town — without a large ant and #14 black beetle pattern (see Milton regulations).

# Stream Facts: Truckee River

### Characteristics
• The Truckee is a pretty stream of midsize. A wader may cross it easily in the upper sections, occasionally in the lower reaches described, depending on flows. Parts of the river are heavily wooded; elsewhere it runs though through lightly populated areas or barren high canyons. The Grand Canyon of the Truckee is more desolate and difficult to access.

### Getting There
• From the San Francisco Bay area, take I-80 through Sacramento to the town of Truckee, roughly 200 miles.

### Seasons
• Standard trout (see 1997 regulations).

### Special Regulations
• Subject to change. Carefully read the current Department of Fish and Game pamphlet available wherever licenses are sold. What follows here are the truncated California Fish & Game regulations for the 12 miles of wild trout waters:
   (A) From Boca Bridge to the confluence of Gray Creek . . . . . . . . . . . . . . . . Limit 2
   (B) From the confluence of Trout Creek downstream to the Glenshire Bridge and from 100 yards upstream of the Highway 80 bridge at Union Mills downstream to the Boca Bridge (minimum size 15 inches, artificials with barbless hooks only) . . . . . . . . . . . . . . . . . . . . . Limit 2
   (C) From the Glenshire Bridge downstream to 100 yards upstream of the Highway 80 bridge at Union Mills (minimum size 15 inches, flies with barbless hooks only) . . . . . . . . . . . . . . . . . . . . . . . . . . . . . . . . . . Limit 2

### Fish
• Up to 3,600 fish per mile (and as low as 1,300); 55 percent wild browns running to 22 inches, the rest wild and planted rainbows to 19 inches, with a median for both species just under a foot.

### River Miles
• It is 88 miles from Lake Tahoe to Pyramid Lake (in Nevada), with the 12-mile long middle section of special interest to the fly-rodder.

### Camping
• Donner Memorial State Park, 2 miles west of 80 on old US 40 / 530-582-7892
• Tahoe National Forest, take 89 north from I-80 past Truckee; also look for campgrounds on 89 near the river between Truckee and Squaw Valley

## TRUCKEE RIVER MAJOR HATCHES

| Insect | A | M | J | J | A | S | O | N | Time | Flies |
|---|---|---|---|---|---|---|---|---|---|---|
| Little Yellow Stone; *Isoperla; Alloperla* | | ██ | ██ | ██ | ██ | | | | E/D | Glickman Yellow Stone, Yellow Parachute Humpy Partridge & Yellow 12, 14 & 16 |
| Green rock worm *Rhyacophila* | | | ██ | ██ | ██ | | | | Late A/D | Stimulator, Hemingway Caddis, Beadhead Rockworm & BH Sparkle Pupae 12, 14 & 16 |
| October Caddis *Dicosmoecus* | | | | | | ██ | ██ | | E | Stimulator, LF Deep Sparkle Pupae with copper Bead in thorax 6, 8 & 10 |
| Gray Sedge *Hydropsychid* | | | | ██ | ██ | ██ | | | Late A/D | Elk Hair Caddis, Schroeder Parachute Caddis, Beadhead Sparkle Pupae 12, 14 & 16 |
| Pale Morning Dun *Ephemerella infrequens Inermis* | | | ██ | ██ | | | | | SF M/E | Comparadun, Orange Parachute Humpy, Rusty Spinner, Grouse & Orange Foster's Turkey Beadhead 14, 16 & 18 |
| Blue Winged Olive *Baetis, pseudocloeon* | | | ██ | | | | | ██ | A | Olive Comparadun, polypro floating nymph 18, 20 & 22 |
| Carpenter ants | | ██ | ██ | | | | | | — | Milton Monstrosity 6 & 8 |
| Green Drakes *Drunella grandis* | | | ██ | | | | | | Late M & E | Foster's Keeled Paradrake, Quigley Cripple, Beadhead Prince Nymph 8 & 10 |
| Tricos *Tricorythodes* | | | | | ██ | ██ | | | M | Sparkle-winged spinner, black comparaduns 20 & 22 |
| Sulphurs *Epeorus* | | | ██ | ██ | | | | | M & Late E | Sparkle-dun, Partridge & Yellow 12, 14 & 16 |
| March Browns *Rhithrogena* | | ██ | ██ | | | | | | A / E | Royal Wulff, Foster's Turkey Beadhead 12 |
| Golden Stone *Caleneuria pacifica* | | ██ | ██ | | | | | | E | Stimulator, Gray Ugly, Black Rubberlegs 4, 6 & 8 |

HATCH TIME CODE: M = morning; A = afternoon; E = evening; D = dark; SF = spinner fall; / = continuation through periods. © 2004 Frank R. Pisciotta

# Truckee

### Elevation – 6,051 • Population – 10,000

## ACCOMMODATIONS

**The Star Hotel**, 22 South Main, Lodi/ 209-368-4122 / An economical hostel. / $$
**The Truckee Hotel**, Commercial Road and the Bridge / 530-587-4444 / Known for 1900s decor; / $$–$$$
**Richardson House**, 10154 High Street / 530 587-5388 / Bed and Breakfast with an ideal location / $$
**Alpine Country Lodge**, Interstate 80 & Donner Overpass, Truckee, CA 96160 / 530-587-3801 / Allows dogs and other pets. / $$
**Best Western Truckee Tahoe Inn**, 11331 State Route 267, Truckee, CA 96161 / 530-587-4525 / $$
**Donner Lake Village Resort Hotel**, 15695 Donner Pass Rd, Truckee, CA 96161 / 530-587-6081 / $$$
**Loch Leven Lodge**, 13855 Donner Pass Rd, Truckee, CA 96161 / 530-587-3773 / $$–$$$
**Super 8 Lodge Truckee**, 11506 Deerfield Drive, Truckee, CA 96161 / 530-587-8888 / $$

## CAMPING

**Donner Memorial State Park** (largest) / 800-444-7275
**Goose Meadows** / 800-280-CAMP
**Silver Creek** / 800-280-CAMP
**Granite Flat** / 800-280-CAMP

## RESTAURANTS

**The Treat Box**, "Old Highway 40," 530-587-6554 / for pastries, lemon meringue / $
**Ponderosa Deli**, 10068 Donner Pass Road / 530-567-3555 / Good deli foods and good wine selection. / $
**Truckee Bagel Company**, 11448 Deerfield Drive, Truckee / 530-582-1852 / Try their bagel of the week—fresh, warm. / $
**The Squeeze Inn**, 10060 Donner Pass / 530-587-9814 / for omelets / $$
**La Bamba**, 11760 Donner Pass Road / 530-587-3516, try #17, the Chile Verde / $$
**Taco Station**, 10100 West River Street / 530-587-8226 / for huge tacos / $
**Tahoe Taps**, Highway 287 / 530-587-7777 / for calzone, pizza, live music and dancing / $$
**The Passage**, The Truckee Hotel on Commercial Row / 530-587-7619 / for fine dining / $$$
**Cottonwood**, Highway 267 / 530-587-5711 / with a patio and view of town / $$$

## FLY SHOPS

**Mountain Hardware and Sports** (see Tom), 11320 Donner Pass Road /
530-587-4844 / Has excellent fly selection
**Bud's Hardware/Sporting Goods**, 10043 Donner Pass Road / 530-587-3177

See also Transit Cities: San Francisco Bay Area, Sacramento, Reno

## HOSPITAL

**Tahoe Forest Hospital**, Truckee, CA 96161 / 530-587-7607

## AIRPORT

**Truckee Tahoe Airport District**, 10356 Truckee Airport Road, Truckee, CA
96161 / 530-587-4119

## AUTO RENTALS

**Airport Auto Rentals** / 530-587-2688
**Hertz** / 530-550-9191

## AUTO SERVICE

**Truckee Automotive** (ask for Jerry), 11410 Deerfield Drive, Truckee / 530-587-
5705

## FOR MORE INFORMATION

Truckee Chamber of Commerce
12036 Donner Pass Road
Truckee, CA, 96161
530-587-2757

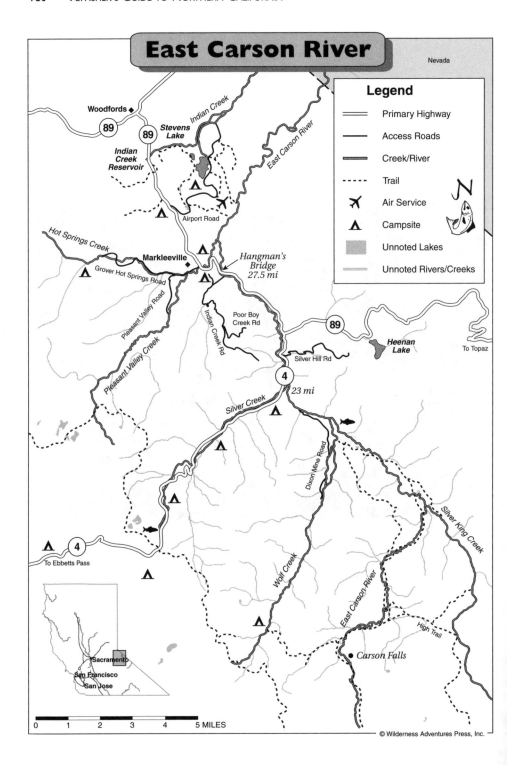

# East Carson River

Nevada

## Legend

| | |
|---|---|
| ═══ | Primary Highway |
| ─── | Access Roads |
| ═══ | Creek/River |
| ----- | Trail |
| ✈ | Air Service |
| ⛺ | Campsite |
| ▓ | Unnoted Lakes |
| ░ | Unnoted Rivers/Creeks |

Woodfords ◆
89
89
Stevens Lake
Indian Creek
East Carson River

Indian Creek Reservoir

⛺
Airport Road

Hot Springs Creek
Markleeville
⛺ Grover Hot Springs Road
⛺
Hangman's Bridge 27.5 mi

Pleasant Valley Road
Indian Creek Rd
Poor Boy Creek Rd
89
Heenan Lake
To Topaz
Silver Hill Rd

Pleasant Valley Creek
4
23 mi
Silver Creek
⛺

⛺

Dixon Mine Road

Silver King Creek

⛺

⛺
4
To Ebbetts Pass
⛺

Wolf Creek

East Carson River

High Trail

⛺

Sacramento
San Francisco
San Jose

● Carson Falls

0   1   2   3   4   5 MILES

© Wilderness Adventures Press, Inc.

# East Fork of the Carson: Plunge to the Desert

*by Jim Crouse*

The East Fork of the Carson River originates from a spring 10,000 feet up in the Carson/Iceberg Wilderness. It plummets down the eastern slope of the Sierra, then slices a deep canyon before joining with the major tributaries of Wolf and Silver creeks near the juncture of Highways 4 and 89. From Hangman's Bridge, two miles south of Markleeville, the river winds its way through high desert, between steep, multicolored walls of stone, ultimately exiting California to continue its journey into Nevada. Over this 40-mile course, an angler can cast his or her favorite imitation to wilderness trout in a high Sierra stream, then in a roadside fishery, and finally, in a Wild Trout river of considerable size.

Along the way, the East Carson earns a reputation as one of California's blue ribbon waters. Though decades of overharvesting have taken a toll, revised regulations are improving conditions somewhat. Make no mistake about it — native trout swimming this river are beautiful, robust specimens, especially in the lower stretches. Any angler who makes the trip to tangle with these trout will have the best of reasons to urge careful stewardship for their home — and to return soon.

## Upper River Access

The Carson River was once a tributary to the ancient Lake Lahontan, an inland sea covering much of the present state of Nevada. Lahontan cutthroats are still found on the east Sierra slopes. In the upper, creek-like reaches of the East Carson, a population of rare Paiute cutthroats, (*Oncorhynchus clarki seliris*), is now listed under the Endangered Species Act. The endangered designation invokes special measures for protection and provides allocation of funds to preserve and restore stream habitat. Since Carson Falls acts as a barrier that isolates the Paiute from downstream species, the water above it is closed to all fishing.

Below Carson Falls the stream begins to cut its way through volcanic and granite landscape, gaining in size as many small tributaries add to its volume. The area upstream from Wolf Creek is the most isolated stretch of the East Carson and the least frequented. Well out of range of hatchery trucks, it has the highest population of native rainbows, as well as wild browns and a few Lahontans.

Access to this part of the river is available by hiking or riding in on horseback. To reach the southernmost point of departure, take Little Antelope Pack Station (elevation 8,800 feet), take Mill Road, which turns west off Highway 395 between the towns of Coleville and Walker, then climbs a steep grade ( trailers not advised). There are several trailheads here. You can reach the headwaters of the East Carson by taking the one marked "Dumont Meadows," which ends just below Carson Falls, a hike of about eight miles. To access the Carson downstream, take the Silver King trail to where

*What it's all about: a leaper on the East Carson. (Photo: Kyle Giampaoli)*

it meets the river (after traveling along Silver King Creek), also about eight miles. Whichever route you choose, expect a very long walk.

On either trail, be sure to take a topographical map. Also make sure to check the Department of Fish and Game Regulations carefully. The river may be closed above Carson Falls. Likewise, Silver King Creek and tributaries are closed to all fishing above Llewellyn Falls.

Another route to the river is through Wolf Creek Meadows, where you will find a trailhead that will get to more fishable water in less time. Take Highway 4 south from Markleeville for eight miles and turn onto Wolf Creek Road. You will cross Silver Creek and follow that stream for a few miles. The pavement stops and the road becomes steep — not terribly rough, but slippery when wet. Topping a hill, you'll have your first splendid glimpse of Wolf Creek Meadow.

As you near the meadow, a road leads off to the left . Turn there and cross a little bridge over Wolf Creek, where you will see a parking area at the east end of the meadow. Pass this, and continuing on this winding road not suitable for trailers for approximately half a mile. At the top of the hill, you will find another parking area for the High Trail trailhead. From here you can walk the High Trail, which actually veers away from the river , and prepare for a rugged hike down to the water wherever the passage looks likely.

You can also drive, continuing down the backside of the hill to a flat area. Park and walk down the road to the confluence of Wolf Creek and the East Carson, about a five-minute hike.

Once down at the river, anglers have a good chance at those wild rainbows, browns, and cutts. Rainbows predominate, and the fish here generally run small, seldom over 14 inches. Some browns break that rule, as will the occasional, curiously featured whitefish — surprise!

### Tackle for the Upper River

Lighter gear is appropriate here. The upper river is a place to bring your favorite small-creek rod, 7 to 9 feet long, in a weight from 3 to 5. This is also good water for basic dry fly patterns: Adams, Mosquito, Humpy, Elk-Hair Caddis, and October Caddis. Excepting the October imitation, most of these should be size 14 or smaller. Nymphs should include the Golden Stone, Little Olive Stone, Hare's Ear, and A.P. Black. You can try a Muddler or a Crystal Bugger, but when the water is low, it is best to leave them in your fly box.

Be careful wading when the water is high. The upper river is quite susceptible to the effects of melting snowpack above. From early to midseason in years with good water, this stretch cannot be traversed in spots, making it difficult to fish.

In years of drought, on the other hand, the fish population suffers severely. That fact, along with unfortunate overharvesting (this wild fish water has a "put-and-take" limit of five fish) can blight angling opportunities.

### The Middle River

Between Wolf Creek and Silver Creek, the East Fork of the Carson is more accessible to those who have limited time to fish. The river still contains some native rainbows and wild browns, along with some imports: a share of Fish and Game stockers, and some heftier rainbows (to four pounds) planted by Alpine County. There's also a novelty item. In the spring, usually May, the DFG "spawns" Lahontan cutthroats for its program at Heenan Lake, then releases brooders into the middle section of the East Carson. They can weigh from two to five pounds.

The best access to this stretch begins less than a mile downstream from the confluence of the East Carson and Silver Creek, where Highway 4 crosses the Centerville bridge. From this point to six miles downstream the highway parallels the river. The fisher will find more company here than anywhere else. Powerbait and worms are the preferred patterns of many, but flyfishers have an advantage with wild fish that won't eat bait but will take some of the offerings listed below.

### Tackle for the Middle River

Popular dry flies include the Parachute Adams, Elk-Hair Caddis, Royal Wulff, Humpy, and Stimulator. Productive nymph patterns include the Golden Stone, Dark Stone, A.P. Black, Hare's Ear, and Caddis Pupa. And here is the place where Crystal Buggers, Zonkers, and Muddlers also work well (see techniques).

Rods can be 8 to 9 feet long, from 3- to 6-weight. A longer and heavier rod is preferable, because this stretch of the river can get windy.

Wade with caution. Rocks are slippery, especially during drought years. Felt-sole boots are highly recommended, and if you have a wading staff, bring it. Warning: wading (and fishing) can be adversely affected when small reservoirs upstream release runoff into the local tributaries of Silver and Monitor Creeks . An angler seeing blue skies may not expect these flows. Suddenly the current increases and sediment and silt discolor the water.

The last "put-and-take" part of the East Carson ends at Hangman's Bridge, a landmark that deserves its name. On April 17, 1874, Ernst Reuch was traveling in custody to trial in Bridgeport for the murder of E. T. Erickkson. He never made it. Masked vigilantes intercepted his party and dispersed his escort. Ernst was knotted into a hangman's noose and cast off the bridge.

The loop was very tight.

### The Wild and Scenic Lower River: Hangman's Bridge to Nevada

From Hangman's Bridge to the Nevada state line, the East Carson is designated a California Wild and Scenic River. The gradient decreases in this section, and the canyon widens. Markleeville Creek is the last major tributary. From just below that confluence, the river leaves the road. It will not come close again until it brushes Highway 395 south of Gardnerville, Nevada, some 22 miles downstream.

The lower river is characterized by isolated pools and long barren stretches. East-slope, high-desert vegetation covers the canyon slopes. Piñon pines and sage scent the air. There are virtually no trees streamside, leaving ample room for backcasts and no shade. The river is at its highest volume here. During spring runoff, flows of nearly 2,000 cubic feet per second are common below Markleeville Creek. At that level it is often best to leave the river to kayakers.

Fishing improves when flows drop below 700 cfs. However, you should always allow plenty of time to fish this section, due to the long walks between productive places. It's a wise move to explore this area with someone who knows the venue well. This is an area with far fewer fish per mile than other California blue ribbon waters, and you'll work for them. Which may well be worth your time. Rainbows predominate, as elsewhere, and may run to 20 inches. Once again, you might see a big Lahontan cutt and browns here.

Most fishers hike upstream from the bridge, where there is an access off Highway 89, about 2.5 miles north of Markleeville. The turnoff is for Indian Creek Reservoir and the airport. The runway of the latter is visible just over 2.5 miles down the road, straight ahead as the pavement veers to the left. Head for the runway, looking for a dirt road to the right. Park in one of the pullouts.

The dirt road eventually turns into a path, and the hike from there down to the river is variously estimated at a mile to 1.5 steep miles. If you are over 40 years old, less than svelte, and accustomed to a lower altitude, it will feel like 12 miles on your way out. Take water and take your time.

*Spiderman (aka the Editor) with an East Carson brown. (Photo: Seth Norman)*

Because there are so few places to reach the E. Carson in this area, don't count on solitude when you reach the river. However, you will have less company than on other stretches.

### Tackle for the Lower River

A larger volume of water and frequently windy conditions suggest a heavier system on this stretch. A 9-foot rod, 5- or 6-weight, is recommended. Lighter outfits are fun until the wind comes up, then frustrating.

Flies that work in the upper parts of the river also work well here, with two considerations. In this wider canyon, fish see more terrestrials, so consider carrying hoppers, beetles, and ants. The isolated pools fish much like still waters. Conditions in the latter demand more exact imitations, so parachute patterns, comparaduns, and floating nymphs are good choices. Midges also come into play, some as small as size 26. So do streamers — another reason for the bigger rod.

### Techniques for the East Carson

On the wooded and willowy upper sections of the East Carson River a fisher will need the roll, steeple, and possibly even slingshot cast. Flies should be presented both up and downstream, using a parachute or serpentine technique to sneak in enough slack for longer drifts.

*Wet wading the East Carson. (Photo: Seth Norman)*

Casting conditions improve as the canyon widens in the middle section. The larger volume of water also dictates a change in presentation. High stick and upstream methods are the most effective for nymph anglers. Although not a fan of bobber-fishing, a strike indicator may well help here. One of the more effective set-ups uses a tuft of polypropylene yarn, with weight above or below the fly.

During high flows, as in the early season, many dry fly presentations have to be across stream. Employ a quick upstream mend to get a few more seconds of natural float.

Bait fish in the East Fork comprise a significant portion of the trout's cuisine — thus the streamers suggested previously. A note about fishing these is in order, from one who has watched anglers try streamers for many years.

Many people struggle to cast these lures because fly rods are designed to throw the weight of fly line. A heavily weighted streamer disturbs this balance. Compensating for this requires a change in technique. Begin by angling the tip of your rod farther off to the side than usual on the backcast; then, on the forward cast, raise the tip toward vertical. This will open the loop, and minimize bounce. Avoid false casting whenever possible; a simple pick up and lay down should do. As with all casting, it is important to begin the backcast with a tight line — no slack — but with streamers it is particularly important to generate high line speed so that the fly does not drop behind you. Also, shooting line is easier with the rod properly loaded. Tougher than laying out an Adams, certainly, but streamers can be valuable tools. Remember to try them up and across, as well as down and across. Try every angle, since a change in presentation can make a big difference.

# Stream Facts: East Carson River

## Seasons
- Last Saturday in April through November 15

## Special Regulations
- East Fork and tributaries: closed above Carson Falls Carson Falls to Hangman's Bridge, 5 fish, no size restrictions.
- East Fork from Hangman's Bridge to the Nevada State Line, only artificial lures, limit 2, minimum size 14 inches.

## River Characteristics
- The East Carson begins in springs at 10,000 feet on the eastern slope of the Sierra Nevada Mountains. It runs through the Carson Iceberg Wilderness on its journey north and east into the State of Nevada. By the time it meets Wolf Creek, it's a wooded freestone stream. Below the meeting with Markleeville Creek it becomes a major river cutting its way through a high desert canyon. The best fishing is on the stretch near the town of Markleeville in Alpine County.

## Trout
- A few Lahontan cutthroats are distributed throughout the system, both wild fish and DFG plants of brood stock to 25 inches and some wild browns. Native and stocked rainbows predominate, averaging 12 inches, with some fish over 20. A small population of endangered Paiute cutthroats resides in the extreme upper river, which is closed to fishing.

## River Miles
- There are approximately 40 miles of river from the upper reaches to the Nevada border. The wild trout section is about 12 miles long, from Hangman's Bridge to the Nevada state line.

## River Flows
- These vary enormously from the headwaters to the lower section. The upper beat is subject to inflows of snowmelt and opens later in the season. Fishing the middle section may be affected by releases from reservoirs. The lower section is fishable when the flows, as measured at Garderville, Nevada are below 700 cfs (best at about 350cfs). Call the Irrigation District for conditions at 702-784-5241.

## Hub Cities
- South Lake Tahoe is the closest city of size, about 40 minutes from the best river access.
- Woodfords is a small community on the way (8 miles from Hangman's Bridge).
- Markleeville is 1.7 miles from Hangman's Bridge where the wild trout section begins (34 miles from South Lake Tahoe).

## EAST CARSON RIVER MAJOR HATCHES

| Insect | A | M | J | J | A | S | O | N | Flies |
|---|---|---|---|---|---|---|---|---|---|
| **Stoneflies** | | | | | | | | | |
| Golden Stone<br>*Acroneuria californica* | | ■ | ■ | ■ | ■ | | | | Nymph: Gold Beadhead Stone<br>Dry: #6–8 Yellowstone or Yellow Madame X |
| Salmon Fly<br>*Pteronarcys californica* | | | ■ | | | | | | Nymph: Park's Stone Fly<br>Dry: #6–8 Orange Stimulator or Bird's Stone |
| Little Yellow Stone<br>*Alloperla pacifica* | | | | ■ | ■ | ■ | | | Nymph: Light Hare's Ear<br>Dry: #14–18 Yellow Elk Hair Caddis or Yellow Humpy |
| Little Brown Stone | | ■ | ■ | ■ | | | | | Nymph: Dark Hare's Ear<br>Dry: #10–14 Brown Bucktail Caddis or Red Orange Humpy |
| Little Green Stone | | | | | ■ | ■ | | | Nymph: Olive Hare's Ear<br>Dry: #16–18 Light Green Elk Hair Caddis or Pale Green Humpy |
| **Caddisflies** | | | | | | | | | |
| Rock Worm<br>*Rhyacophila* | | | | | | | ■ | | Nymph/Emerger: Tan Caddis Larva; Dark Tan Sparkle Pupa<br>Dry: #10–16 Tan Elk Hair Caddis |
| Spotted Sedge<br>*Hydropsyche cockerelli* | | ■ | ■ | ■ | | | | ■ | Nymph: Green Rock Worm<br>Dry: #10–16 Gray or Tan Deer Hair Caddis |
| October Caddis<br>*Dicosmoecus atripes* | | | | | ■ | | | ■ | Nymph: #8 Orange Woolly Worm<br>Dry: #8 Orange Stimulator |
| Turtle Case Makers | | | | ■ | | | ■ | | Nymph: #16–20 Cream Caddis Pupa<br>Dry: #16–20 Tan Elk Hair Caddis |
| Grannom | | | | | ■ | | | | #14–16 Tan Elk Hair Caddis or Green Peeking Caddis |

## EAST CARSON RIVER MAJOR HATCHES (CONT.)

| Insect | A | M | J | J | A | S | O | N | Flies |
|---|---|---|---|---|---|---|---|---|---|
| *Baetis* | | ▮ | | | | | | ▮ | Baetis Nymphs, Baetis Parachute, Baetis Comparadun #16-20 |
| Pale Evening Dun *Ephemerella inermis* | | | | ▮ | ▮ | ▮ | | | Dark Hare's Ear, Black; Lt. Cahil, Pali Evening Dun #12-16 |
| Pale Morning Dun *Ephemerella infrequens* | | | | ▮ | ▮ | ▮ | | | Olive Brown Hare's Ear, PMD Nymph, PMD Parachute #14-18 |
| Tricos *Tricorythodes* | | | | | ▮ | | | | Trico Dun, Trico Spinner #22 |
| Little Yellow May | | | ▮ | ▮ | ▮ | ▮ | | | Dark Hare's Ear, Grizzly Wulff, Ginger Quill #12-16 |
| March Brown *Rhithrogena* | | | ▮ | | | | | | Brown Hare's Ear, Brown Soft Hackle, March Brown #10-12 |
| Midges | | ▮ | ▮ | ▮ | ▮ | ▮ | ▮ | ▮ | Griffith's Gnat, Gray Midge, Black Midge #20-26 |
| Craneflies | ▮ | | | | | ▮ | | | Gray/Olive Wooly Worm, Darbee Crane Fly #8-10 |
| Grasshoppers | | | | ▮ | ▮ | ▮ | ▮ | | Henry's Fork Hopper; Hopper X #8-12 |
| Ants | | ▮ | | | ▮ | ▮ | ▮ | | Black Flying Ant #12; Black Ant #12-16 |

# A Fragile Fishery

With rainbows running to 20 inches, the East Carson would seem to qualify as a blue-ribbon fishery. In fact, in the early 1970s, anglers averaged 2 to 3 fish per hour. Today it fishes between .5 and 1 per 3 hours.

Department of Fish and Game estimates of trout per mile in east slope Sierra streams suggests why it's so low: Hot Creek, 11,414; East Walker, 9,356; Lower Owens, 5,750; Truckee River, 2,499; East Carson, 363. Of those few, just over 100 fish per mile measure more than nine inches.

What happened here, and what is happening now?

There are many causes for decline in trout numbers. The Advent of river rafting's popularity was the first noticeable sign, in an "artificials only" piece of water, crude rodholders and entrails found in the stream tell the story. Commercial outfitters are probably not the problem. Many individuals float the river, with a few violators causing most of the damage. In the lower canyon especially, there is little enforcement because of access problems.

Another problem can be found 12 miles below Hangman's Bridge, where the East Fork crosses into Nevada. The state line is the end of the wild trout section. Downstream is "catch-and-keep," according to Nevada regulations. This means that when rafters exit the river in Nevada with a load of fish, there's no way of knowing where they were caught. Rafters know this, making restrictions in the wild trout section virtually impossible to enforce.

A solution for part of this problem is obvious on its face. The East Fork of the Carson is designated a California wild trout River, but the current regulations allow anglers to kill two fish over 14 inches. This was innovative policy when instituted in 1984 but no longer. Trout numbers continue to decline. With the river now sustained primarily by a relatively few sizable rainbows, it is critical to protect the broodstock, if the fishery is to survive, make the Carson kill limit 0, period.

Flyfishers are often the only constituency wild fish have. It will take our efforts and attention to loosen that noose below Hangman's Bridge.

# South Lake Tahoe

## Elevation – 6,200 • Population – 20,000

Most of the East Carson discussed here runs through Alpine County, the least populated county in California. Much of the best fishing is near the town of Markleeville. While services are limited here, it is only 32 miles to the mountain city of South Lake Tahoe, California, which borders Stateline, Nevada, a major gambling and resort area.

There is an airport at South Lake Tahoe but no commercial service at this time. Most travelers from the east fly into Reno, Nevada, or San Francisco. From Reno the drive to the East Carson takes less than two hours; from San Francisco one should allow five. Sacramento, California, also has some commercial air service. It's a two hour drive to the river.

The South Tahoe/Stateline area has over 12,000 rooms available — motels, cabins, condos, and glittery casino hotels. With prices ranging from $25 to over $200, there is lodging available to suit anyone's pocket book. Private and public campgrounds are also in the vicinity.

From San Francisco, take Highway 50 east through Sacramento. Highway 50 crosses Echo Summit. With Lake Tahoe visible in the distance, the road descends Meyers Grade. At the bottom of the hill, Highway 89 south intersects Highway 50. Take Highway 89 to Luther Pass approximately 12 miles to the junction of Highway 88. Turn left on Highway 88 (also Highway 89 for the next six miles) drive six miles east to Woodfords. Turn right on 89 where it branches off from 88 at the sign reading Markleeville, six miles. About 1.7 miles past Markleeville, the highway crosses the East Carson and parallels the river several miles.

From Reno, Nevada, Highway 395 south takes you through Carson City to the town of Minden Nevada. As you start to enter town, Highway 88 veers off to the west. Take Highway 88 to Woodfords, California. At the juncture of Highway 88 and Highway 89 (also Highway 4), turn south and drive six miles to Markleeville. You will encounter the East Carson River at Hangman's bridge,1.7 miles south on this road, which is the upper end of the wild trout section (see also airport access).

## MARKLEEVILLE AREA

### ACCOMMODATIONS

**Carson River Resort**, 3 miles south of Markleeville at 12399 Highway 89 / 530-694-2229 / Cabins, campground, store, gas, fishing, sporting goods / $-$$

**Hope Valley Resort**, 5 miles west of Woodfords, / 800-423-9949 / $ / Tent cabins, camping and cafe

**J. Marklee Toll Station**, downtown, 14856 Highway 89, Markleeville, CA 96120 / 530-694-2507 / $-$$ / Motel, cafe

**Sorensen's Resort**, Hope Valley Highway, Markleeville, CA 96120 / 916-694-2410 / Cabins, restaurant, bed & breakfast, conference area, flyfishing school (private lessons & guide trips by Jim Crouse and Judy Warren) / $$$

**Woodfords Inn**, Highway 89, Markleeville, CA 96120 / $-$$ / Motel, hot tub

## CAMPING
For information on the following Carson District Campgrounds, call 800-444-CAMP   Markleeville Campground is located .5 miles south of Markleeville on 89. Hope Valley Campground is located 6 miles west of Woodfords, off HWY 88. Silver Creek is located 7 miles souith of Markleeville on HWY 4.

For information about Wolf Creek campgrounds, call Bureau Land management, 702-882-1631

For information about Grover Hot Springs Campground, call CA State Parks, call 800-444-CAMP

## RV PARKS
**Carson River Resort**, 530-964-2292

## RESTAURANTS
**Alpine Hotel and Cutthroat Saloon,** downtown Markleeville / 530-694-2150 / $-$$
**Steamers Bar & Grille,** 2236 Lake Taho Blvd. / 530-541-8818
**The Deli,** downtown Markleeville / 530-694-2410 / $
**Divided Sky,** 3200 US HWY 50 / 530-577-0775

## GROCERIES
**East Fork Resort,** 3 Miles south of Markleeville on 89
**Sierra Pines General Store,** in Markleeville

## FLY SHOPS
**Alpine Fly Fishing Shop,** downtown Markleeville, inside Grover's Corner, 14841 Hwy 89 (right across from Cutthroat Saloon) / 530-542-0759 / Jim Crouse's store

## AUTO REPAIRS
**Woodfords Auto Service**, Woodfords, CA 96120 / 530-694-2916 / Repairs and towing

## FOR MORE INFORMATION
Alpine County Chamber of Commerce
PO Box 265
Markleeville, CA 96120
530-694-2475 / www.alpinecounty.com

## SOUTHLAKE TAHOE/STATELINE AREA

## ACCOMMODATIONS
The South-Tahoe-Stateline area has over 12,000 rooms; motels, cabins, condos, glittery casino hotels. With prices ranging from $25 to $200, there's lodging available to suit anybody's pocketbook. Private and public campgrounds are also in the vicinity. What follow are only a few of the lodging choices.
**Best Western Hotels,** 3 locations / 530-541-6722 / $$

Harvey's Resort Casino, 800-553-1022 / $$$+
Harrah's Casino Hotel, in Stateline / 800-648-3773
Holiday Inn Express, 3961 Lake Tahoe Boulevard / 530-544-5900
Inn by the Lake, 3300 Lake Tahoe Boulevard / 530-542-0330
Travelodge, 3 locations / 530-541-5000

## RESTAURANTS

The South Lake Tahoe area also offers a wide variety of culinary choices: fast food
  places, breakfast establishments, family restaurants and gormet dining.
The Cantina, Hwy 89 at 10th St, (a mile north of Junction at 50) / 530-544-1233 /
  Popular Mexican / $-$$
Passarettis, 1181 Emerald Bay Road (Hwy 89/50) south of Y / 530-541-3433 /
  Family Italian / $-$$
Chase's Bar & Grill, 1901 Airport Rd / 530-544-2739
Brewery at Lake Tahoe, 3542 Hwy 50 / 530-544-2739
Evan's American Gormet Cafe, 536 Emerald Bay Rd / 530-542-1990

## FLY SHOPS

Tahoe Fly Fishing Adventures, 3433 Lake Tahoe Boulevard, South Lake taho 96150
  / 530-541-8208
The Sportsman, 2556 Lake Tahoe Boulevard, South Lake Tahoe 96150 / 530-542-
  3474

## AIRPORT

South Lake Tahoe has no commercial services, see Sacramento, CA, and Reno, NV

## HOSPITALS

Barton Memorial Hospital, 2155 South Avenue, South Lake Tahoe, CA
  96150 / 916-541-3420
Carson Valley Medical Center, 1107 Highway 395, Gardnerville, NV 89410 / 702-
  782-1500

## AUTO RENTALS

From Reno, NV, and Stateside, NV (bordering South Lake Tahoe
  Hertz / 800-654-3131
  Avis / 800-831-2847

## OTHER ATTRACTIONS IN AREAS

There is a vast vacation industry built around Lake Tahoe, and gambling at
  Stateline. For information, call South Lake Tahoe Chamber of Commerce, 916-
  541-535 or the Lake Tahoe Visitors Authority, 800-288-2463. The Visitor's Center
  can book rooms and trips.

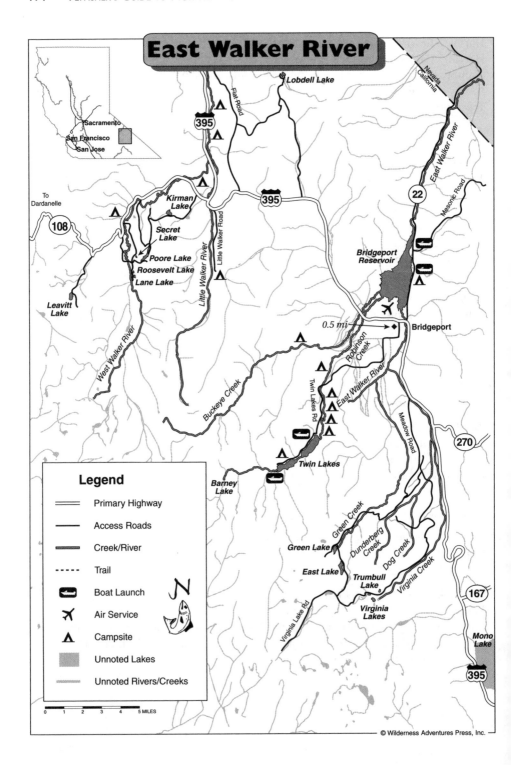

# East Walker River

Lobdell Lake

Nevada
California

Flat Road

395

To
Dardanelle

108

Kirman
Lake

Secret
Lake

Poore Lake
Roosevelt Lake
Lane Lake

Leavitt
Lake

West Walker River

Little Walker River

Little Walker Road

395

22

East Walker River

Masonic Road

Bridgeport
Reservoir

0.5 mi

Bridgeport

Robinson
Creek

Buckeye Creek

Twin Lakes Rd

East Walker River

Meadow Road

270

Twin Lakes

Barney
Lake

## Legend

| | |
|---|---|
| ═══ | Primary Highway |
| ─── | Access Roads |
| ─── | Creek/River |
| - - - | Trail |
| ⬅ | Boat Launch |
| ✈ | Air Service |
| ⛺ | Campsite |
| ▓ | Unnoted Lakes |
| ~~~ | Unnoted Rivers/Creeks |

N

Green Creek

Green Lake

Dunderberg
Creek

Dog Creek

Virginia Creek

167

East Lake

Trumbull
Lake

Virginia
Lakes

Mono
Lake

Virginia Lake Rd

395

0  1  2  3  4  5 MILES

© Wilderness Adventures Press, Inc.

# East Walker River

### by Kate and Bill Howe

*Meat and Potatoes Fishing:* There's nothing surprising about the East Walker River, save perhaps how good it is — how many fish, how big.

Cradled in the high Sierra at 6,500 feet lies the historic community of Bridgeport. Surrounded by mountains — the Bodie Hills to the east and the Sawtooth Ridge to the west — the Bridgeport Valley offers some of the finest trout waters in California. Within minutes of town an angler can cast to large rainbows from a float tube on Bridgeport Reservoir, wade the sand bar at Upper Twin Lakes, or pick his way down the meadow sections of Robinson Creek, looking for wary rainbows in crystal-clear water.

If this sounds like a flyfisher's utopia, it is, and the East Walker River is one of the best reasons to visit, a place to stalk browns and rainbows from willow-lined banks.

It's not such a long cast away: from San Francisco the drive takes six hours, east via Highway 108, over Sonora Pass and down into Bridgeport. This is a stunningly beautiful road, although a tad rough on the brakes. (Alternative, but less direct routes over the Sierra include Highway 50 to the north and Highway 120 to the south.) Driving time from Los Angeles is longer, nearer to eight hours: Highway 395 takes you north through the desert, past Mt. Whitney and along the eastern slope of the Sierra.

If planning a trip from either metro area, you might also consider flying into Reno and renting a car. From there, the drive south to Bridgeport is only 2.5 hours— if you don't stop to fish.

## Upper Section

The headwaters of the East Walker drain mountains in the southeast corner of the valley, including Green Creek, Summers Creek, and other small tributaries. Not all that water stays in the river, however; the Walker is a major source of irrigation for the ranches through which it flows on the way to Bridgeport Reservoir. Most of the upper river above Bridgeport is on private property, but there is public access in the town itself, and along a stretch about a half-mile above where it enters the lake.

Through town, the East Walker is a typical meadow stream, with a channel wide and deep, flowing slower than it does in the lower canyon. Although this stretch gets a lot of pressure, it can produce some incredibly large fish, especially in the autumn when the brown trout spawn. It's only a short walk from most Bridgeport hotels, so it can make for some fine "after dinner" fishing.

Access is from the bridge on Highway 395 at the south end of town. Walking downriver from this point is fairly easy, but be prepared to exit the stream after about a quarter-mile, where a bridge blocks wading. Beyond the bridge you'll find a good stretch of water that runs for another quarter-mile. Note: the banks here are private property. Be courteous, mindful of no-trespassing signs, and careful of livestock — especially the bulls, which are dangerous.

*Admiring a prime East Walker rainbow  (Photo: Edgar Yeechow)*

The last section just above the reservoir is fishable, but also private ranchland; this area is better left alone.

Wading gear is essential for the town section. Wear hip boots or chest-highs with felt-soled wading boots when fishing during cool weather, shorts and wading boots for hot summer days.

### Fishing the Upper River

About that meat-and-potatoes approach: there can be evening hatches in this area, courtesy of large burrowing mayflies and several types of caddis, but the big fish here tend to favor noninsect, subaquatic food forms: leeches in black, olive and brown; streamers that resemble the fry of trout, carp, and other rough fish; crayfish imitations in brown and orange. Carry sculpin patterns tied in both natural shades of brown and tan, and in bright attractor versions — orange and yellow. Opt for wool heads rather than deer-hair; wool soaks up water and sinks rapidly, so is better suited for fishing deep. Match the size of these flies to the naturals, using hooks with smaller gapes — the authors prefer 8s—to minimize damage to fish you intend to release.

Nine-foot rods designed for 4- to 6-weight lines are appropriate for the East Walker above Bridgeport Reservoir. A reel should be loaded with at least 150 yards of 20-pound Dacron backing — not only to handle the runs of larger fish, but because extra backing adds diameter to the spool, speeding retrieves by allowing maximum pick-up of line with each turn of the reel. This is a must when trying to turn big browns in current.

Use long leaders, 10 feet to 12 feet tapered to 3X (or 4X for low water), and unweighted flies. To get your presentation down to the feeding zone, apply weight to your leader several inches above the fly. Doing so will put the fly on the bottom, where it needs to be, but also will allow it to drift with the current in a life-like manner.

## Lower Section at Big Hole

The lower East Walker is one of California's most incredible fisheries — and one of the most accessible. From the dam at Bridgeport Reservoir, it flows northward to the Nevada border, an eight-mile distance. Nearly all of this water lies only a few steps from your car door.

This is not to say the entire river corridor has easy access. Quite the contrary; willows and shrubs line much of the stream right up to the bank and lay in wait to entangle the unsuspecting flyfisher. But with a little caution, you can avoid the pitfalls and instead enjoy a rewarding fishing experience.

At the base of the reservoir dam is the aptly named "Big Hole," where the waters of the lake exit into a huge circular basin carved deep into the river bed. Although the river slows somewhat before it hits the channel neck and continues downstream, don't let the placid appearance fool you; this is one of the most difficult stretches of the East Walker to fish well with fly gear. Converging and opposing currents run side by side, creating back eddies and seams every three or four feet. These very conditions attract big trout to the Big Hole.

The prime times to fish the Big Hole are in early spring (right after opening day) and again in late autumn, when brown trout come up to spawn. Although trout hold here all season long, fishing this section midsummer can be a frustrating experience.

## Fishing Big Hole Area

Preferred tackle for the Big Hole differs somewhat from gear appropriate for the rest of the river. Rods should throw at least a 7-weight line and measure nine or more feet in length; you will need to mend and control line in heavy current. Reels should have plenty of backing, for the reasons stated above. Although floating lines have some application for shortline nymphing (with long leaders and split-shot) and for occasional dry-fly action along the edge of the pool and at its tailout, sinktips are better suited to most of this water. Just the ticket are five-foot tips with a #6 sink rate, or heavy minitips (self-built or store-bought). Fullsink lines are not recommended because they are impossible to mend once under water.

That last point must be stressed: line control is crucial when fishing the Big Hole. Start with as little line out of your rod as possible and try to keep direct contact between your stripping hand and the fly. The Hole is full of snags that eat flies; get careless and you'll end up fishless and flyless.

*Gotcha! A big, East Walker rainbow in the net! (Photo: Edgar Yeechow)*

When fishing a floating line with large nymphs and streamers, use a 9- to 10-foot leader that tapers to 2X or 3X. Leaders for sinktips should be no longer than two feet — anything longer may allow currents to force your fly toward the surface and out of the feeding zone.

Don't devote a whole lot of time to the Big Hole. Fish it in the early morning until the sun is fully on the water, and in the evening during the last hour before dark. These are the prime times, period.

Only a few types of flies are needed here. Streamers and nymphs should be large to ensure visibility. Marabou patterns in sizes 4 through 8 work quite well, especially in colors black and white, black and yellow, and all-white. Round out your selection with Montana-type nymphs, rubberlegs, A.P. nymphs (black), and hare's ears or Bird's nests, all in sizes 8 through 12. These patterns can also be used in a few spots elsewhere on the river.

The distance from the Big Hole down to a section known as Murphy's Pond (the widest piece of water aside from the Big Hole) is about three miles. There are enough parking spots along the highway that an angler could easily limit his fishing to these alone, traveling by car between them. Hoofing the whole stretch, however, can be exhausting. Some of the water is marginal or nonproductive, so you'll need to use your river-reading skills to find the trout.

*The East Walker's brush-choked banks at Big Hole
below Bridegeport Reservoir Dam. (Photo: Kate Howe)*

Murphy's Pond is very tough to fish — silty and difficult to wade. But it contains some huge brown trout. Keep this spot in mind if you enjoy a real challenge.

### Murphy's Pond to State Line

From Murphy's Pond the river runs another five miles to the Nevada state line. This is the section of the East Walker where the authors spend the most time. You'll find riffles and runs one right after the other, interrupted occasionally by some of the most intriguing pocket water anywhere. There are plenty of fish in the Murphy's-to-Nevada stretch, but you have to work for them. Shortline presentation of streamers and nymphs is by far the most productive approach.

The river's channel here can be both narrow and meandering. Break it up into small sections: fish each with determination, methodically hitting all the water from bank to bank. Make sure to probe all depths. Fish may change location from hour to hour, depending on hatch, weather, and water conditions. (As a tailwater fishery, however, flows and water temperatures on the lower East Walker remain fairly constant, fluctuating only when the lake is drawn down for irrigation or spring runoff flood control.)

## Wading

The lower East Walker has a reputation for being a treacherous wading stream, and this reputation is well deserved. Gear must be in good shape. Chest waders are a must. Water levels can change from ankle deep to neck high (or higher ) in a matter of a few steps. Tight-fitting neoprene waders are great but uncomfortable in the hot summer months. If you opt for cooler fabric waders, wear a wading belt to avoid shipping too much water when you fall.

The river bottom is rocky. (We once heard wading the Walker described as walking on mucus-covered bowling balls. Take that to heart.) Tie your wading shoes tightly and make sure you have studs or cleats for traction. Use a wading staff.

## More Tackle: Flies

Appropriate rods, reels, lines, and terminal tackle are much the same as those used for the upper river. Add some caddis and mayfly nymphs (as well as some conventional generic nymphs, such as hare's ears) to your fly box, tied beadhead style in sizes 10 through 16.

Dries should include generic forms of caddis (sizes 10 to 18), mayflies (sizes 14 to 18) and stoneflies (golden stones, little yellow stones, and brown stones, in sizes 12, 14, and 16). As summer progresses, terrestrials become important. Hopper imitations bring aggressive strikes, as will the woolly bear caterpillar, a local pattern.

Don't forget to bring sculpins, as these small fish are an important food item here. Colors should range from light tans and browns to dark olives. Sizes can start as small as #10.

In addition to the browns and rainbows, you may also encounter Lahontan cutthroat. These are the only trout indigenous to the Bridgeport Valley and have been recently reintroduced by the Department of Fish and Game.

# Stream Facts: East Walker River

### River Characteristics
- On the stretch from Bridgeport to the lake, this is a meadow stream with a deep channel, rough fish for forage, some big browns, especially in the Fall.
- Just below the dam is the Big Hole, a wide part of the river with complex currents.
- Farther down toward Nevada, you will find riffles and runs one right after the other, interrupted occasionally by intriguing pocket water.

### Seasons
- The trout season is open from the last Saturday in April until October 31, and you may fish from an hour before sunrise to an hour after sunset.

### Special Regulations
- From Bridgeport to State Highway 182 Bridge, 1 fish, minimum 18 inches, artificial lures with barbless hooks only.
- From the State Highway 182 Bridge to Nevada state line, 2 fish, minimum 14 inches, artificial lures with barbless hooks only.
- Be certain to check regulations.

### Trout
- Browns from 12 inches to 8 pounds, rainbows average 12 to 16 inches. This is "traditional brown trout water," but rainbows are the most often caught. (*Editor's note:* DFG estimates have run as high as 9,000 per mile.)

### River Miles
- From Bridgeport to Bridgeport Reservoir, less than .5 miles.
- From the dam below Bridgeport Reservoir to Nevada state line, eight miles.

### River Flows
- Flows fluctuate, dictated by runoff and irrigation needs downstream. Water in the East Walker belongs to the Walker River Irrigation District. Call Ken's Sporting Goods for conditions.

### Hub City
- Bridgeport

# EAST WALKER RIVER MAJOR HATCHES

| Insect | A | M | J | J | A | S | O | N | Flies |
|---|---|---|---|---|---|---|---|---|---|
| Baetis | █ | █ |  |  |  |  | █ | █ | Nymph: Pheasant Tail Nymph #18<br>Dry: Tan Paradun Olive Cripple #18–20; Tan Spinner #18–20 |
| Epeorus |  | █ | █ | █ | █ |  |  |  | Humpy #16–18; Sparkle Dun #14–16; Pheasant Tail Nymph #14–18; Dark Hare's Ear #14–18 |
| E. tibialis | █ |  |  |  |  |  |  |  | Nymph: Bird's Nest; Pheasant Tail<br>Dry: Bruisable Dun #14–17; Humpy |
| Pale Morning Dun<br>Ephemerella infrequens |  |  |  |  |  |  | █ | █ | Nymph: Hunchback Infrequens<br>Dry: PMD Paradun; PMD Emerger |
| Caddis<br>Rhyacophila |  | █ | █ | █ | █ |  | █ |  | Nymph: Mercer's Z-Wing Caddis #16–18; Beadhead Caddis #16–18<br>Dry: Olive Cripple #16; Tan Elk Hair Caddis |
| Spotted Sedge<br>Hydropsyche |  | █ | █ |  |  |  |  |  | Nymph: LaFontaine's Deep Pupa Green; Olive Z-Wing<br>Dry: Elk Hair Caddis; Hot Creek Caddis |
| Caddis<br>Glossosoma |  | █ | █ |  |  |  |  |  | Nymph: Cream Soft Hackle; Bird's Nest #16–18<br>Dry: Olive Cripple #16; Elk Hair Caddis |
| Grannom<br>Brachycentrus |  |  |  |  |  | █ |  |  | Nymph: Bird's Nest #12–18<br>Dry: Olive Cripple #12–18; Elk Hair Caddis #12–18 |
| Microcaddis<br>Hydro |  |  |  |  |  |  |  |  | Nymph: Soft Hackles #16–24 (many colors and sizes) |

## EAST WALKER RIVER MAJOR HATCHES (cont.)

| Insect | A | M | J | J | A | S | O | N | Flies |
|---|---|---|---|---|---|---|---|---|---|
| Golden Stone *Calineuria or Acrineuria* | | | | | | | ▇ | | Nymphs: Rosborough's Golden Nymph #4–10<br>Dries: Stimulator #4–10, Sofa Pillow #4–10 |
| Olive Stone *Alloperla* | | | | | | ▇ | | | Nymphs: Light Olive Hare's Ear #12–16<br>Dries: Light Olive Stimulator #10 |
| Little Yellow Stone *Isoperla* | | | | | ▇ | | | | Nymphs: Partridge and Yellow #10–12, Burk's Yellow Orange Stone #10–12<br>Dries: Yellow Stimulator #12, Parachute Stone #12, Bucktail Caddis #10–12 |
| Brown Stone | | | | | | ▇ | | | Brown Bucktail Caddis #10–14, Dark Hare's Ear #10–14 |
| Baitfish | | | | | | | | ▇ | |
| Carp, Trout Fry & Sculpin | | | | | | | | ▇ | Streamers: Muddler Minnows, Matukas |
| Chubs, Dace | | | | | | | | ▇ | Black/White Marabou, Black/Yellow Marabou, Woolly Buggers |

# Bridgeport

## Elevation – 6,500 • Population – 500

## ACCOMMODATIONS

**Best Western Ruby Inn**, N. Main Street, P.O. Box 455, Bridgeport, CA 93517-0455 / 760-932-7241 / $-$$

**Bridgeport Inn**, South Main Street, P.O. Box 426, Bridgeport, CA 93517 / 760-932-7380 / $-$$

**Cain House** (B&B), N. Main Street, P.O. Box 454, Bridgeport, CA 93517 / 760-932-7040

**Chalet Motel and RV Park**, Highway #395, P.O. Box 1010, Bridgeport, CA 93517 / 760-932-7488 / $-$$

**Mono Village Resort**, 1000 Twin Lakes Road, Bridgeport, CA 93517 / 760-932-7071 / $-$$ / At the far western end of Upper Twin Lakes. Also offers camping, RV parking, store, restaurant, marina, rental cabins

**Redwood Motel and Gift Shop**, N. Main Street, P.O. Box 543, Bridgeport, CA 93517 / 760-932-7060 / $$

**Walker River Lodge**, 100 Main Street, Bridgeport, CA 93517 / 760-932-7021, 800-688-3351, Fax 760-932-7914 / $$-$$$ / Family units, on the river, pool, small pets okay, senior discount

**Virginia Creek Settlement**, 1 Main Street, Bridgeport, CA 93517 / 760-932-7780 / $-$$ / Five miles south of Bridgeport, this place is an experience in itself; restaurant serves the best food around, motel facilities are extremely clean; the campground however, was designed as an Old West town — choose from tent cabins or sleep in a teepee

## RESTAURANTS

**Rhino's Bar and Grill**, 266 Main & Sinclair, Bridgeport, CA 93517 / 760-932-7345 / $-$$ / Lunch, dinner, pizza, beer/full bar and sandwiches...satellite TV

**Virginia Creek Settlement**, Highway 395, 6 miles south of Bridgeport / 760-932-7780 / $$ / Great food and atmosphere...Italian/American and the best pizza in the West, beer/wine

**Bridgeport Inn**, South Main St., Bridgeport, CA 93517 / 760-932-7380 / $$-$$$ / Fine dining in the heart of the Sierras: steaks, seafood, prime rib, $ bar

**Hays Street Cafe**, South end of town, Main St., Bridgeport, CA 93517 / 760-932-7141 / $$ / Breakfast, lunch...good hearty meals in a country atmosphere... reasonably priced; beer

## RV PARKS

**Falling Rock Marina** , Highway 182 (2 miles SW of Bridgeport), PO. Box 338, Bridgeport, CA 93517 / 760-932-7001

**Twin Lakes Resort** , Twin Lakes Road (10 miles SW of Bridgeport) PO. Box 248, Bridgeport, CA 93517 / 760-932-7751

**Willow Springs Motel and RV Park** (7 miles south of Bridgeport on Highway #395), P.0. Box 1040, Bridgeport, CA 93517

## CAMPING

There are five public campgrounds southwest of Bridgeport, all off Twin Lakes Road, between 9 and 12 miles from town. There are none on the lower river from the dam into Nevada, though a private campground, **Paradise Shores**, is located on Bridgeport Reservoir / 760-9327735.

Much of this area is in the **Toyabe National Forest**, where "dispersed camping" in unimproved areas is allowed with a fire permit. Call (late in the day is better) or write for extensive information: Bridgeport District, Toyabe National Forest, P.O. Box 595 / 760-932-7070

## Sporting Goods and Fly Shops

**Ken's Sporting Goods**, Main Street, Bridgeport, CA 93517 / 760-932-7707 / Flies, flyfishing tackle, camping supplies, Bridgeport area fishing information

## HOSPITALS

Mammoth Lakes: **Mammoth Hospital**, P.O. 660 Mammoth Lakes, CA 93546 / 760-934-3311

## AIRPORT

**Bryant Field** (Bishop Airport) / 760-932-7500 / No commercial flights; difficult conditions. Mammoth Lakes is closest.

## OTHER ACTIVITIES

For a list of the many great activities available in this area, contact the Bridgeport Chamber of Commerce 760-932-7500

## FOR MORE INFORMATION

Bridgeport Chamber of Commerce
85 Main Street
Bridgeport, CA, 93517
760-932-7500

# Lower Owens River

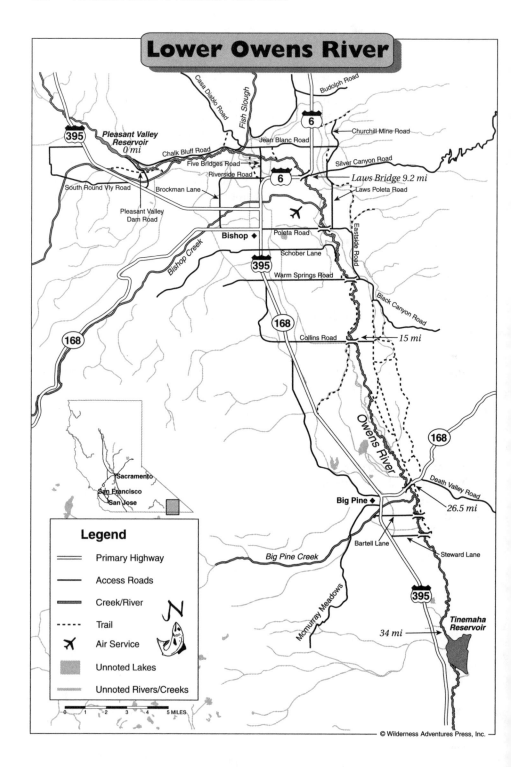

Casa Diablo Road

Fish Slough

Budolph Road

**395**

**6**

Churchill Mine Road

**Pleasant Valley Reservoir**
*0 mi*

Chalk Bluff Road

Jean Blanc Road

Five Bridges Road

Silver Canyon Road

Riverside Road

*Laws Bridge 9.2 mi*

South Round Vly Road

Brockman Lane

**6**

Laws Poleta Road

Laws Poleta Road

Pleasant Valley Dam Road

Eastside Road

**Bishop ♦**

Poleta Road

Bishop Creek

Schober Lane

**395**

Warm Springs Road

Black Canyon Road

**168**

**168**

Collins Road

*15 mi*

Owens River

**168**

**Sacramento**

**San Francisco**
**San Jose**

Death Valley Road

**Big Pine ♦**

*26.5 mi*

## Legend

Bartell Lane

Steward Lane

═══ Primary Highway

**Big Pine Creek**

── Access Roads

Mcmurray Meadows

═══ Creek/River

⤳ Trail

✈ Air Service

**395**

Unnoted Lakes

*34 mi*

**Tinemaha Reservoir**

Unnoted Rivers/Creeks

0  1  2  3  4  5 MILES

© Wilderness Adventures Press, Inc.

# Lower Owens River: Meadow Stream under the Mountains

## by Kate and Bill Howe

*Chestnuts roasting on the open fire, season's closed on favorite streams.*
*Beginning to feel a bit like Christmas — must be time to fish the Owens.*

Few of California's great trout waters are open to angling year-round; of these, the Lower Owens River is one of the best. That this is not more widely known among northern California anglers reflects the fact that from a flyfishing perspective, the Eastern Sierra is really another country, a new frontier for anglers accustomed to Hat Creek and rivers like the Pit and McCloud. Especially foreign are the wide horizons of high desert plateau, where runoff from the alkaline soil nurtures water life but supports few trees to obscure a view toward peaks. When you do see a line of willows in Owens Valley, or perhaps an enormous, ancient cottonwood planted by settlers to break gales, there's water and some seriously good trout fishing.

At an elevation of about 4500 feet, the Owens Valley is often windy, warm in summer, temperate in spring and fall. Bishop temperatures can be near-zero in winter — or so comfortable on December days that, even with the sky full of snowy mountains, you'll remove your sweater to fish in shirt sleeves. At such times it might not be just the temperature that makes you warm, however. Angling challenges here are often distinct from more northern or western venues. And the abundance of aquatic life in the Owen's food chain can bewilder the amateur. In a single day, for example, you may see hatches of several species of mayflies, the hucks of streamside stoneflies, and ovipositing caddis. Add to these craneflies Dobson and Alder, water beetles and a healthy scud population; then midges, which abound all year and are especially important in the colder months; terrestrials during summer months; and consider also the various baitfish that live in or move through the river.

What this wide range of trout feed reveals is a sophisticated system — so complex, ironically, that impressionism is usually a better bet than attempts to exactly match a hatch. This rule does not, however, relieve an angler from an obligation to make a keen and fluid assessment of what's up in the water.

Or reading whether the water's up. Flows moving down the lower Owens River fluctuate on a seasonal and even daily basis, as one might expect of a main artery delivering water south to Los Angeles. Both spring runoff and power generation at Pleasant Valley Reservoir also factor into the equation. But such swings should not suggest a canal environment — rather that fishing this river in flux is a fact of life. Feeding patterns of fish are certainly affected by the changes. Interestingly enough, some of the best angling occurs during high water periods, when the Owens trout are more likely to leave bankside cover to feed in midriver current lines and seams.

*Owens River brown trout. (Photo: Edgar Yeechow)*

Complicated conditions, often, but the fish of this river make careful study worthwhile. The Owens is home to both planted and wild rainbows, *Salmo gairdneri*, some grown to very large sizes; and there's black bass thoughout the system, beginning with the first backwaters below Pleasant Valley Campground. But the prime fly-rod adversary here is the brown trout, especially in the DFG-designated special-regulation section where *Salmo trutta* predominate. While studies in the mid-1980s put combined trout populations at over 11,000 per mile, current Department of Fish and Game electroshock and creel surveys provide only a rough idea of total trout numbers and biomass. Suffice it to say that a competent flyfisher can reasonably expect to catch 30 or more fish a day, with most in the 5- to 14-inch range. The wild trout section in particular has long held a fine population of 11- to 14 -inch fish, with many in the 15- to 19-inch class. In addition, there are enough trout better than 19 inches — to 25 and 30 — justify the belief that the Owens offers the best chance anywhere in California to take trophy browns in a spring creek environs. All that's required to catch them is timing, luck, knowledge, and a significant amount of skill.

While the upper section of Owens from Big Springs to Crowley Reservoir now contains some of the largest fish, especially during spawning migrations from Crowley Lake, it is open to the public for only a few hard-hit miles and only during the standard season. The part of Lower Owens open all year includes the water downstream from Lake Crowley, abut 30 miles; but the section through the canyon to

*Floating the Owens. (Photo: Kate Howe)*

Pleasant Valley Reservoir is a stretch both unique and, to the visiting angler, dicey to approach in winter, if it can be approached at all. By comparison, the Lower Owens beneath Pleasant Valley Dam is accessible for more than 30 miles on the way to Tinemaha Reservoir. It may be fished all year both by regulation and by a practical standard of access.

### Fishing the Lower Owens

The water here is seldom discolored or too chilly. Although parts of the river-bottom consist of deep holes and sand pockets, wading is relatively easy — you can always find places where you can cross to reach holding zones on the opposite bank. This is easiest in winter, when flows are lower and more stable than during spring and summer. At any time of year, however, sand and holes can cause problems, so consider walking the shore and entering the water only when necessary. Watch where you put your feet on the banks, as these are riddled with holes dug by animals for dens.

While fishing this river you will find many places where streamside vegetation has overgrown the banks. Some of this descended from flora planted by early settlers: salt cedar and giant cottonwoods. Willows, buck brush, and tulles often create a snarl of greenery, sometimes what seems an impenetrable wall. Such barriers may have you scratching your head, wondering if humans have ever set foot beyond it. Yes, they have, and you, too, can find a way in and a way out. Don't skip these spots as so many anglers do; they are productive precisely because they are rarely fished. Naturally, such bushwacking has a few drawbacks, and the authors have lost many pairs of waders in the process. This is less of a problem along the special-regulation section of the river, where trees and shrubs are not as prevalent as elsewhere. (*Editor's note*: if you ever had the chance to watch the Howes, it would soon be clear that their "bushwhacking" approaches are made carefully, for the sake of safety, in order to not alarm the fish, and by way of doing the absolute minimum damage to vegetation. Some types of flora, like cattails, grow — or recover — very slowly.)

Because large areas of the far downstream river cannot be reached by road, you can find solitude and relatively untouched sections by using a watercraft. A float from Five Bridges Road to East Line Street will reveal many miles of great flyfishing water. Because of constrictions in the river, however, such a trip is best made in a small McKenzie boat (12 feet or less in length), a stout raft like an Avon, or a small aluminum johnboat.

Before you set off on such an adventure, check your planned put-in and take-out areas for vehicle access. Also, be sure to pack food, fresh water, a first-aid kit, a flashlight and any other incidentals you might need for nighttime comfort, as it is a long hike out to the road should any mishap occur. Be prepared to walk your craft — the river narrows in spots and there are shallows and turns not navigable with a boat. Obviously, novices should not tempt fate. Although the river is small, it is still dangerous and has some very technical water.

Hikers and boaters will find many side channels that meander through the valley. Don't ignore these either, since they offer persistent anglers opportunities for hooking very large fish. Near Tinemaha, sloughs also hide an occasional largemouth bass — heavyweights that will eat trout flies when provoked.

Whether floating or wading, keep water fluctuations in mind. Heads up.

## Tackle

For most of the techniques important on the Owens, a nine foot, 4-, 5-, or 6-weight rod with medium-action, rigged with a double-tapered floating line are preferred. Lines and rod weights lighter than these are difficult to cast during the windy afternoons that prevail in the valley.

Leaders should be long, 10 feet to 12 feet, tapering to 3X or 4X for fishing streamers. Count on adding four feet of 4X, 5X, or 6X tippet when using smaller dries, nymphs, and soft-hackle flies. Tippet diameter should be determined by fly size and water clarity. Such long leaders and tippets not only help create a drag-free drift, but allow a wet fly to swim deeply.

They also require particular care. When fishing finer lines, as when dead drifting nymphs on a light tippet, a slight tension is all that's needed to check for a fish. Modest pressure serves a second purpose: it often causes a trout to clamp down hard on the fly, turn away, and hook itself. Violent reactions to strikes are not only unnecessary but frequently disastrous. Many anglers break off big fish with overaggressive yanks, especially when presenting soft-hackle patterns down and across. Remember,

*Successful nymph fisher on the Owens. (Photo: Bill Howe)*

if you properly maintain contact with your fly, avoiding slack in line or leader, all that's required to set the hook is a slight and steady raising of the rod.

Wading gear should be adapted to the season you're fishing. Wear neoprene when the temperature is cold. As the air warms you can downgrade to hip boots, even shorts and wading shoes during the heat of summer. Boots should have felt soles to help prevent slipping. While a wading staff is not necessary to negotiate the Owen's current, it will come in handy when probing for secure footing around the river's many undercuts and dropoffs.

No angler should be caught here without insect repellent. The authors prefer to use noncaustic Avon Skin-So-Soft, which is effective, yet gentle to both your skin and your tackle.

### Tactics and Flies

*Caddis* — Never mind the dams — the alkaline Lower Owens is really the eastern Sierra's largest spring creek, and hosts an incredible population of insects, with good hatch activity year-round. Caddis are often the most conspicuous of these. Let's look at emerging caddis first.

One of the best imitations for a caddis pupa on its way to the surface is the soft-hackle fly. These can be either dead-drifted, or swung down and across the river. When tying or buying soft-hackles for the Owens, choose sizes #16 to #20, preferably

*A sexy curve on the Owens. (Photo: Kate Howe)*

on a light wire hook. Bodies should be dubbed in such naturalistic colors as light olive, dark olive, tan, brown, and gray, although a pearl crystal hair body, reverse-wrapped with thin copper wire, will also attract strikes. If tying your own fly, apply dubbing sparsely, taper the body so it thickens toward the front of the hook, and wrap a collar of Hungarian partridge or soft hen hackle. Any good fly-tying book will present instructions for soft-hackle patterns, which are among the easiest flies to tie.

Seldom will soft-hackles fail to bring healthy, rod-jarring strikes when fished carefully in the subtle currents and eddies of the Owens. These simple patterns suggest such caddis species as *hydropsyche*, also known as the spotted sedge — use hare's-ear dubbing and brown partridge hackle; and *rhyacophilia*, the green sedge, which you may tie with green thread, a green body and gray partridge hackle.

The authors favor such flies in their favorite method of fishing here: to probe each run with a dead-drifted soft-hackle, covering all the water methodically, sometimes making each successive cast only six inches from the last. This approach may seem time-consuming — it is — but pays off because many runs hold fish from the top of the water column down to the bottom; so a methodical, observant angler can literally hook a dozen trout in less than 30 feet of river. The trout are there, believe it, and an impatient approach can lead to a long walk down many miles of river with relatively few fish caught. That's why knowledgeable Owens River flyfishers pick each run apart and practically vacuum it. In fact, the authors have spent many hours on little more than a couple of hundred feet of river, not visiting the same water twice in a month. It's an intense way to fish, certainly. But it's not only productive, but wonderfully educational, revealing just how rich this river is. And it hones angling tactics.

During winter, when the metabolism and aggression of trout have cooled with the water temperature, the fly must be presented in as slow a manner as possible. While small soft-hackles and spring-creek-type nymphs lend themselves to this type of presentation all season long, they are especially effective in this season. (Note that soft-hackles can also imitate the swimming nymph of Baetis , the blue-winged olive, which appear in the river year round. For these use a gray body and blue-dun hen hackle.)

*Streamers* — Streamer fishing on the Owens can be a thrill. One of the most productive patterns is probably already in your fly box: the venerable muddler minnow. For winter and early spring, muddlers in sizes 8 through 14 are hard to beat. Insect hatches during this time of year are sparser, so the trout are looking for food that will provide a lot of calories. Appropriate colors for muddlers include black, various shades of olive, and natural deer hair. If tied unweighted this fly may be fished in the surface film. Add a split-shot or two in order to probe depths for larger browns.

In addition to muddlers, other useful streamers include woolly and crystal buggers, Byford's zonkers, deer-hair and wool-head sculpins. Most or all of these will be available at your favorite fly shop. Sizes should range from #6 to as small as #14. Include dark flies for fishing when the water is off-color or during low-light periods, lighter versions for clear-water and midday angling.

*Other Bugs* — Flyfishers in general can become too intent on finding some specific, usually elusive, seasonal hatch. To obsess on the Owens may lead to missing the great angling that's always available — keep in mind that the temperature of tailwaters remains relatively consistent throughout the year, insuring an abundance of insects. That's one reason the authors urge an impressionistic approach, either with soft hackles discussed, or with generic nymphs and emergers. And while so doing they have enjoyed many productive hours on this river even when nothing was hatching; or, more intriguingly, after an intense hatch, when you would expect to find the trout already gorged.

On the Owens and elsewhere, there's often a need to look beyond the obvious and try something new. Consider, for example, carrying patterns to imitate the following food items:

Alder flies: The young of this insect hatches midsummer. Adults hang about streamside vegetation, and are often mistaken for caddis — which means, of course, that you can use a caddis dry fly to imitate the adult. Alder fly larva can be imitated with brown woolly worms in sizes 10 through 14.

Dobson flies: The larvae of Dobson flies are a mouthful for trout, and are usually referred to as hellgrammites. A useful imitation is Doug Prince's hellgrammite in sizes 6 through 10. Like the Alder fly, the metamorphoses takes place midsummer.

Water beetles: Two species of water beetles are found in the lower Owens, the water tiger (*Dytiscidae*) and the water scavenger beetle (hydrophildae). If you wish to imitate these try to catch some naturals, so that you can precisely match size. These insects swim, so give flies a semblance of life with a slow retrieve.

Crane flies: Although they look like giant mosquitoes, crane flies are not blood-suckers. An appropriate if somewhat abstract imitation of the adult insect, which is available to trout spring and autumn, is the Ginger variant in sizes 10 through 16. For the cranefly's sub-aquatic larvae fish a muskrat nymph in sizes 10 through 16.

Scuds: Frequently considered a last resort, these crustaceans are plentiful in the weedy sections of the lower Owens. Fish them in sizes 10 through 20, in colors that imitate the naturals — shades of olive, tan and cream.

For winter fishing in the Owens, pack a variety of nymphs in sizes 14 through 20. Pheasant Tails will seduce fish, so do gold- or copper-ribbed hare's ear nymphs. Other useful patterns include hunch-back Infrequens, poxy-back Baetis, Bird's nest, Burk's leg nymph, AP nymphs in a variety of colors, li'l yellow stone nymph, drifting flashback nymphs and various pupae imitations.

Don't worry if you can't find some of the above in your local fly bin. A standard collection of searching patterns and generic imitations will serve you well on the lower Owens; conversely, these favorite Eastern Sierra flies have caught fish for the authors all over the world. Again, while a few lakes and streams have unique hatches for which you need local information and patterns, the Owens is not one of these. Here, pattern takes a back seat to presentation.

***Dry Flies*** — Many dry-fly patterns function extremely well on the lower Owens, though usually for smaller fish. The stoneflies found here include the golden stonefly (*Calineuria*), little yellow stonefly (*Isoperla*), brown stonefly (*Hesperoperla*), and the little green stonefly (*Sweltsa borelis*). To imitate the adult insects try stimulators in various colors and sizes, as well as Andy Burk's CDC stones in sizes 14 and 16.

For adult caddis, carry elk- and deer-hair caddis patterns in sizes 14 to 18. Simple as that.

Mayfly patterns should include blue-winged olives, pale morning duns and the Adams, all in sizes 14 to 18, and preferably tied for slow water in parachute- or thorax-styles.

If fishing during summer and autumn, take a few terrestrial patterns: grasshoppers in sizes 10 and 12, beetles in 14 and 16, and ants sized 16 to 20.

When fishing dry flies on the lower Owens you'll often have to use a downstream presentation that lets the trout see the fly before it sees anything else. If you "line" these wary trout, you'll spook them, and they may stay down for hours. Always strive for a drag-free drift. If you get refusals with good drifts, switch to a smaller fly.

### Access

To reach the wild brown trout water of the lower Owens, go northwest on the Pleasant Valley Dam Road off Highway 395 (seven miles northeast of Bishop). Drive about a mile until you reach the river, where you will find a campground. Across the

*A prime, deep Owens River run. (Photo: Kate Howe)*

river and beyond the campground, a gravel road runs right; this will parallel the river along the northeast side to Five Bridges Road, a distance of approximately six miles. A network of dirt spurs leading off the right offer excellent access. While some have big dips — proceed with caution — the sandy soil can usually be navigated by a passenger car.

Special regulations begin below Pleasant Valley Reservoir and continue downstream for about 4.4 miles to the Department of Fish and Game sign on Chalk Bluff Road. With some slight changes to these boundaries, this section has been managed as a wild fishery for many years. The brown trout remain pre-eminent here despite heavy stocking of rainbows downstream, occasionally extreme low water conditions, and heavy angling pressure. Their success is possible because this section of the river lends itself well to their particular needs: meandering meadow water flows over a gravel bottom ideal for brown trout spawning. Bigger fish lurk beneath the many miles of undercut banks, hiding in the shadows of overhanging willows. Both fry and adults take full advantage of slower side channels.

If you proceed on Pleasant Valley Dam Road roughly .7 miles past the campground, and veer left at the fork — you can't get lost here — you'll arrive at a small parking area. A walk along the trail will bring you to a stretch of water immediately below Pleasant Valley Dam. Close by you will find an artificial spawning channel, running about .8 miles downstream.

*Prime cutbank run on the Owens. (Photo: Kate Howe)*

Of course the spawning channel is closed to fishing all year. But a walk of a mile will bring you to a fishable stretch. This is an easy place to drown. The river is rougher here than in the Wild Brown Trout section, and subject to radical fluctuations in flow. Because you need to wade down into the river, where the banks are often steep, you may be caught when water is shot out from the system above. Bill Howe, a big man, was washed downstream here, and considers it a "Close call."

To reach Five Bridges Road, go north on Highway 6 off 395, jog left at the Five Bridges sign: you'll reach the river in a few hundred yards. If you stay on Highway 6, it will also cross the Owens two miles and east of this juncture, give or take a dime, at Laws Bridge. At this time no decent driveable track follows the river downstream from Five Bridges, so access on the way to Tinemaha Reservoir is available from various roads that branch off 395 in the town of Bishop. These include a maze of access roads, some paved, some not. While the water along the river is all owned by Department of Water and Power, Los Angeles, be aware that you may need to cross private property to get there. Courtesy is the rule here; ask permission. The easiest to find on your map — you need one — are Poleta Road, East Line Road, and Warm Springs Road; on each of these, proceed east. South of Bishop, the river can be reached from Collins Road. About 15 miles south of Bishop, in the town of Big Pine, both Bartell Road and Steward Lane will meet the stream.

*Classic, brushy small stream water on the Owens. (Photo: Kate Howe)*

Although the lower Owens below the special-regulation water contains wild trout, it is also stocked by the Department of Fish and Game. This means that some fish are easy to catch and you may not feel guilty about knocking one on the noggin. It also means you're likely to run into crowds fishing the places where the trout are planted: at Laws Bridge on Highway 6, Collins Road, Westgard Pass Road (also called Highway 168) and Steward Lane.

**Travel Information and Local Contacts**

The Owens River runs through Mono and Inyo counties on the eastern side of the Sierra. Its route is paralleled, albeit at some distance, by Highway 395. The town of Bishop is an excellent spot for a base camp. Driving time from Los Angeles to Bishop via Highway 395 is about 5.5 hours. Access from the San Francisco Bay Area during summer is via the highways that cross the Sierra (80, 50, 4, 108, 120) and lead to Highway 395. In winter, Northern California travelers should use either Highway 80 to Reno, then turn south on Highway 395; or take Highway 99 south to Highway 58 (Tehachapi Pass), then 395 north.

# Stream Facts: Lower Owens River

### Seasons and Special Regulations
- From Pleasant Valley Dam downstream to the footbridge at the lower end of Pleasant Valley campground: All year, artificial lures with barbless hooks only, 2 fish limit with maximum size 12 inches. ( note: artificial spawning channel about .8 miles down from Pleasant Valley Dam is closed to all fishing.)
- From footbridge at lower end of Pleasant Valley Campground downstream 4.4 miles to Fish & Game sign on Chalk Bluff Road: All year, artificial lures with barbless hooks only, 0 limit.
- From sign on Chalk Bluff Road downstream: Open all year, no restrictions, five fish limit.

### River Characteristics
- The Lower Owens is a classic Eastern Sierra spring creek of medium size; chopped into segments by dams, it's also a tailwater. The alkaline water is rich with life; caddis predominate. Mostly open shoreline; larger fish often hold below undercut banks.

### Trout
- Planted and wild rainbows, salmo gairdneri, some grown to very large sizes; but the prime fly-rod adversary here is the brown trout, especially in the DFG-designated special-regulation section.

### River Miles
- 30 miles from Pleasant Valley Dam to Tinemaha Reservoir.

### River Flows
- Regulated by dams and manipulated from 150 to 800 cfs. Three hundred to four hundred cfs is the level favored by the author, but as with any tailwater, the consistency of flow is what's most important, low or high.

### Boat Ramps
- No developed launches: you must use a craft you can carry, drag and drop.

### Hub Cities
- Bishop, also Mammoth Lakes (see Hot Creek)

# LOWER OWENS RIVER MAJOR HATCHES

| Insect | J | F | M | A | M | J | J | A | S | O | N | D | Flies |
|---|---|---|---|---|---|---|---|---|---|---|---|---|---|
| Baetis | | | ■ | | | | | | | ■ | | | Nymphs: Pheasant Tail Nymph #18<br>Dries: Tan Paradun Olive Cripple #18–20, Burk's Painless Baetis #18–20 |
| Epeorus | | | | | ■ | | ■ | | | | | | Humpy #16–18, Sparkle Dun #14–16, Pheasant Tail Nymph #1418, Dark Hare's Ear #14–16 |
| E. tibialis | | | | | | ■ | ■ | | | | | | Nymphs: Bird's Nest, Pheasant Tail<br>Dries: Bruisable Dun #14–16, Humpy #14–16 |
| Pale Morning Dun Ephemerella infrequens | | | | | | ■ | ■ | | | ■ | | | Nymphs: Hunchback Infrequens<br>Dries: PMD Paradun, PMD Emerger |
| Caddis Rhyacophila | | | | ■ | | | | ■ | | ■ | | | Nymphs: Mercer's Z-Wing Caddis #16–18, Beadhead Caddis #16–18<br>Dries: Olive Cripple #16, Tan Elk Hair Caddis |
| Spotted Sedge Hydropsyche | | | | | | ■ | | ■ | | | | | Nymph: LaFontaine's Deep Pupa Green, Olive Z-Wing<br>Dries: Elk Hair Caddis, Hot Creek Caddis |
| Saddle Casemaker Glossosoma | | | | | | ■ | | ■ | | | | | Nymphs: Cream Soft Hackle, Bird's Nest #16–18<br>Dries: Olive Cripple #16, Tan Elk Hair Caddis |
| Grannom Brachycentrus | | | | | | ■ | | ■ | | | | | Nymphs: Bird's Nest, Soft Hackle<br>Dries: Olive Cripple #12–18, Elk Hair Caddis #12–18 |
| Microcaddis Hydro | | | | | | ■ | | | | | | | Nymphs: Soft Hackles #16–24 (many colors and sizes) Beadhead Caddis<br>Dries: Parachutes #16–24, Tiny Elk Hair Caddis #16–24 |

## LOWER OWENS RIVER MAJOR HATCHES (cont.)

| Insect | J | F | M | A | M | J | J | A | S | O | N | D | Flies |
|---|---|---|---|---|---|---|---|---|---|---|---|---|---|
| Golden Stone *Calineuria or Acroneuria* | | | | | | | | | | | ▮ | | Nymphs: Mercer's Poxyback Stonefly Nymph #6–10 Dries: Stimulator #4–10, Sofa Pillow #4–10 |
| Olive Stone *Alloperla* | | | | | | | | | ▮ | | | | Nymphs: Light Olive Hare's Ear #12–16 Dries: Light Olive Stimulator #10 |
| Winter Stone Black, Red, Brown | ▮ | | | | | | | | | | | | Nymphs: AP Black #12–16, Timberline Brown #12–16 Dries: Red & Dark Brown Stimulators #14–16, Black Elk Hair Caddis |
| Little Yellow Stone *Isoperla* | | | | | | | ▮ | | | | | | Nymphs: Partridge and Yellow #10–12, Burk's Little Yellow Orange Stone #10–12 Dries: Yellow Stimulator #12, Parachute Stone #12, Bucktail Caddis #10–12 |
| Brown Stone | | | | | | | | | ▮ | | | | Brown Bucktail Caddis #10–14, Dark Hare's Ear #10–14 |
| Slow Water Mayflies | | | | | | | | | | | | | |
| *Callibaetis* | | | | ▮ | | | | | | | | | Nymphs: Poxyback Callibaetis, Pheasant Tail Dries: Parachute Adams |
| Tricos *Tricorythodes* | | | | | | ▮ | | | | | | | Nymphs: Pheasant Tail, Poxyback Trico #20–22 Dries: Trico Spinner, Bruisable Dun |
| Baitfish | ▮ | | | | | | | | | | | | Streamers: Woolhead Muddlers, Woolly and Crystal Buggers #6–14, Sculpins |
| Scuds | ▮ | | | | | | | | | | | | #6–14 |

## Owens Hatch Chart Caveat

Hatch charts are subject to the vagaries of so many conditions — and on the Owens that's true in spades. Consider the following: the Owens is both spring creek and tailwater — actually a double tailwater; the alkaline waters are enormously rich; some parts are stony and quick, others connected to ponds, sloughs and lakes; and the weather in the area is prone to extraordinary changes. Factor in ten or a dozen mayflies, including burrowers in the slow sections, half a dozen species of stoneflies at least, unknown numbers of caddis, terrific populations of midges, craneflies, alder flies (especially at the mouth of Rock Creek), cressbugs, and scuds…add water beetles, water boatman (when hatching, these are often mistaken for caddis) and backswimmers — and realize that any one, two, six, or eight beasts may be active and available to trout at a single point in time, never mind the sculpin, other baitfish, and fry…

Obviously, any graph or pattern that emerges from such errata will be anything but simple, straightforward, and predictable — so what is revealed on the chart on the preceding pages is more a "best guess, it's anybody's game" plan. This much can be said: the authors have seen these bugs and beasts on the Lower Owens, within the time frames identified, one year or another. So be prepared. Now you understand why we prefer impressionistic flies.

*Note:* the Howes tie their own variations of flies, which are not commercially available. At their request, the editor has mixed some of these selections.

# Bishop

## Elevation – 4,147 ft. • Population – 3,474

Bishop, located in the high desert along Highway 395, is less of a tourist destination than the Mammoth Lakes area north of the Lower Owens but is closer to the river and has many accommodations and services. At 4,147 feet, compared to Mammoth Lakes 7,800, it also has a significantly different winter climate (for Mammoth services and accommodations, see Hot Creek chapter).

## ACCOMMODATIONS

In Bishop the authors' favorite place to stay:

**Lakeview Lodge**, 2296 N. Sierra Highway, Bishop, CA 93514 / 619-873-4019 / $–$$ / Clean rooms, family units, kitchens, AC, cable TV, off season weekly rates / Owners: Dennis and Barbara Nichols

*Also in Bishop:*

**Best Western Holiday Spa**, 1025 N. Main Street, Bishop, CA 93514 / 619-873-3543, 800-528-1234, Fax 619-872-4777 / $–$$ / AAA, 89 units, pool, spa, group rates, small pets, nonsmoking rooms, refrigerators, microwaves, in-room coffee, lower summer rates

**Bishop Sierra Gateway**, 51 Units, 155 E. Elm St. (at Main St.), Bishop, CA 93514 / 619-873-3548 / $–$$ / Pool, bus parking, small pets, cribs, off season rates

**The Chalfant House Bed & Breakfast**, 213 Academy Street, Bishop, CA 93514 / 619-872-1790 / $$–$$ / AAA, 7 rooms, private baths, gourmet breakfast/evening refreshments, antique store

**Creekside Inn**, 725 N. Main St., Bishop, CA 93514 / 619-872-3044, 800-273-3550, Fax 619-872-1300 / $–$$ / AAA, 89 rooms, pool, spa, 12 rooms with fully equipped kitchens; rooms available for pet owners, 4 creekside patios w/BBQ & tables, senior discount, tour & group rates, free continental breakfast, Bishop airport van pickup

**Elms Motel**, 233 E. Elm Street, Bishop, CA 93514 / 619-873-8118, 800-848-9226 / $–$$ / AAA, 19 units, clean, quiet, off highway, lawn area w/BBQ, access to city park, in-room coffee, fish cleaning & freezing facilities

**Lakeview Motel**, 2296 N. Sierra Hwy, Bishop, CA 93514 / 619-873-4019 / $–$$ / 12 units, kitchens, off-season rates, family units, weekly and monthly rates

**The Matlick House Bed & Breakfast**, 1313 Rowan Lane, Bishop, CA 93514 / 619-873-3133 / $$$ / AAA, 5 rooms, country breakfast, sitting room with fireplace, evening wine & hors d'oeuvres, private baths

**Mountain View Motel**, 730 W. Line Street, Bishop, CA 93514 / 619-873-4242 / AAA, 35 units, fax, patio with BBQ, fish cleaning & freezing, ample parking, senior & off-season discounts

**Paiute Lodge Motel**, 796 W. Line Street, Bishop, CA 93514 / 619-873-6391 / $–$$ / 16 units, quiet, clean, nonsmoking rooms, telephones, kitchenettes, color TV, coffee bar, electric heat/air conditioning, patio, lawn, BBQ, fish cleaning and freezer

**Sierra Foothills**, 535 S. Main Street, Bishop, CA 93514 / 619-872-1386, 800-776-9710 / $–$$ / AAA, 43 units, pool, spa, small pets, handicap rooms, in-room coffee, free HBO

**Biship Creek Lodge**, 760-873-4484

**Best Western Bishop Holiday Spa Lodge,** 1025 N Main St / 760-873-3543

**Thunderbird Motel**, 190 W. Pine Street, Bishop, CA 93514 / 619-873-4215, Fax 619-873-6870 / $ / AAA, 23 units, senior discount, group rates, bus parking, small pets, refrigerators, microwaves, free continental breakfast

## RESTAURANTS

In addition to various fast food and restaurant chains , Bishop has the following:

**Bar-B-Q Bill's**, 187 South Main Street, Bishop, CA 93514 / 619-872-5535 / $ / Open daily from 11AM / Western-style dining specializing in BBQ beef, ribs, ham & chicken, salad bar, charbroiled hamburgers & chicken; food to go, catering

**Bishop Creek Lodge**, Hwy. 168,16 miles west of Bishop on South Lake Road, Bishop, CA 93514 / 619-873-4484 / $$$ / Nestled in the High Sierra, serving breakfast, lunch & dinner, cocktails, banquet facilities

**Bishop Grill**, 281 N. Main St., Bishop, CA 93514 / 619-873-3911 / $ / Family style coffee shop w/counter, home style cooking…traditional breakfast and luncheon fare, a Bishop tradition

**El Charro Avitia**, 970 North Main Street, Bishop, CA 93514 / 619-872-5516 / $$ / Open 11:30AM Monday–Friday, 4PM Saturday & Sunday / Authentic Mexican, steak & seafood, buffet court with over 100 items, dancing, cocktail lounge, pool tables, Happy Hour 4PM to 6PM Monday–Friday, banquet facilities

**Glacier Lodge**, 11 miles west of Hwy. 395 at Big Pine Creek, Bishop, CA 93514 / 619-938-2837 / $$$ / Gourmet meals, breakfast 7:30AM to 9AM, & dinner 6PM to 10PM / Foreign & domestic wines / Reservations preferred

**Imperial Gourmet Chinese Restaurant**, 785 North Main Street, Bishop, CA 93514 / 619-872-1144 / $$ / Mandarin cuisine, daily specials / Early bird specials 2:30–5:30 Monday–Thursday, cocktails / Sunday brunch 11:30AM–2:30PM / Open 11:30AM–10PM

**Inyo Country Store**, 177 Academy St., Bishop, CA 93514 / 619-872-2552 / $ / Open daily at 8AM / Breakfast and lunch Monday–Saturday / Dinner Thursday–Saturday from 5:30PM by reservation / Wine & beer, excellent food, great homemade desserts & cappuccino

**Jack's Waffle Shop**, 437 North Main Street / 619-872-7971 / $ / Open daily 6AM–10PM / Family restaurant, complete meals, sandwiches & food to go, home-made pies & cakes, hearty breakfasts, prime rib Friday evenings

**The Matlick House**, 1313 Rowan / 619-873-3133 / $$$ / Lunch by reservation only, wine

**Pete & Al's Airport Cafe**, 703 Airport Road / 619-872-4420 / $$ / Open Tuesday–Sunday 8AM–2PM / Great breakfasts & lunches, fresh fish every Friday

**Petite Pantry**, 2278 N. Sierra Hwy / 619-873-3789 / $ / Open Monday–Saturday 7AM–10PM, Sunday 7AM–4PM / Breakfast, lunch & dinner, homemade pies

**Whiskey Creek**, 524 North Main Street / 619-873-7174 / $$ / Open daily from 7AM, cocktail lounge opens at 4PM / Coffee Creek Cafe serves cappuccino & pastries on the patio in the morning. Family style breakfast, lunch, & dinner; banquet facility, outside seating available

*Delis:*

**Erick Schat's Bakery**, 763 North Main Street / 619-873-7156 / $ / Open daily 6AM–10PM, winter hours 7AM–6PM / Home of the World Famous Sheepherder Bread since 1938; fancy pastries, fresh ground coffee, gifts, soup, sandwich & salad bar

**Manor Market**, 3100 West Line Street / 619-873-4296 / $ / Open Monday–Saturday 6AM–9PM and Sunday 6AM–8PM / Bishop's largest selection of wine & microbrewed beer; take-out sandwiches, chicken, potatoes; picnic tables

**Meadow Farms Country Smokehouse**, 2345 North Sierra Hwy / 619-873-5311 / $–$$ / Open daily 9AM–6PM / Famous mahogany smoked meats & jerky since 1922

**FLY SHOPS IN AREA** (see also Mammoth Lakes, Hot Creek)
Most sporting goods shops in Bishop are all tackle. There is a collection of fly shops in Mammoth Lakes (see Hot Creek) for anglers coming from the north, and one on the route up from Los Angeles, off Highway 395 at the town of Ridgecrest:

**High Sierra Flyfisher**, 337 W. Ridgecrest Blvd., Ridgecrest, CA 93555 / 619-375-5810

*In Bishop, the following stores carry some supplies:*

**Brock's Sporting Goods**, 100 N. Main St., Bishop, CA 93514 / 619-872-3581 / Probably the best Bishop source.

**Culver's Sporting Goods**, 156 S. Main St., Bishop, CA 93514 / 619-872-8361

**Mac's Sporting Goods**, 425 N. Main St., Bishop, CA 93514 / 619-872-9201

**AIRPORT** (see also Mammoth Lakes, Hot Creek)
**Inyo County Airport** / 619-872 2971 / No commercial flights

**AUTO RENTALS** (see Mammoth Lakes)

**HOSPITALS**

**Mammoth Hospital** (Centinela), P.O. 660, Mammoth Lakes, CA 93546 /
   619-934-3311

**CAMPING**

The Lower Owens has a campground right on the water, beside the wild trout section. Drive seven miles northeast of Bishop on 395, take a right on Pleasant Valley Dam Road; head toward the mountains (the turn is toward the northeast, but the road will bend north-northwest). It's roughly a mile to the river and campground.

*For more campground information, see Hot Creek chapter, or contact:*

**Inyo National Forest Headquarters**, 873 N. Main St., Bishop, CA 93514 /
   619-873-5841
**California Department of Fish and Game**, 406 West Line St., Bishop, CA
   93514 / 619-872-1171

**FOR MORE INFORMATION**

Bishop Chamber of Commerce and Visitor Center
690 N. Main St.
Bishop, CA 93514
619-873-8405

**OTHER ATTRACTIONS**

Plan to spend some time during your visit in nonfishing pursuits. In addition to skiing at Mammoth Lakes, the Owens Valley offers one photo opportunity after another, and side-trips are well worthwhile. Check out the Tule Elk Preserve in Independence (south on Highway 395), for example, or spend an afternoon photographing the wildlife in the Owens corridor, where you may see ringtail cat, beaver, mule deer, sage hen, and California quail.

Of course, the crowning glory of this area is the magnificent Sierra Nevada range that appears to rise straight up from the valley floor and touch the sky. The Owens Valley has incredible vistas and unbelievable contrasts in terrain.

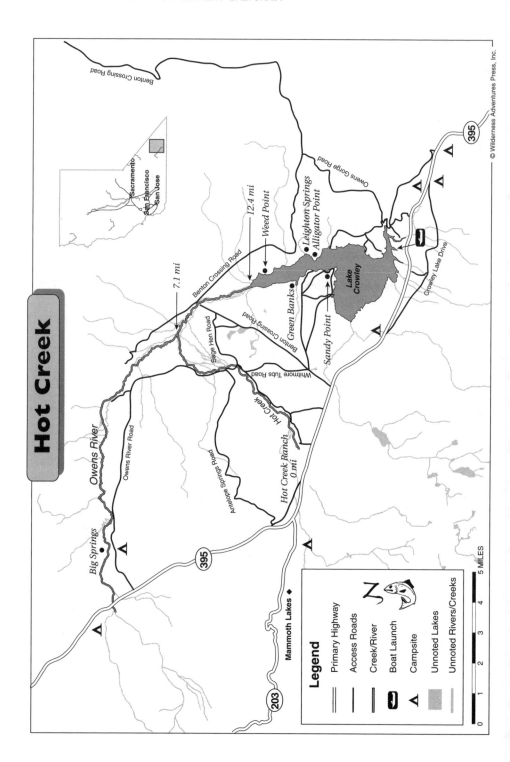

Hot Creek

Benton Crossing Road

Owens Gorge Road

12.4 mi

Weed Point

Leighton Springs
Alligator Point

7.1 mi

Benton Crossing Road

Sage Hen Road

Benton Crossing Road

Whitmore Tubs Road

Green Banks

Sandy Point

Lake
Crowley

Crowley Lake Drive

Hot Creek

Owens River

Owens River Road

Antelope Springs Road

Hot Creek Ranch
0 mi

Big Springs

Mammoth Lakes ◆

395

203

Sacramento
San Francisco
San Jose

Legend

Primary Highway

Access Roads

Creek/River

Boat Launch

Campsite

Unnoted Lakes

Unnoted Rivers/Creeks

N

0    1    2    3    4    5 MILES

# Hot Creek: Miracle Miles

### by Dan Gracia

Hot Creek is an unusual piece of water: 7,000 feet above sea level it bubbles out of springs at the upper end of one of the deepest valleys in the United States — a true alpine spring creek. While subject to the greatest fishing pressure in the entire state of California, this small water sustains one of the greatest concentrations of trout of any river in the country — unusual, at least. Arguably unique.

## Overview

How Hot Creek got to be that way is a cataclysmic story, beginning when an underground ocean of magma erupted out of the ground to hurl up the White Mountain range. Land collapsed into the bed where that lava ocean once lay, creating a caldera and, ultimately, the Owens Valley, defined on one edge by the White Mountains and along the other by the eastern scarp of the Sierra Nevada.

At the town of Bishop, Owens Valley is 10,000 feet deep from the top of the mountains to the valley floor. The views are as awe-inspiring for some as the trout fishing also found here. Visitors who can tear their stares away from the mountains and steal their attention from trout will discover abundant wildlife: birds of prey migrate through in summer and fall, in numbers apparently dependent on the populations of chipmunk, golden mantled ground squirrel, and Belding's, the "picket pin" ground squirrel (for which the picket pin nymph was named.) Some years you can't leave a car or tent door open without some rodent squirreling in. Identifying the various raptors can be difficult because of the many color phases in evidence, but harriers, sharp shinned hawks, prairie falcons, and kestrels make up shares of the population; and golden eagles can be spotted as small black dots riding the thermals high above. While the presence of sea gulls may seem incongruous in this high desert valley, fully one-third of the West Coast's sea birds nest at Mono Lake, less than an hour's drive north of Hot Creek.

There's plenty of life at ground level as well. During the day you may spot a marmot around the rocks; at dawn-glow and dusk, deer appear; and at night the strained counterpoint of wailing coyotes may keep you counting stars, wondering if you really want to fall asleep…just…yet.

Then there's the creek and all those fish….

Hot Creek is formed by seven separate springs — some scalding, some cold — that rise up out of the ground about 3 miles upstream from the main public access area. These springs ensure a year around temperature of 56 to 60 degrees— prime conditions for producing trout. Although there is a state hatchery built around the springs, none of the trout raised there are released into the creek, but planted in nearby venues. Hot has been managed as a wild trout fishery since 1973.

*Stealth pays dividends on Hot Creek. (Photo: K. Giampaoli)*

Immediately below the hatchery is a small stretch of meadow meander that is open to the public. Fish are not as plentiful here, and you have to hunt for access, but it is a legal option.

The next few miles of stream are privately held by Hot Creek Ranch. There's some excellent fishing on this property, but there's a caveat: the Ranch imposes a "dry fly only" rule upon its guests, reminiscent of those elite, turn-of-the-century fishing clubs in England. In fact, when the facility was sold some years ago, the "dry fly only" proviso was reputedly included in the contract. Local lore recalls tales of "nymphers" returning to their cabins after indulging forbidden rites, only to find themselves locked out, with their luggage on the door step. Such stories suggest that the rule has teeth. In fact, however intimidating as the rule may seem, dry fly fishing on Hot Creek is a fine, even efficient technique.

*Hot Creek know-how: keep low and work the banks. (Photo: K. Giampaoli)*

Public access begins again as Hot drops into a canyon which just so happens to remain one of the most geothermally active areas. (Isn't that how it goes, though?) This two-mile section is the stretch that receives serious fishing pressure. It's also where fishers can find a fantastic concentration of trout: more than 11,000 per mile — 11,414, to be exact, according to a Department of Fish and Game electro-shock survey in 1985, with browns outnumbering rainbows by roughly 7 to 1.

Electroshocking is never exact, of course, but even if the numbers are off by half, the result is still staggering; Hot isn't a river — you can often cast across it. But look carefully, a long time, and keep counting, scratching numbers in the dirt, piling pebbles. Start with a second abacus —

Of course, just because they're here doesn't mean they're yours. To succeed on Hot Creek, you have to do everything right.

Hot Creek is also famous for the springs which give it its name. The earth's crust is thin throughout this region, conspicuously so. Small hot seeps and fumeroles dot the landscape, particularly terrain near the creek, and in the bed itself. Watch your step, as these will make muddy, hot, slippery messes out of parts of the trail. In places, super-heated water bubbles and boils from the earth, and the location of these emergences changes from time to time.

In some spots the springs can't make up their mind: sometimes the water is clear and quiet, sometimes cloudy, reeking of sulfur. Fits of temper are common; part of the path at the end of the bridge had to be roped off, due to the sudden appearance of a new boiling pot, which dripped frosty blue, mineral-laden water across the trail and into the creek.

Two of the springs in this section are relatively consistent, however, constantly pulsating hot water. These are popular with Hot Creek bathers (see Other Attractions), but veteran "springers" are careful not to get too close to the center of either, because of sudden, unexpected surges of scalding water; but approached with caution they can provide a welcome and relaxing way to end a hard days fishing. Occasionally you will even see trout rising along the north side of the upper one, as a thin stream of cold water from the creek above clings to the edge of the bank. The trout just do it to taunt you.

## Fishing Hot Creek

The river enters the public section from the Ranch through a barbed wire fence. The gradient is fairly mild here; this is a typical slow, clear spring creek. You can reach this upper portion of the river by parking at the first paved lot and walking down the "Fisherman's Trail."

This upper area features the widest section of Hot Creek and harbors some of the biggest fish in the river. It also demands the most skill.

After the creek passes a stand of the few trees found here, it turns the corner to the right, narrows, and picks up speed. From this point to the base of Fisherman's Trail (where it comes down the cliff), the stream remains skinny, but holds plenty of trout.

The water slows again as you pass the junction of Fisherman's Trail and start to move farther into the canyon. A pair of narrow throats between here and the hot springs, about 1.5 miles below, necessitate either wading through the creek — carefully, along the edges — or climbing up and around rocks.

Throughout this middle section the water speed varies. Weeds and some mid-river rock formations break up and accelerate the flow. Access may be had by walking in from either end of the canyon or by parking at and descending from any of the interim dirt lots located on the road above, the most strategically placed are between the uppermost "Fisherman's Trail" and the bottom-most paved lot, at the lower hot springs (the only place with restrooms).

As the river emerges from the last constriction of the canyon, it pours into the deepest part of Hot Creek. This "meat hole" holds good quantities of easily seen but rarely caught trout. Currents are convoluted in this pool, entering from both sides

*Hot Creek magic: a big rainbow and scenery galore. (Photo: K. Giampaoli)*

around a boulder the size of a small house. Churning water creates ever-changing "challenges" to proper line control.

Perhaps to escape this, adventurous flyfishers (usually young ones) sometimes climb on top of the big rock in the middle of the creek, only to find that they are in the worst possible place to get a natural drift. Should they happen to hook a fish, they're also in the worst position to land and release it unharmed, as the law requires.

Below this pool, downstream past some rocks in the middle of the creek, the flow slows up a bit again. This is the lower section. Sometimes thick with picnickers near the hot springs, it is also dense with trout.

The creek creates one last pool before spilling into the first hot spring and mixing with its worshippers. Fishing downstream from here is usually futile: not only do the springs heat the water but they secrete the occasional doses of arsenic. Don't arrive here thirsty.

## Techniques

Normally on a small spring creek like this, where an angler must expect to make short casts to fish tiny flies on fine tippets and dead drifts are an absolute necessity, a 3- or 4-weight rod would be a good choice. And so it is, right up until about 1:00 in the afternoon, when the wind claims the canyon for its own. It howls — if you are not throwing at least a 5-weight by then, you're liable to eat your cast.

Even with a heavier rod, anglers may have trouble, however, here are some suggestions: In windy conditions many flyfishers casting into the wind try to add more power by pushing the rod harder and faster. Unfortunately, this usually drives the rod tip down — which opens up the loop, wastes energy, and gives the wind more surface area on which to push back. You'll know this is what happened when some other fisher — not you, naturally — observes "M-m-m-m, tasty weight forward, maybe next time I'll eat a double taper."

Try this instead: concentrate on obtaining a tight loop with your cast and on tilting the casting angle (or arc) so that the loop opens up only inches above the water instead of feet above it. Remember that the shorter the distance a fly is in freefall, the less likely that wind can blow it off target.

Another effective method is to use a sidearm cast, as there is less wind near the surface of the water than 10 to 15 feet above it. The drawback here is that such casts are less accurate, and you'll often hook the weeds on the bank behind or beside you.

## Tackle

Medium to long leaders are the norm for dry fly fishing here, with leaders under nine feet rarely seen. Tippets are typically 6X and 7X, although 5X leaders can be used with larger flies. Longer leaders with light tippets allow better drifts in slow, clear water and keep the opaque fly line away from the trout. When the wind comes up, however, cut down the tippet to deliver more power to the end of the leader, helping to turn the fly over in the face of adversity. If presentations absolutely require a longer tippet, you can add butt section to your leader (two knots to tie) and accomplish the same result. This makes a longer leader with a proportionally shorter tippet, thus delivering more power to turn over the fly.

Dry fly fishing is most effectively practiced upstream at Hot Creek. Place as much of the line as possible in the same current as the fly for the best drifts. Casting above and slightly to the side of the fish will allow the fly to float over without lining him. Slightly overpowering casts, with the rod lowered to an angle of 45 degrees (semi-sidearm), will throw a curve in the end of your line reliably and repeatedly. Note that the farther you cast across these intricate currents, the lower your chance of success. And the weeds will further complicate matters. Sometimes, downstream drifts are the only possible way to present your fly to the fish.

As tough as some of this sounds, Hot is probably one of the best dry fly streams in the country, with plenty of hatches and willing fish.

## Nymph Fishing

Normally when nymph fishing, you want your fly to be right down on the bottom for maximum effectiveness. Hot Creek is unusual in that the water here is very shallow (often little more than knee deep), so trout tend to rise more readily than in other venues. This allows you to set your nymph about 12 inches below an indicator on most of the creek, thereby catching fish while avoiding most of the bottom weeds.

*Hot Creek's scenery is tough to beat. (Photo: K. Giampaoli)*

You will need to readjust that depth for the deepest sections of the creek, but much of Hot can be fished surprisingly close to the surface.

The "hinged-nymphing method" of fishing developed by Dean Schubert and Dave Hickson (originally published in *Fly Fisherman* Magazine) is very effective for presenting flies in this manner. To rig this system, tie a dime-size piece of polypropylene yarn (coarse and shiny) to the end of a 7-foot, 3X leader with an improved clinch knot. Then, using another improved clinch knot, tie a short piece of 6X tippet around the leader, abutting the yarn.

An important note about indicators: the most successful anglers on this creek usually don't depend on their strike indicator to signal a take, because it often won't budge in the sort of quick sequence common in slow water: fish sucks in fly — fish expels it. Instead, smart anglers take the time to spot fish first, then present the fly using the indicator primarily to judge the position of the drift — to show when the fly is in range of a feeding move. Thus the indicator is more of a presentation tool than a simple bobber. When the trout's head snaps from the side back to center or moves quickly to one side and stops — or when there's that telltale white flash of an opening mouth — strike!

Of course, presenting your fly to fish comes after the first step — finding them. Hot Creek is the perfect place to hone observational skills. Blindcasting will produce trout here but not nearly in the numbers possible with practiced sight fishing.

*A big, Hot Creek rainbow. (Photo: K. Giampaoli)*

One key to learning the latter is not to expect to see the whole fish at once: look for parts first. Realize that there are a very few vertical lines in a trout stream, especially in Hot with all the streaming weeds, so verticals are exactly what to look for, like the edge of a square tail. Find that, then slide your view along (what might be) a horizontal body; look for a fin sticking out to the side. Odds are, that if there's a shadow underneath such a fishy looking formation, you are indeed seeing "Mr. Trout."

Even without spotting a "sure thing," there are a few easy rules to help you locate fish at Hot Creek. First, anyplace you can see rocky bottom through the weeds, there's a trout lurking nearby. Then, anything that breaks up current here will create a place for a trout to hold.

The last rule concerns an exception to most other venues: in most moving waters, anglers look for the greatest delivery of current, as that also delivers the largest quantity of food. That found, they search for "soft spots" nearby where fish may hold. This pattern also works at Hot; however, there is so much food in the stream that trout occupy not only obvious lies but marginal positions that would not attract them in less fertile places. With this in mind, take care to walk softly along the edges of the creek, as many of the biggest fish can be found in 8 to 12 inches of water, often only inches from the bank.

## Trout Foods

The weed growth in Hot Creek creates perfect habitat for aquatic insects — bug hotels if you will. Blue-winged olives are here by the ton, along with several other species of mayflies, caddis, midges, snails, and lots of scuds. Trout have an abundance of naturals to choose from, never mind your imitations. And, as noted, the long stringy weeds not only produce the insects but also hide the fish and complicate presentations.

Midges hatch throughout the season, as do the blue-winged olives (*Baetis parvis*). Populations of pale morning duns (*Ephemerella infrequens* and *Ephemerella inermis*), mahogany duns (*Paraleptophlebia*) and the western slate-winged olive (*Ephemerella flavelina drunella*) come off June through August. Tricos (*Tricorythodes*) also appear in August and often generate good spinner falls early mornings into October. Caddis are a mainstay, with turtle case makers (saddle case makers — *Glossosoma*), little green rock worms (olive sedge — *Rhyacophila*) and net spinning caddis (spotted sedge — *Hydropsyche*) providing fishable hatches from June through August. The Grannom (*Brachycentrus*) and October caddis (*Dicosmoecus*) hatch in the fall. Most of these insects with the exception of the October caddis, are small, ranging from 16 down to size 22.

Aquatic water beetles also make their home in the weeds, along with scuds. The latter are a real favorite. Normally found deep inside the bright green weedbeds, Hot Creek's scuds are so prolific that you will often find them when you're picking up rocks to check "The Daily Special."

One of more entertaining sights you will see here is a flyfisher casting to what he thinks are rises, when what's actually breaking the surface are trout's tails, thrust up as fish root out scuds with snouts buried in the weeds.

This is somewhat less entertaining when you realize you're doing it yourself.

## Line Control Techniques

Along with all its other challenges, Hot Creek is also a great place to sharpen line control skills. There's a wide variety of water "types" in this little creek, and you need every trick to successfully fish them. It's a complicated place: although you can generally cast across the creek, doing so will catch very few fish — there's too many convoluted currents to lay a drift 45 feet away. So save the long hauls and consider Hot a microcosmic laboratory in which to practice and perfect techniques.

Using aerial mends will increase success in any moving water, and Hot Creek is no exception. The key to this feat is to recognize that once the loop is formed by stopping the rod, you can literally paint the mends you want with the tip of the rod. As long as you don't overpower your cast by moving the rod too abruptly, the line will fall on the water behind the fly in any design you execute (after the stop). Yes, it is a question of practice.

A last Hot Creek tip: experienced anglers here sometimes defeat intricate currents by using the very floating weeds that make life so hard. To do this, they lay the mid-section of line on top of the beds, allowing only the front few feet and the leader to drift into the target area. Of course, sometimes the line hangs up on the weeds when you don't want it to. That is called "fishing."

### Etiquette

As elsewhere, etiquette on Hot Creek is not set in stone but fluid to a point. Fishing territories shrink when more anglers arrive, but it is never OK to fish the water another angler is covering: if the first fisher is casting to areas 30 feet above and below where he is standing, he is entitled to do so unimpeded. And never fish closer than a cast's length above or below another angler. If both your lines are covering the same water, you are too close.

The above may sound rather obvious to most flyfishers, but with the abundance of trout on Hot Creek, people become so involved with their own space they become oblivious to others.

When walking to another spot on the creek, be sure to step well back from the water. As noted, many fish hold close to the bank and are often easily spooked. Also, please don't be a Hole Hog! One of the creeks' regulars stakes out a tree on the upper section and will fish only that section for as long as he's there. He often casts clear across to the far side of the creek, evidently intent on impressing anglers with his ability. Since most anglers know that a decent drift is impossible at that distance, they may marvel at how safe the trout are.

### Wading

Wading is permitted on Hot Creek, although some self-styled streamkeepers will insist otherwise. They do have a valid concern: in any stream, creek, or river in which you wade, you do destroy insects and damage their habitat. This is especially true in spring creeks, with their proliferation of rooted vegetation; so step lightly and as seldom as possible.

That said, the fact is that with such complex currents, wading is often necessary to effectively present your fly. When this is the case, wade into position as needed, then wade back out instead of continuing through the stream. Use the trail to move to the next spot, not the creek "highway." And take great care when moving around weeds, as they are easily uprooted and washed downstream; step over and around, not through it. By planning your route carefully, you can have minimum impact on the stream without risking life and limb.

With forethought and proper attention, it is possible to fish Hot Creek while looking out for its safety and protection, allowing the stream to support large numbers of both trout and anglers. That combination has rarely worked as well elsewhere as it does here.

Perhaps that only makes ironical an observation about this unusual, perhaps unique fishing venue: Hot Creek winds through an arid landscape, a sparkling ribbon full of life, coursing a gorge to join the Owens River for a long journey south. And ultimately, one of the country's most exciting streams — water that is an elixir for nurturing trout — pours out of faucets in downtown L.A.

# Stream Facts: Hot Creek

## Location
- Hot Creek is located near the middle of the state on the eastern side of the Sierra, above Bishop, just outside the town of Mammoth Lakes.
- From the Bay Area or Sacramento, travelers may come via Highway 50 or Interstate 80 or when Tioga Pass is open, then drive south on Highway 395 past the junction of highways 395 and 203 (Mammoth Lakes turnoff). Just before the Mammoth Lakes Airport, turn east into the southern entrance of the Owens River Road. (Don't confuse this with the northern entrance to Owens River Road, which is located north of the junction of 395 and 203. You want the south one, beyond the airport.)
- When traveling from points south, take the same turn, which will come up 30 to 35 miles north of Bishop, just before you reach the junction of 395 and 203. (Watch for the airport on your right.)
- From the southern entrance of Owens River Road, continue driving toward the fish hatchery. Turn right just before the entrance, proceeding past the driveway to Hot Creek Ranch. After this point, the road bends left and is no longer paved.
- Follow the gravel up the hill as it turns right and passes through the gate to the Hot Creek area. This gate opens at sunrise and closes at sunset. The road is paved again for a very short section here, and the parking lot to the "Fisherman's Trail" is immediately to the left. This trail provides access to the upper section of the public water.
- If you continue past the first parking lot, you will see other dirt roads, which also begin trails down to the middle section of Hot Creek.
- The last lot, paved, is the main parking area for the Hot Springs bathers. It has restrooms. A paved trail from here heads down into the canyon. A historical marker overlooking the edge of the canyon describes the process by which this caldera was formed. Note: this section is the most geologically active area of Hot Creek, with a number of sections fenced off. For good reason—those who jump them may be parboiled.

## Seasons
- Hot Creek is open to fishing from the last Saturday in April through October 31.

## Special Regulations
- Artificial flies only with single, barbless hooks, catch and release, zero kill limit.

## River Characteristics
- Hot is a short, alpine spring creek usually narrow enough to cast across, with the highest density of trout per mile of any stream in the United States and the highest density of fisherman in California. The largest section of public access water runs through a small gorge. Expect wind in the afternoon.

## Trout
- According to the Department of Fish and Game, catch rate averages right around one fish per hour, but a flyfisher skilled in sight fishing can catch 20 to 30 per day. Average sizes run 10 to 14 inches, with both 8- and 16-inchers turning up regularly. Fish 18 inches and over are rarely caught here: they exist, but the skill level demanded to entice and land them is high. Many of the biggest keep their heads firmly planted in the weeds, rustling up scuds.

## River Miles
- About six miles altogether, three of which are open to the public.

## Hub City
- Mammoth Lakes

## Favorite Flies
- **Dry Flies**
  #18 Olive Hot Creek Caddis
  #16 Quick Sight Ant
  #10 Dan's Hopper (late summer)
  #16 Quick Sight Beetle
  #18 Blue Winged Olive Parachute
  #16 & #18 Parachute Adams
  #16 & #18 CDC Caddis
  #16 Olive Cripple
  #16 Tan Cripple
  #20 Sparkle Wing Trico Spinner
  #18 Rusty Spinner
  #16 Sulfur Spring Creek Dun

  **Streamers (when all else fails):**
  #12 Olive Leech
  #10 Olive Woolly Bugger

**Nymphs**
#16 & #18 Pheasant Tail
#16 Olive Sparkle Pupa
#12 Ginger Sparkle Pupa
#18, #20, & #22 Brassie, preferably tied
  with a muskrat fur thorax
#20 Black Midge Pupa
#16 & #18 Peacock Bead-Head Caddis
#12 Hare's Ear Bead Head Caddis
#16 & #18 Partridge & Green Soft Hackle
#14 Partridge & Orange Soft Hackle
#12 & #16 Flashback Scud

# HOT CREEK MAJOR HATCHES

| Insect | A | M | J | J | A | S | O | N | Time | Flies |
|---|---|---|---|---|---|---|---|---|---|---|
| Blue Winged Olive<br>*Baetis parvis* | █ | █ | █ | █ | | | █ | | O | Nymph: #18 Pheasant Tail<br>Dry: #18 BWO Parachute, #16 Olive Cripple |
| Pale Morning Dun<br>*Ephemerella infrequens / inermis* | | | █ | █ | █ | | | | M | Nymph: #16 Pheasant Tail<br>Dry: #16 Sulfur Spring Creek Dun, #16 Tan Cripple |
| Mahogany Dun<br>*Paraleptophlebia* | | | | | █ | █ | | | A / E | Nymph: #16 Pheasant Tail<br>Dry: #16 Parachute Adams, #16 Tan Cripple, #18 Rusty Spinner |
| Western Slate Winged Olive<br>*Ephemerella flavelina drunella* | | | █ | █ | █ | | | | O | Nymph: #16–18 Pheasant Tail<br>Dry: #16–18 BWO Parachute<br>#16 Olive Cripple |
| Tricos<br>*Tricorythodes* | | | | | █ | █ | █ | | M (~65°) | #20 Sparkle Wing Trico Spinner |
| Turtle Shell or Saddle<br>Case Makers<br>*Glossosoma* | | | █ | █ | █ | | | | | Nymph: #18 Peacock Bead Head Caddis,<br>#18 Partridge & Green Soft Hackle<br>Dry: #18 Hot Creek Caddis, #18 CDC Caddis,<br>#16 Olive Cripple |
| Little Green Rock Worm<br>*Rhyacophila* | | | █ | █ | █ | | | | | Nymph: #18 Peacock Bead Head Caddis,<br>#18 Partridge & Green Soft Hackle<br>Dry: #18 Hot Creek Caddis, #18 CDC Caddis,<br>#16 Olive Cripple |

HATCH TIME CODE: M = morning; A = afternoon; E = evening; O = overcast and low light conditions

## HOT CREEK MAJOR HATCHES (continued)

| Insect | A | M | J | J | A | S | O | N | Time | Flies |
|---|---|---|---|---|---|---|---|---|---|---|
| Net Spinning Caddis / Spotted Sedge *Hydropsyche* | | | ▓ | ▓ | | | | | | Nymph: #16 Peacock Bead Head Caddis, #16 Partridge & Green Soft Hackle<br>Dry: #16 Hot Creek Caddis, #16 CDC Caddis, #16 Olive Cripple |
| Grannom *Brachycentrus* | | | | | | ▓ | ▓ | | | Nymph: #18 Peacock Bead Head Caddis, #18 CDC Caddis, #16 Olive Cripple<br>Dry: #18 Peacock Bead Head Caddis, #18 Partridge & Green Soft Hackle |
| October Caddis *Dicosmoecus* | | | | | | | ▓ | | | Nymph: #14 Partridge & Orange Soft Hackle, #12 Ginger Sparkle Pupa, #12 Hare's Bead Head Caddis<br>Dry: Often not important before close of season |
| Midges *Chironomidae* | ▓ | ▓ | ▓ | ▓ | ▓ | ▓ | ▓ | ▓ | | Nymph: #20 Black Midge; #18, 20 & 22 Brassie<br>Dry: #18 Parachute Adams; #18, 20 & 22 Brassie (floated in the film) |
| Scuds (Scud life cycle is entirely aquatic but they are important throughout the season) | ▓ | ▓ | ▓ | ▓ | ▓ | ▓ | ▓ | ▓ | | #12 and #16 Flashback Scud |

# Mammoth Lakes

## Elevation – 7,800 ft. • Population – 4,785

Mammoth Lakes is a 15-minute drive from the upper end of Hot Creek. A popular ski resort as well as a pretty and busy mountain town, it has a variety of flyfishing shops and an abundance of hotels, motels, lodges, and condominiums for rent. The fishing season is off-peak, so prices are reasonable. You can spend anywhere from $20 to $200+ a night, or rent a condo for the week. Information is available on the Mammoth Lakes web page at http://www.visitmammoth.com.

### ACCOMMODATIONS

**Econo Lodge Wildwood Inn**, .25 mile west of Old Mammoth Rd. on Main St., Mammoth Lakes, CA 93546 / 800-845-8764 / Continental breakfast, coffee in room; some rooms with refrigerators; some with views; pets accepted; offers ski plans; ask about lower summer rates / $–$$

**Quality Inn**, 3537 Main St., Mammoth Lakes, CA 93546 / 800-874-4949 / Complimentary continental breakfast; coffee in room; free cribs; business services available / $$

**Shilo Inn**, 2963 Main St., Mammoth Lakes, CA 93546 / 619 934-4500 / Free airport transportation; coffee and complimentary breakfast; meeting room and business services; whirlpool, sauna, and weight room; indoor pool; pets accepted with some restrictions / $$$

**1849 Rentals**, 70 Condos located at Warming Hut II, Mammoth Lakes, CA 93546 / 619-934-7525; 800-421-1849; Fax 619-934-6501 / Courtesy van; walk to ski lifts; midweek specials; recreation area; spas, sauna, pool, tennis; fireplaces; VCRs; laundry room; lower summer rates / $$–$$$

### CAMPING

There are many public camping areas close to Hot Creek and the Mammoth Lakes/June Lake Loop area. The closest to Hot Creek is at **Convict Lake** — take Hot Creek Road (from the lower end of the creek) to 395 for 1.5 miles, and cross the highway to Convict Lake Road. Follow signs to the lake and campground. Another campground is at **Lake Mary**: Exit Highway 395 at Highway 203. There is a private campground just outside Mammoth Lakes: Mammoth Mountain, 619-934-3822.

### RESTAURANTS

You want Italian? French? Mexican? Seafood? Steaks? Sushi? Burgers? McDonalds? Burger King? Pizza? Sports bar that specializes in selling special drinks in test tubes? Dancing to live music at Whiskey Creek? The most expensive supermarket (Von's) in the state of California?? Mammoth Lakes has it all. Here are a few:

**Aspen Grill,** 202 Old Mammoth Road, Mammoth Lakes, CA 93546 / 760-934-2537 / formerly known as The Rafters / Monday night Football Fever at 5:30PNT includes touchdown shooters, low cost drinks, and comp buffet; a $10 "drafter's" card gets unlimited $1 draughts and other club benefits; Happy Hour runs 5:307:301'N1 weekdays, featuring $1 Margaritas and food and rink specials / $$$

**Giovanni's Restaurant & Lounge,** located in Vons Center at Old Mammoth Road and Meridian, Mammoth Lakes, CA 93546 / 760-934-7563 or 934-3463 / Voted Mammoth's best pizza in the Mammoth Times readers' poll / Small, 2-topping pizza with soup or salad lunch special for only $4.65 Monday-Saturday from 11:30AM-4F'M; Large-screen TV; happy hour is Sunday-Thursday from 4:306: 301pM, Friday from 4:30-6:00 'u; 12 beers on tap; hot pizza slices I $-$$

**Grumpy's Saloon and Eatery,** 37 Old Mammoth Road, Mammoth Lakes, CA 93546 / 760-934-8587 / Popular, smoke-free family restaurant / Several large-screen TVs for sports fanatics; pool, shuffleboard, and pinball / Drink specials and test tube shots / $$-$$$

**Goats Bar,** located in the Red Rooster Mall on Main Street, Mammoth Lakes, CA 93546 / 760-934-4629 / Popular watering hole and game mecca; large screen TVs; features a wide selection of blues on CD; pool table, darts, and great food; happy hour is 1 LAM-71'M daily / $$-$$$

**La Sierra's Cantina,** Main Street, Mammoth Lakes, CA 93546 / 760-934-8083 / Mexican food / $$-$$$

**Mammoth Stonehouse Brewery & Restaurant,** 361 Old Mammoth Road (next to Alpenrose), Mammoth Lakes, CA 93546 / 760-934-6196 / Smoke-free serves delicious meals, including steaks, chicken, and vegetarian dishes; microbrew selections; $9.95 winter dinner special Monday-Wednesday; full cocktail bar with pool tables and live music / $$-$$$

**Ocean Harvest, Old Mammoth Road, Mammoth Lakes,** CA 93546 / 760-934-3970 / Try CheapsEats, great food at a great price, starting at 6eM on Sunday, Tuesday, Friday, and Saturday, with drink specials and food for $5.95 or less / $$-$$$

**Shogun Japanese Restaurant,** Sierra Center Mall (upstairs) on Old Mammoth Road / 760-934-3970 / Traditional sushi bar (excellent); bar and cocktail lounge / $$-$$$

**Slocums Italian Grill & Bar,** 3221 Main Street, Mammoth Lakes, CA 93546 / 760-934-7647 / Tasty burgers, great sandwiches, and delicious salads / Happy hour 4-61'NT / Dining room opens at 5:301'M / $$-$$$

**Stonehouse Brewery,** Old Mammoth Road next to Alpenrose, Mammoth Lakes, CA 93546 / 760-934-6196 / Smokefree and serves delicious steaks, chicken, and vegetarian dishes, as well as excellent microbrew selections / $$-$$$

**Whiskey Creek,** Corner of Main Street and Minaret Road, Mammoth Lakes, CA 93546 / 760-934-2555 / Smokefree; happy hour weekdays from 3-6PM, with $1 microbrewed drafts from Mammoth Brewing Co.

## SPORTING GOODS AND FLY SHOPS
**Kittredge Sports,** 3218 Main St., Mammoth Lakes, CA 93546 / 619-934-7566

**High Sierra Products,** 123 Commercial Dr. / 760-924-3723
**The Troutfitter,** Shell Mart Center #3, Mammoth Lakes, CA 93546 / 619-924-3676

## AIRPORT

**Mammoth Lakes Airport,** Mammoth Lakes, CA 93546 / 619-934-3813 / Commercial flights from Long Beach airport via Mountain Air Express (800-788-4247) services the Mammoth Lakes Airport once a day, Thursday through Sunday, and charters are available. Equipment is a Merlin Turboprop. The airport is also available to general aviation for private planes. It's located about 15 minutes out of town on Owen's River Road on the way to Hot Creek. (Note: Some lodgings will transport — see accommodations.)

## HOSPITALS

**Mammoth Hospital,** PO 660 Mammoth Lakes, CA 93546 / 619-934-3311

## AUTOMOTIVE REPAIRS

Available in Mammoth Lakes.

## AUTO RENTALS

**U-Save Car Rental,** located at airport / 800-207-2681
**Mammoth Shuttle,** taxi service / 619-934-3030

## FOR MORE INFORMATION

Mammoth Lakes Chamber of Commerce
Box 123
Mammoth Lakes, CA
619-934-2712

Mammoth Lakes Visitor Center
Highway 203 (Forest Service Building)
800-367-6572

## OTHER ATTRACTIONS IN AREAS

Dedicated hot springers can find a variety of sinks in which to indulge themselves in this area. For information about these, call the Mammoth Visitor Center Ranger Station, 619-924-1094. This is also the place to inquire about camping, 619-924-5500.

The Devil's Postpile, a local geological wonder, is located "just over the hill" from Mammoth, near the Middle Fork of the San Joaquin River (which also has some good and technically less difficult fishing). Ask at the visitor center listed above.

# Private Waters

There have long been private fishery operations in California, but the last few years have seen a boom in their development, especially in those that are open to the paying public. The reasons for this surge are varied — and some worrisome — but there is clearly a market for alternatives to often overcrowded destinations.

Some of the private fisheries described below are on streams or creeks, others are stillwaters; some have both. New operations emerge monthly, however, and the absence of any resort should not be interpreted as a deliberate exclusion. Likewise, the intent was neither to promote, nor to damn with faint praise, but to give anglers a sense of what to expect, which varies by site, season, weather, an angler's skills and attitude. It would pay prospective guests to ask specific questions.

The editor gamely offered to visit those sites he had not seen — this did not happen — and in every case sought reports from reliable people who had. Owners or managers were also invited to describe their operations (in a case or two, the "greatest," "biggest," and "best" superlatives were edited out).

Along those lines: nobody paid to get in this book, and it is not an "advertising vehicle."

## ALPERS RANCH
### North of Mammoth Lakes, off Highway 395

The Alpers Ranch is a quiet and uncrowded resort located on the crystalline headwaters of Owens River, just below Big Springs (and just above the Arcularius Ranch), with views across rolling hills into Long Valley and the White Mountains. It consists of three distinct venues: the meandering creek, small but with deep pools and undercut banks hiding large wild rainbows; a canal with stocked fish; and a stocked pond managed as a separate fishery. The accommodations have been described as "rustic and reasonable" — nine modest cabins, some older than others, all clean, with ample hot water. Guests return to fish here year after year, so call well in advance to make reservations.

Stealth is required on the river. The larger fish tend to stay in pools at the bends; these can be quite deep — to 10 feet or more. Though the insect life may be somewhat sparser than on the lower Owens, there are good populations of caddis, assorted mayflies, and golden stones. The ranch's cattle are fenced away from the banks.

**Alpers Ranch** (call for current rates)
760-648-7334

## CLEAR CREEK
**Off 299, above French Gulch**

The Clear Creek operation is part of the Kutras Ranch, a vast spread along a canyon in the Trinity Alps, eight miles above the town of French Gulch. The Kutras family has maintained this property thoughtfully enough to earn the Forest Service Stewardship Award from the state of California.

The creek deserves such care: longest in California, a freestoner fed by tributaries and springs, it's also one of the richest in insect life, with abundant mayfly, caddis, midge, and stonefly populations — including *Pteranarcys californica*, the salmonfly giant — as well as sculpin up to four inches long (and turtles and frogs). All these are fodder for a mix of large stocked and small to midsize wild rainbows, along with the rare brown or two. The stocked fish average 14 to 18 inches, though some of the holdovers now run to 24 or 26. Wild fish sometimes will top a foot and tend to hold in the faster water.

The big fish take the pools, some of which are 100 yards long here, shadowed by the oak forest common to 1,800-foot elevations, and by islands of elephant ears. Casting is challenging — a fisher who approaches with stealth will be far, far more often rewarded.

The ranch has three beats, each with roughly two miles of stream. The upper and lower have four-bed (two bunks) cabins built on decks above small pools where the wisest fish rise during dinnertime barbecues. There are also propane stoves, cooking utensils, gas generators, running water for washing, bottled for drinking, and separate shower and flush toilet facilities. Middle beat guests stay in a modified A-frame with a loft, carpeting, and more amenities, including a microwave and TV. On any of the three sections of stream, odds are that visitors will see no one, save perhaps a member of the Kutras family, a ranch hand, or a caretaker stopping by to make sure all's well.

**Rates:**
$200 per angler per day, three beats (two anglers per beat)
$310 to reserve a beat and cabin (two fishermen, minimum two-night stay)
$25 per day non-angler fee

**Season:** May 1 to November 15

**Kutras Ranch**
Contact: Duane Milleman
The Fly Shop
Redding, CA
1-800-669-3474; www.theflyshop.com

## HENDERSON SPRINGS
**Three Miles from Big Bend (northeast of Redding)**

Henderson Springs is a lodge on 500 wooded acres, just off the Pit River. It has four lakes ranging in size from five to 20 acres and a half-mile of spring creek, all

*A dandy Clear Creek 'bow. (Photo: Seth Norman)*

surrounded by forests of pine, fir, spruce, and oak. The ponds vary in appearance: Frog is a wild-looking water, with downed trees and shallows; Clear is a deep basin with giant blood midges; Big Lake has stands of flooded timber on one side, flats on another, as well as channels and mossy islands. Expect callibaetis, midges, scuds, damsels, and dragons. Float tubes or pontoon craft are a must on these stillwaters — no prams or small boats.

The fish are a mix of several stockings, rainbows and browns, some brookies in the larger lake, maybe some wild travelers up from the river. The average is 17 to 20 inches, and there are bigger browns to 24.

The main lodge is a large, seven-bedroom, four-bath house, with a 25-foot vaulted ceiling in the main room and a deck overlooking a creek (now fishing for a mix of rainbows and brookies). The housekeeping cabin nearby is spacious and light, with unusual woodwork. The downstairs bedroom has a double bed, and there are four single beds in an upstairs loft. Kitchen amenities and a barbecue are supplied.

**Rates (per day):**
$240 per person for lodging and meals
$160 per person for lodging in guest cabin with kitchen facilities
$140 per person for flyfishing only
$125 per person for non-anglers with lodging and meals provided

**Season:** September 15 to day before Thanksgiving; February 1 to June 1

**Henderson Springs**
P.O. Box 220
Big Bend, CA 96011-0220
1-888-337-0788 or 530-337-6917; www.hendersonsprings.com

## RIVERSIDE ON FALL RIVER
### On the Fall River just downstream of Island Bridge

This property has nearly a mile of private access to the famous Fall River. There is a four-bedroom house with a well-equipped kitchen, and there are three boats available for guest use. (See Fall River chapter for more information on this fishery.)

**Rates:** $495 per night with a maximum of four couples or six individuals

**Season:** Last weekend in April to November 15

**Riverside on Fall River**
Contact: Duane Milleman
The Fly Shop
Redding, CA
1-800-669-3474; www.theflyshop.com

## EAST PEAK LAKE
### Near South Lake Tahoe at Heavenly Ski Resort

East Peak Lake is somebody's good idea. Its location at the base of a Heavenly Ski Resort run suggests its primary purpose — storage for snowmaking operations. Fed by springs (and, presumably, runoff from the slopes), it is surrounded by conifers and granite, with flooded timber along parts of two sides. The manager of the hatchery that produces the fish insists they are derived from the last pure strain of Mt. Whitney trout. They run between 16 and 28 inches and likely spend much of their time hunting dragonfly nymphs, which in this location grow to the length of a thumb. There are some hatches during the short season — this is 8,000-plus feet — and the fish hunt below the trees for hapless terrestrials.

East Peak Lake is a day-use-only venue, managed by and booked with a system that offers season passes, day and half-day rates. The number of fishers is limited, and all day visits are guided. Float tubes are necessary and can be rented at the store, along with other tackle and gear. Transportation to the lake from South Lake Tahoe can be arranged at no additional cost. Transportation to the casinos — 10 minutes away — is something else again.

South Lake Tahoe is well situated for expeditions to the east and west branches of both Carson and Walker Rivers and scores of smaller lakes and streams.

**Rates (full day):** $250 one angler; $325 two anglers

**East Peak Lake**
Contact: Victor Babbit
Tahoe Flyfishing

*Beautiful East Peak Lake. (Photo: Seth Norman)*

3377 Lake Tahoe Blvd.
South Lake Tahoe, CA 96150
530-541-8208; www.tahoeflyfishing.com

## FIVE DOT RESERVOIR
### 17 miles north of Susanville

Located north of Susanville at 5,322 feet, Five Dot is a large reservoir (400 acres when full) situated in the transition zone between forested mountains and high desert plateau, on an active cattle ranch with 6,000 head. The impoundment supports a tremendous biomass: summer-stocked fingerlings are said to grow to two pounds in a year. The rainbow/steelhead variants are raised nearby and average five pounds with many in double digits.

Five Dot has mature weed growth. Anglers may expect damsels, leeches, scuds, water boatman, and callibaetis hatches in season. The lake can be waded or fished from float tubes, prams, and small boats (no motors). Flocks of migrating and nesting waterfowl share the water, and most days, resident bald eagles make an appearance.

**Rates:** $125 per angler

**Season:** mid-April through June; mid-September through October

**Five Dot Reservoir**

*Work Goodrich Creek's banks with a low profile. (Photo: Seth Norman)*

530-253-3164

## GOODRICH CREEK
### East of Lake Almanor, off Highway 36

Goodrich is a spring creek, here flowing through wide McKenzie Meadows, part of an active ranch. At its upper end, the stream doubles back on itself in a series of oxbows; the lower end has slightly more current and is thready in places, with undercut banks. The stocked rainbows run to 25 inches, with rare wild browns up to 27.

Goodrich's stream life is lush: mahogany duns, green or gray drakes, trico, baetis, callibaetis, hexagenia (the early summer hex hatch can be frightening), several caddis — including October — midges, leeches, and minnows. For much of the summer, trout feast on grasshoppers blown into the creek from the meadow, providing excellent dry fly action, although some fish eventually get so twitchy they even reject naturals.

Goodrich is booked as a day-use or overnight fishery.

**Rates:** $125 per angler (one to four anglers) or $100 per additional angler for overnight stay in cabins;
$150 per person (no overnight stay)

**Season:** May through October

**Goodrich Creek** (email: information@goodrichcreek.com)
Reno Fly Shop (exclusively booked through)

294 E. Moana Lane #14
Reno, NV 89502
775-825-3474; www.renoflyshop.com

## HAT CREEK RANCH
**50 miles southeast of Redding off Highway 299, near the town of Hat Creek**

Hat Creek Ranch contains a half-mile of rehabilitated (upper) Hat Creek, a pond of an acre, another of about four, and a restored farmhouse-cum-lodge with a tying desk in the downstairs foyer, a main room for meetings, and a dining table with a view across the creek to the smaller impoundment. Beyond that, pasture land runs to the mountains, but the sight of big trout snouts scooping midges often obscures the horizon and has rushed many meals.

Here, Hat Creek is much smaller than the broad reaches below Powerhouse 2 but also contains prolific insect life, with substantial hatches of green drakes and other mayflies, caddis (including October), and significant numbers of stoneflies. Parts of the banks are open enough for easy back casts, but this is mostly a stalking stream where wading is discouraged. There are also wild browns in the stream, particularly in late autumn, with the very largest arriving in mid-November.

The unobstructed banks around the ponds make them attractive to beginning casters — that, and the cruising trout. By midseason, however, the fish get wary, and presentation becomes increasingly important. The size of the stocked rainbow/steelhead variants presents problems, especially when conditions demand long, light tippets and size 20 flies. The fish average 16 to 18 inches, but holdovers may now go 10 pounds. The weed beds shelter damsels, dragonflies, midges, callibaetis, PMDs, and caddis. Float tubes are not necessary but are provided.

The ranch is operated as a day fishery, but there are many nearby lodging choices. Lassen and Burney Falls parks are close by, as are the Pit, Hat, and Fall Rivers.

**Rates:** $125 per person, per day; $75 per half day; $75 per child 16 years or younger; $75 per day
during the off season; maximum six anglers

**Season:** year-round except the creek, which is open from late April to November 15

**Hat Creek Ranch**
Contact: Duane Milleman
The Fly Shop
Redding, CA
1-800-669-3474; www.theflyshop.com

*Hat Creek Ranch offers challenging trout in small water.*

## HOT CREEK RANCH
### Just east of Mammoth Lakes, off Highway 395

Hot Creek Ranch is one of the oldest private-water venues in California. Once upon a time, fee anglers could kill 20 fish per day; but for decades this part of the spring creek has been catch-and-release, no wading, dry fly only. The latter rule allows cripples and any fly you can see on the surface.

The ranch contains 2.25 miles of Hot Creek, meandering through 250 acres in the evening shadows of the Sierra. As noted in the Hot Creek chapter, this is a phenomenally rich alkaline water. Though the ranch streamkeeper considers the Department of Fish and Game estimate of 11,000-plus fish per mile somewhat high — "more like 7,000" — there's no question that plenty of wild rainbows and browns lay up in the weeds, eating scuds, mayflies, and a variety of caddis (see Hot Creek chapter for hatches).

The accommodations include nine cabins on the creek, each with one bedroom and both a double and queen-size bed. All cooking utensils are provided, also linens, towels, etc. The porches have views and barbecues, and each cabin has a covered garage. A guide service and fly shop are located on the premises.

Reservations for Hot Creek should be made a year in advance.

**Rates:**

Monday through Thursday: $182 per night, two people, minimum two-night stay

Full week rate (Monday to Monday): $1070
Friday to Monday: $545 two people
Only three rods allowed per cabin; guide service rates are $300 for a full day or
$200 for a half day

**Season:** Last Saturday in April through November 15

**Hot Creek Ranch**
Route 1, Box 206
Mammoth Lakes, CA 93546
1-888-695-0774 or 760-924-5637; www.hotcreekranch.com

## MT. LASSEN TROUT
### 20 miles northeast of Red Bluff, off Highway 36

Mt. Lassen Trout is a low-elevation, cool-weather venue, open October through
May, with two impoundments of roughly two and five acres. Part of a large, private
hatchery operation, the mixture of fish includes giant triploids — desexed rainbows
that do not dedicate energy to developing eggs or milt, and thus, put weight on
quickly. All fish are raised to at least four pounds before they are stocked and run to
16 or more. They feed on damsels, midges, and callibaetis. Hatches in fall and early
spring are reliable enough that there is some opportunity for dry fly fishing most
days.

The area is part of the lava-strewn moonscape below Mt. Lassen, surrounded
by oak and scrub oak. Anglers can float tube, though it's usually not necessary. The
onsite resources include picnic table and sanitary facilities. Note that before fishing
the ponds, anglers must disinfect waders, boots, float tube, and fins in a mild chlo-
rine solution.

**Rates:** $200 per person per day

**Mt. Lassen Trout**
28125 Hwy. 36E
Red Bluff, CA 96080
530-597-2222; www.monstertrout.com

## OASIS SPRINGS FLYFISHING RESORT
### 28 miles east of Red Bluff off Highway 36

Oasis Springs is another private-water venue located in the low oak and lava
hills below Mount Lassen. The lodge has access to a long stretch of Battle Creek in
a section where it is mostly contained in a narrow canyon. Guests can hike up or
downstream; many choose to fish a riffle in front of the lodge for both stocked and
wild rainbows and a few browns over 20 inches.

This resort has more recreational activities for families than those venues solely
oriented to fishing, including a tennis court and pool. The latter is certainly an
advantage during midsummer; the area gets warm.

Instruction is available, as are tackle rentals and meal packages. There are also frequently promoted specials, usually involving longer stays, which reduce the per-day cost.

**Rates:**
Private stream access fee: $155
Guided stream enhancement: $172 (one or two anglers, up to four hours, lodging guests only)
Guide service: $320 (one or two anglers, eight hours)
Lodging Sunday to Thursday: $165.00 to $205 for creek-front suite
Lodging Friday, Saturday, and holidays: $180.00 to $225 for creek-front suite
Meal package: $55 (three meals)

**Oasis Springs Flyfishing Resort**
1-800-239-5454 or 530-474-1487; www.oasisflyfishing.com

## ROCK CREEK LAKE (Canyon Creek Ranch)
### 35 miles east of Red Bluff

Rock Creek Lake is the third venue located in the foothills south of Mount Lassen, but it sits at a somewhat higher elevation — about 1,800 feet, well into the conifers. The nine-acre impoundment is deep, streamfed, and wooded all around, with stocked rainbows to 27 inches and browns to 29. The latter have lived in the lake for many years, spawning in the feeder stream.

Limited casting may be done from the dam and from the shallows near the outlet, but this is primarily float-tube water. Weed banks harbor a variety of insects and forage, including damsels, mayflies, caddis, and midges. Rock Creek Lake is available for day-use or overnight stays. There is a comfortable two-bedroom cottage right on the lake, with a well-equipped kitchen.

**Rates:** Daily fishing fee is $125; two-bedroom cabin onsite (four beds) rents for $95 per night

**Season:** End of March to November 31

**Rock Creek Lake**
Contact: Duane Milleman
The Fly Shop
Redding, CA
1-800-669-3474; www.theflyshop.com

## LAKE CHRISTINE
### East of Red Bluff, near well-known Rock Creek Lake

Lake Christine is located less than an hour from Red Bluff or Redding. The lake covers approximately seven acres, with a lot of shallow water and weed beds. You'll need a float tube to cast to the browns and rainbows here, but sight fishing is the norm. The same Rock Creek that flows through Rock Creek Lake also flows through Lake Christine. Target the area where the stream channel enters the lake and around the weed beds along this current of water. Contact the booking agent for lodging recommendations in the area.

**Rates:** $100 per person per day

**Season:** Late March through November

**Lake Christine**
Contact: Duane Milleman
The Fly Shop
Redding, CA
1-800-669-3474; www.theflyshop.com

## BAILEY CREEK LODGE
### Within an hour of Red Bluff

Bailey Creek and Rock Creek rise from the same ground and tumble down the mountainside for only a few miles before crossing Twin Creeks Ranch. The riffles and pools of these freestone streams are filled with fish and covered with a canopy of streamside trees. Rainbow and brown trout run to trophies in the 20-inch range. The relatively low elevation gives the area a temperate climate, and the creek hosts prolific insect hatches and fast-growing fish. There is also a small lake on the property with some very large rainbows that can be cast to from shore.

The lodge at Bailey Creek has five bedrooms and a second-story dining room and deck that overlook the nearby creek. A pool and sauna are also available.

**Rates:** $235 per day (meals, lodging, and fishing); $125 per day for non-anglers

**Season:** Last Saturday in April to November 15

**Bailey Creek Lodge**
Contact: Duane Milleman
The Fly Shop
Redding, CA
1-800-669-3474; www.theflyshop.com

## BATTLE CREEK CANYON
### 45 minutes from Redding or Red Bluff

Five miles of private water on Battle Creek are now available to anglers on historic Battle Creek Ranch. This little freestone creek averages 20 feet across and moves through a canyon of riffles and pools full of wild rainbow trout. Fish run 10 to 14 inches, with a few running two to three pounds.

Anglers can also fish over a mile of spring-fed Baldwin Creek on the ranch. Baldwin's deep pools hold some nice rainbows. The Coleman Ditch is available here, as well, with spring creek–like qualities that provide excellent trout habitat. All fishing is catch-and-release with barbless hooks. The ranch is open for day-use fishing only, but anglers can stay in nearby Redding or Red Bluff.

**Rates:** $125 per angler, per day

**Season:** May 1 to November 15

**Battle Creek Ranch**
Contact: Duane Milleman
The Fly Shop
Redding, CA
1-800-669-3474; www.theflyshop.com

## SUGAR CREEK RANCH
### West of Weed, near Callahan, off Highway 3

Sugar Creek Ranch is located at the confluence of Sugar Creek and the Scott River, about 45 minutes west of Weed, something under an hour from Dunsmuir. There are seven ponds up to five acres in size on the 150-acre ranch, which is open to catch-and-release flyfishing for large rainbows year-round. (No California fishing license required.) Sugar Creek is near the Trinity Alps, in something of a climatic "banana belt." While wet flies work well, the summer dry fly action is excellent. Common hatches include midges, callibaetis, tricos, BWOs, PMDs, caddis, damsels and dragonflies, and little yellow stoneflies, along with a variety of terrestrials.

Anglers can stay in the two-story cedar lodge on the property or opt for a motel in the town of Etna, about eight miles from the ranch. Etna also has several restaurants. Callahan has a small store and a bar that serves sandwiches.

**Rates:**
Daily rod fee: $150 per guest
Master suite: $200 (double occupancy) or $250 (single occupancy)
Standard room: $190 (double occupancy) or $230 (single occupancy)

**Sugar Creek Ranch**
P.O. Box 1531
Callahan, CA 96014
530-467-5213; mike@sugarcreekranch

## ANTELOPE CREEK LODGE
### North on I-5, then east on Highway 97 out of Weed

Antelope Creek traverses this 328-acre ranch on the northeast side of Mt. Shasta, offering a mile and a half of fishing for midsize rainbows and browns. This is a typical meadow stream with many undercut banks, flats, pools, and tailouts. There are also two lakes on the property that have plenty of trophy-sized rainbows and browns. The larger lake can accommodate two or three float tubes.

The lodge has four bedrooms and five baths and can accommodate up to eight anglers. The ranch sits at 5,000 feet, with a mix of meadows and forests of aspens, pines, and cottonwoods.

**Rates:** $235 per angler; $125 for non-angler; $270 for single angler; minimum two-night stay

**Season:** Mid-May through October

**Antelope Creek Lodge**
Contact: Duane Milleman
The Fly Shop
Redding, CA
1-800-669-3474; www.theflyshop.com

# Tackle, Gear, Cautions, etc.

Each of the authors in this book makes recommendations for tackle specific to the river or stream they fish, techniques employed there, and their own preferred styles. In many chapters, particular rigging systems are important — leaders, indicators, methods of attachment — and described in detail. Some overall trends:

Three- and 4-weight rods are fine until the wind comes up; then an angler will be grateful for a 6-weight. A 5-weight, or sometimes a 6, is a fair to good compromise.

Rods of 8 to 9 feet are usually adequate; a 9-footer is often suggested in order to extend the reach when high-stick nymphing, to better mend casts, or more effectively control line in tangled currents.

In bigger waters with big fish, a good reel with a smooth drag and plenty of backing will "save the day." Reliability is the key. Also, a filled spool speeds a retrieve.

A floating line is standard. On most venues authors advise also carrying fullsink or sinktip lines for fishing nymphs and streamers deep. Some favor weight-forward construction, others double taper. Several like sinktips, because the floating section may be mended; but some writers feel only fullsink lines fish streamers properly.

Leader systems vary radically by author, tactic, and river. Except when high-stick nymphing, lengths tend to be 10 to 14 feet. Tippets lighter than 6X were rarely suggested, except on spring creeks and glides, partly because the heavier tip allows for quicker landing of fish, and thus, better survival when released. Proper tippet selection (and leader construction) is as important for proper casting — turning over of the fly — as for fooling and fighting fish.

While a variety of indicator systems are discussed, coarse polypropylene yarn is mentioned often. Several writers suggest the "hinge" method of rigging attributed to Dave Hickson and Dean Schubert. See Index to locate pages where instructions may be found.

Safe wading is a subject of concern — sometimes intense concern. Felt soled boots are the bare minimum; cleats help or are invaluable in the bigger freestone streams. Wading staffs are advised when current is strong, the river bottom irregular or slimy. California waters are cold, even when the ambient air temperature is oppressively hot. Neoprenes, or lightweight waders with insulation, are needed most of the time — almost always on tailwaters.

California weather is a player everywhere — unpredictable, and variable to extremes. Be prepared with the clothing you choose. Don't be caught cold and wet; and forced marches in neoprenes under a blazing sun are flat-out dangerous. Carry fluids.

## Other Necessary or Handy Items

- Polarized sunglasses (a must)
- A selection of fresh tippets and leaders
- Hat or protective headgear
- Insect repellent

- Sunscreen
- Thermometers for checking water temperature
- Devices for collecting or sampling insect specimens
- A net, if you use one.
- Spares of anything fragile which, if broken ends a trip.
- Likewise, spares for anything critical which might be lost.

## Various Cautions

Poison oak is present in many places — learn to identify it. Waders offer protection in the areas they are worn but be careful to rinse them off.

Keep alert for the relatively rare rattlesnake as well as the occasional bull (bees kill more people due to anaphylactic shock than any other animal in the United States, followed by range cattle.)

# Trout of These Waters

## by Seth Norman

*"Anglers of the Western World, you, as the lamented Power would have said, 'Are born to good luck.' Your lot is cast in a land of many waters and many fishes."*

"The Fish and Fishing of the United States," anonymous, 1885

One can argue that California once had a lion's share of North America's native trout species, from the various goldens and cutthroats of the Sierra to the McCloud's Dolly Varden and a host of vigorous and distinct strains of rainbow. One can argue that we still do. Since the 1800s, however we have proceeded to blithely transplant, overharvest, isolate from habitat, and occasionally exterminate the original races even while importing others to compete and commingle. What's left today is a mixed blessing of mongrelized locals and successful immigrants.

Fish from those two categories comprise the vast majority of trout available in the venues described in this book, and in the state as a whole. Only in a few remote waters, with names not to be mentioned, may populations still be found in which the helix of Little Kern Goldens and Paiute cutthroats isn't "bent" by hybridization. Almost everywhere else, the native trout have exercised options we made available; when it comes to breeding, cutthroats, goldens, and rainbows, including steelhead, lack discrimination. At least they do in the sort of artificial circumstances presented when settlers, miners, sheepherders, and sports folks carry fish from one drainage to another, or when politicians pass out piscine versions of pork barrel payoffs (which keeps some hatcheries open and explains how carp came to and conquered this country). Part of the reason biologists are so urgent about protecting the few pure-strain remnants is that every major river system has long since been corrupted.

Or worse. As noted in the Truckee River chapter, Lahontan cutthroat that spawned in that river, once caught to 41 pounds in Pyramid Lake, are extinct, likely due to the dual impact of dams and hyperaggressive commercial netting. Likewise, it's probably all over for McCloud River Dolly Varden. Our only homegrown char was cut off by dams, then put head to head with Old World brown trout that fill the same niche in a stream. As for steelhead and salmon stocks…disasters.

On the other side, of course, flyfishers have reason to hail the newcomers, and pay respect to those that endured, however altered.

### Salmo trutta (brown trout)

Brown trout are wild here but not native to the continent, much less this country. Their home waters range from Europe to parts of Asia and the Atlas Mountains of North Africa. In many places they run to the ocean — the "sea-trout" of England are also the fish called "salters" by Down Easters — in other systems they don't . At times scientists have split browns into more than 30 "species," including touts

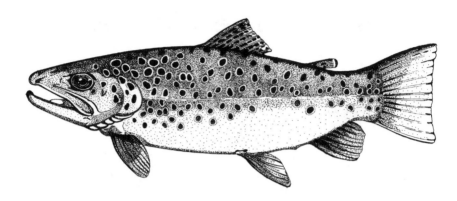

*Salmo trutta (brown trout)*

"Dalmatian," "Hungarian," "Caspian," "Fordridge," and "Galway"; see also "gilla-roo," "sewin," "phinnock," "whitling," and "truff." In the Systema Naturae, however, Linnaeus reduced this abundance to three, classified by the environs where they lived: small brooks, large rivers, the ocean.

In California we usually distinguish two types that might be the same: German browns, imported from that country and found frequently; and Loch Leven, some-what rarer, of Scotch origin. The latter are often believed to be anadromous fish in rivers like the Trinity, where they are conspicuously silvery and pale with few spots — coloration typical of browns coming up from estuaries and the ocean. (Note that on the Trinity and elsewhere the idea that our browns might be seaworthy is a hot-button issue. If they are anadromous, current law requires that they receive more protection than now offered.)

What's true of all browns is that they have Vormerine teeth, sharp ones raised on the roof of the mouth. What's almost always true is that they have yellow fins and red (or orange) and black spots with light halos, mostly above the lateral line and absent on tail, pectoral and ventral fins. Males get a hooked-jawed "kype" in the fall when they look wolfish.

In habits, browns, especially the large fish, tend to be more nocturnal than other trout, though they may be caught all day, even on dries (see North Fork of the Yuba). Browns often lay deep, in slower water, and are tolerant of warmer temperatures. When the two species share a venue, browns are caught less often than rainbows, so seem "warier," though at least one writer insists they simply aren't as quick. Lunkers are aggressive piscivores. By reputation, they also have a taste for the meat of birds and small mammals. Some Midwestern bait fishers angle them with whole or chunked moles, voles, and ground squirrels (sold in shops everywhere?) It's reported that a notorious "brown-killer" of the eastern Sierra was arrested while fishing them with live mice.

Aliens though they may be, brown trout are the favorite of many California fishers. If whirling disease, now reducing some rainbow populations in Montana and Colorado, strikes as hard here, they might soon become the favorites of many more.

The state record is 28 pounds plus. Fish of that size are often lake dwellers that may enter moving water to spawn. Of the rivers described in this book, browns are present in the following: North Fork of the Yuba, McCloud, Upper Sac (less than one percent since the spill, always toward the lower end above Lake Shasta), Fall, Truckee, Trinity, East Carson, both Walkers, Lower Owens, Feather, Hot and Hat Creek (less than five percent).

### Salvelinus fontinalis (brook trout)

Another immigrant doing rather well in California is the Eastern brook trout. A char, brookies can also run to the ocean, and do so in the Atlantic, where they are called "oceanies" around Hudson Bay. As with browns, "speck" sea-runs become silvery.

In California these fish have found a niche at higher elevations, where their ability to spawn in the gravel of alpine lakes has often made them the only viable player. Unhappily, unmolested brook trout rapidly overpopulate and often endure stunted growth rates. Their fecundity also does damage in moving water; they will often push out native cutthroats and goldens, though rainbows generally hold their own.

Brook trout are considered among the most beautiful fish, with short, light wavy lines on dark backs, white-edged fins, and spots of yellow and red. Their tails have no fork, thus the AKA "square tail." Males ready for the fall spawn have brilliant, tangerine-colored bellies edged by black. That dramatic dress is frequently seen on mounted fish, partly because hormone-charged brookies are so vulnerable that the clumsiest angler can often kill the best specimens in a stream.

Brook trout grow quite large, to nearly 15 pounds (less than ten in California), but fish over a pound are rare in the rivers covered by this book. Of these venues

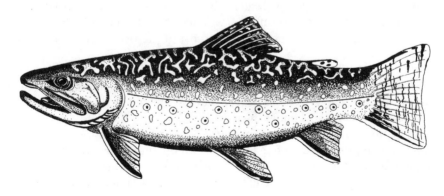

*Salvinelus fontinalis (brook trout)*

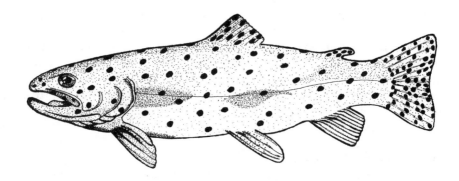

*Lahontan cutthroat*

they are significantly present in the following: Truckee (upper end), East Fork of the Walker, high up on the North Fork of the Yuba and Hat Creek well above where it is described here (high on the flanks of Mt. Lassen).

### Salmo clarki, Oncorhynchus clarki henshawi, Oncorhynchus clarki seleniris (cutthroat)

Cutthroats are mentioned several times in this book, always in reference to conservation issues. Cutt-looking rainbows do come out of the Lower Sacramento, though no one seems to know why. Lahontans, exterminated in the Truckee, are being reintroduced, and there may be some cutts left or newly planted in the west fork of the Walker. California Fish and Game releases cutthroat spawners into the middle section of the East Carson, and tiny specimens of the endangered Paiute strain hang on in the high altitude headwaters of that river, closed to fishing.

In other words, few anglers will catch any. Human avarice, along with the historical inclination to introduce the rainbows, with which cutts will breed, has just about finished these natives as common game in most of the rivers which once held an abundance.

Cutthroats vary considerably in coloration. Generally, they have greenish gold sides. Except for the Paiute strain, they are darkly spotted, though never with red like a brown trout. The characteristic feature, of course, is that for which they are named — a V of orange slash marks under the jaw.

As to habits and temperament, one source believes them "shy," suggesting small dry flies and nymphs fished on fine leaders. Far more often, however, cutts are considered the fools of the trout tribe likely to be hooked over and over, often on gaudy woolly worms tied to 3X tippet. Their fight has been described as dogged or just doggy, though anglers who catch them out of estuaries, from Puget Sound down into northern California, insist that the saltwater makes them fierce.

### Salvelinus malma (Dolly Varden)

Dolly Varden may still exist in the McCloud, but are not even described in California Fish and Game's *Sport Fishing Regulations*. Also a char, also anadromous or at least habitues of estuaries, Dollys have in some quarters the worst reputation of any trout. They are said to "infest" streams and are "ugly, snaky, and rapacious." Growing to upwards of 40 pounds, though not in this state, they are even resented for "smashing" the tackle of anglers fishing for better trout breeds. In other places they are admired for exactly this quality.

Depending on where found, Dolly Vardens may have greenish backs, and sides colored from dark yellow to red. They sport a few red spots, many more in yellow. Sometimes they resemble their cousins, the brookie, but Dolly's backs do not have the wavy light marks, and their tails are somewhat forked.

For most of the time, human beings coexisted with these McCloud fish, they were classified as Dolly Varden, an isolated batch at the extreme southern end of their range. Recent examination of museum specimens suggest they might be instead *Salvelinus confluentus*, the bull trout, which some people still insist is the same as a Dolly Varden. One text asserts that the Dolly is actually an Arctic char, *Salvelinus aplinus*, another that anadromous Dollys are simply confused with these.

For our purpose the fish anglers will not catch on the McCloud because it is probably extinct was a Dolly Varden, unless it is a bull trout, (if they aren't the same), either or both of which could be Arctic char, or at least mistaken for these when found in the sea.

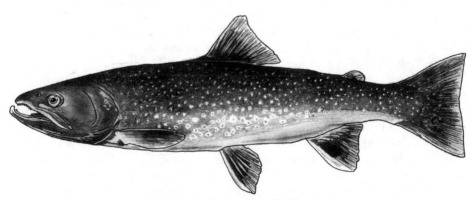

*Salvelinus Malma (Dolly Varden)*

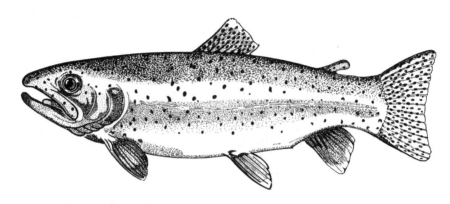

*Salmo gairdneri (rainbow trout)*

### *Salmo gairdneri (rainbow trout)*

Rainbow trout and steelhead dominate the attention and imagination of western flyfishers. Since this book focuses on trout, drawing a distinction between them seems obligatory.

Every single species of trout and char described above (brown, brookie, cutthroat, and Dolly Varden) has some strain that runs to the ocean. Perhaps goldens (not found in any river discussed here), Apache, and lake trout never do, but that still leaves a majority technically "anadromous" in one form or another. It is therefore interesting that hardly anyone argues that sea-going versions should be considered quite as separate from the fresh water sort as steelhead and rainbow trout are often said to be.

California Fish and Game designates any rainbow over 22 inches long, found in a river connected to the ocean, a steelhead. While this may be good policy, size is no reliable distinction: Idaho's Lake Pend Orielle produces rainbows over 30 pounds and a certain landlocked system in Oregon kicked out a fish of 42 (a rainbow, unless descended from some ancient steelhead sealed off from the Pacific Ocean eons ago). Shape and coloration are also poor indicators, unless the steelhead is recently in from the sea; otherwise, it's a job for astrologers.

Clearly, more than anything else, habit distinguishes one creature from the other and the significance of this is enormous. That two fish so similar live such different lives suggests the working of a code more subtle than we know, instinct embedded in the order of proteins in a long enzyme chain. The main import of recognition is this: steelhead runs along the West Coast are so damaged that the fish may soon be listed as endangered, with all the protections and prohibitions that status confers. With that possibility hanging in the balance, it would serve some interests too well if an "all those fish are alike" assessment allowed further depredation of stocks and degradation of habitat.

In the meantime, rainbows appear in every one of these rivers. Miscegenation from decades of stocking has almost certainly eliminated the chance of catching any pure strain. In Latin, they are all *Oncorhynchus* (formerly *Salmo*). Many had ancestors in the system where now found. Add in genes from stockings that stewed together fish from the McCloud, Mount Whitney, Eagle Lake, and elsewhere. (Note: current and ongoing research now indicates that on the Upper Sacramento the wild rainbows found above Simms Flat are remarkably pure; below that, they have mixed somewhat with stocked fish.)

This much these rainbows (usually) have in common: green backs, sometimes bluish, with dark spots that are present even along the top of the head. The interior of the mouth is white and the adipose fin has a black edge. Side coloration runs from pale silver to light green, with a red or pink band that may be faint or, during spawning, deeply colored. Young fish have parr marks, a series of oval "bars" along the lateral line.

Rainbows have a greater affinity for fast water than their brethren, are quicker and more likely to leap when hooked. Their diet is varied, their tastes adaptable. Fresh from the hatchery they will eat anything. Wild fish and those tutored by catch and release anglers can get exceptionally wary. Rainbows typically spawn in the spring — except when they are steelhead, or recently adapted; then they spawn in the fall.

# References

*The Audubon Society Field Guide to North American Fishes*
Alfred A. Knopf, Inc, 1983

*The Complete Brown Trout*
Cecil E. Heacox
Winchester Press, 1974

*Sierra Trout Guide*
Ralph Cutter
Frank Amato Publications, 1991

"The Fish and Fishing of the United States"
Anonymous, 1885

*The Angler's Companion*
Compiled by Brian Murphy
Paddington Press, 1978

*Fishing: An Encyclopedic Guide*
Joseph I. Bates
Outdoor Life Books, E.P Dutton, Inc., 1985

*California Sport Fishing Regulations*
State of California

"Brookies in the Briny"
*Trout Maverick*
Leonard M. Wright, Jr.
Lyons and Burford

*Freshwater Fishes of Britain and Europe*
Alwyne Wheeler Dragon's World Ltd, 1992

"Sea Run Cutthroats"
Roderick L. Haig-Brown reprinted in *The Way of the Trout*
Ted Leeson, Editor
Lyons & Burford

*Freshwater Fishes of California*
Samnal M. McGinnis
University of California Press, 1984

# The Angler in His Environment:
## Observing Streams and Collecting Samples
### by Seth Norman

*"There is no science without careful observation and without it there is also only a primitive form of fishing."*

Nick Lyons, "Water Watching," *A Fisherman's World*

Early season on the Trinity River... I was seining a vast riffle with a kicknet. A pair of flyfishers waded out and asked to see the samples: a half-dozen enormous salmonfly nymphs, *Pteranarcys californica*. One of the pair expressed wonder and surprise at the size of the specimens (several almost three inches long), then described how he had recently killed a brown trout "with his guts just full of those things."

I made what seemed the obvious inquiry. What fly was this fisher using now, and why? An embarrassing question, it turned out. Said fisher had "just guessed" with a size 14 Hare's Ear, because "I didn't know they sold flies that big, and I didn't think about it."

Hiawatha hunting deer would not ignore a hoofprint, salt lick or water source. Studying rivers for stream life is the flyfishing equivalent of tracking game by following spoor: it's a vital tool for the angler, simple to learn, requiring remarkably little time. In a state like California, with waters so diverse, observation will frequently change the fortunes of a day. It makes the difference between understanding and effectively fishing a venue or taking pot shots, best guesses, or depending entirely upon the observations of others, which may or may not be timely.

That's *one* day's fortune. Over years the effect on an angler's experience is incalculable.

I am manifestly biased in this regard: I design and manufacture a kicknet sold by flyfishing shops and entomological supply houses, the "MidStream Riffler." Happily, I have good company to support my prejudice: studying and sampling is advised by a host of flyfishing experts, from David Hughes and Rick Hafele to Randall Kaufmann and Ron Cordes, Charlie Brooks, Gary LaFontaine, Gary Borger, Ralph and Lisa Cutter, Eric Leiser and Robert Boyle, Dave Whitlock, Doug Swisher, Frank Sawyer — the complete list would be rather long, as would the bibliography of works pertaining to trout and their food. Yet the number of anglers who do more than look for an obvious hatch is surprisingly small.

One reason for such neglect is the assumption that "only experts do that," a position made ironic by the fact that an angler with modest knowledge of stream life seems skilled by comparison to one who knows little. Another reason is that, biologically speaking, anglers often confuse the need to know a few orders — those general categories that identify insects in lay terms, like stonefly and caddis — with the more exacting task of learning specific designations of genus and species. While it's true that the subtle refinements come into play on certain venues (see Dick

*Sampling insects on the East Carson. (Photo: Kyle Giampaoli)*

Galland's descriptions of Hat Creek), more general information is usually adequate to a flyfisher's purpose.

That said, note here that this guidebook proceeds with its own assumptions about what the average flyfisher knows about the foods trout eat; specifically, that the fisher has some familiarity with the adult forms of aquatic insects, and can recognize the following:

- A mayfly, drifting on the water while drying its sail-shaped wings, or rising elegantly upward in a direct and stately ascent;
- A caddis fly, with its folded "tent-wings" and moth-like, chaotic flight;
- A salmon or stonefly, a slow and awkward flyer less frequently seen, with broad wings spread flat along its body at rest;
- Midges, usually small or tiny, with a mosquito's profile.

If these insects are not generally known to you, check the bibliography of this book for flyfishers' guides to trout foods, and consider purchasing one of those excellent books to fill you in. Consider also a class from a fly shop or other school.

If those insect forms are familiar, perhaps you also have seen them in their larval or pupa forms. Perhaps not; anglers must search to find these staples of a trout's diet, those items on which fish are usually feeding on when no hatch calls them up.

So how should an angler approach a water, when there's no host of fish rising to "sails?"

The first step is the simplest and most difficult: take time to *see*. Look for shucks, the "skins" some nymphs discard as they climb out to hatch on streamside (and "stream center") rocks. Check the underside of foliage for adult insects waiting in the wings to mate and lay eggs. Slowly turn over subsurface stones; examine the organisms that cling or crawl. Gently sort through moss to see what hides there. Watch shallows for baitfish and fry, or an eddy to look for terrestrials in the scumline, and spinners floating flush in the film. Some of these beasts can only be seen by putting your nose to the water: bend over. Then, look up — for birds hunting insects above you or dragonflies strafing the riffles for prey.

None of these efforts require a single piece of equipment save that with which you come naturally equipped. But note the possibilities: stonefly shucks are fragile. When found, those shucks suggest a recent, probably ongoing emergence — the big nymphs are likely on the move toward banks. Likewise, stonefly adults in the leaves indicate that the clumsy fliers may oviposit — lay eggs — over fast water in the evenings, or fall in by mischance; and that fish, keyed in on the hapless and dead, will take a stimulator even when no rise is evident. Cased caddis live under rocks in cases made of pebbles and debris. Fish will take them stone house and all — thus "dumb enough to eat rocks." Mayfly nymphs clue the angler to proper fly size, shape and color, and though scuds dominate some waters for parts of the year, they are often overlooked. As will be noted by Chip O'Brien about the lower Sacramento, trout gorge sometimes on moss in order to eat the insects, arthropods, and snails living in that soft forest: these lifeforms can also be easily discovered and represented. Plentiful baitfish mean that bigger fish may jump on a streamer-sized meal; a hopper on the path presages strikes in a summer afternoon when the winds rises. "Invisible" spinners can explain many frustrating rises, and sometimes these sexed-to-death creatures will have swarmed high above the stream — that's what the birds were working. Dragonflies, savage skimmers, catch many of the emerging caddis that trout miss; once alerted by "bombers," an angler can sometimes see the flash of fish in the water beneath them.

All that's just a start, a primer for the kinds of payoffs that do more than add fish to memory. Observation is its own reward, engaging the fisher with the wild world in a fashion that is immediate and exciting, full of marvels. Ultimately, wonder about the myriad lives revealed in water that supplies even *more* of the "mystery" that intrigues many fishers than does the "mystical" condition of grosser ignorance.

Perhaps there is a Zen satisfaction to casting a fly you were told to use through hours when it works not at all. But do not neglect the pleasure of sleuthing through the world around you, which is also that of the fish.

## Using Tools to See

Eventually — better sooner than later — a fisher may wish to get a broader and deeper vision into subsurface life, if only because it is well known that trout feed below far more than on top.

A seine is invaluable for this exploration, and a 10-inch by 10-inch square of woven fiberglass window screen mesh, supported on two sides by dowels, will suffice for skimming emergers in the upper edge of the water column. It will also catch drifting adults and spinners, and at times expose masking hatches, revealing a species of insect different from the hatch you see above the stream — and the one that trout really prefer. This can happen on the lower Owens in December, when a fair hatch of medium size white mayflies confuses many fishers because the browns are eating a much smaller blue-winged olive.

Along this line, keep in mind that hatches change during the day, influenced by time, temperature and light, and that you will find different kinds of lifeforms as you move through different types of water. A second or third sampling will catch a new, important organism in the drift.

A larger seine will also serve in the situation described above. But with the traditional kicknet, constructed of two, two-foot "broomstick" shafts supporting a two-foot by two-foot square of mesh, an angler will see another world altogether, populated by nymphs, crustaceans and feed fish. When constructing such a seine on your own, make sure to use mesh strong enough and of the right size ( fiberglass window screen material is perfect, available at most hardware stores). Avoid the kind of micromesh found in women's hosiery and the "no-see-um" screen used in tents: these are so fine they create dams rather than seines, and the majority of significant specimens will be lost.

(Note: the Midstream Riffler is approximately the dimension of the broomstick model, but with substituted collapsible, shock-corded aircraft aluminum shafts for the broomsticks and sleeves sewn to the mesh. The Riffler is slightly superior to the broomstick construction — it's stronger, fits the side pocket of most vests, or hangs from a wading belt, and weighs under four ounces. But the make-your-own version is perfectly serviceable in all other regards.)

To best capture specimens useful to the fisher, proceed as follows: In fast water from 4 inches to 2 feet deep, extend the kicknet with the feet of the shafts pressed hard against the bottom. Stand upstream from the kicknet and shuffle your feet, or stand downstream with one foot extended forward to turn rocks over upstream from the mesh. Dig a few inches through sand or pebbles and vegetation. Wait until the water clears before lifting the net — current will continue to trap specimens in the mesh. Lift the seine while tilting the bottom up at a 45-degree angle, raising it to horizontal as you remove it from the water. Examine your catch carefully; even large lifeforms may be inconspicuous at first. Unless saving specimens for tying purposes, please return all creatures to the water as quickly as possible. When you do, *watch how they move.*

### Seining Slow or Still Water

In slow or still water, extend the seine and walk forward. For bottom-dwelling specimens you may wish to push the feet through sand, mud, and detritus. Make sure you riffle vegetation, particularly the undersides. Gently scrape the shafts (dowels) across the bark of drowned trees and brush. Examine carefully. Again, keep an

*Sampling insects leads to greater success no matter where you fish.*
*(Photo: Seth Norman)*

eye on specimens when you release them to see how they swim or drift away. Tying and fishing tactics should vary with the natural motion of the creature you imitate.

With any of the methods described, remember that you are looking for the prevalent lifeforms on which feeding trout focus. Knowing the Latin or lay name is infinitely less important to fishing than matching size, shape, color, and motion.

That's really all there is to it, at least to begin with, and for most of what you'll ever need to know. But the simple steps involved in collecting will enhance your fishing experience profoundly. As with other aspects of the sport, observational skills evolve: the best of fisher/observers can spot the darkening wing pads on a mayfly nymph and get a fair idea of how close it is to maturity.

The profits from sampling are manifest. An example of this came from a free-stone river in early spring, when a single seine sampling revealed a remarkable collection of 13 dragonfly nymphs, along with a score of tiny mayflies, and perhaps half that many green rockworms (a free-living caddis). I opted for a dragonfly imitation and, in a nice case of symmetry, took 13 rainbows in two hours' fishing.

Returning two weeks later, I was well supplied with fat dragonfly nymphs tied from an actual specimen. Certain that I knew I had the game wired, I only tested the water before fishing out of habit, and so I could gloat.

The first two nets found no dragonfly nymphs at all. The third one revealed a single juvenile — next year's crop. *This* year's had already hatched out…and was now hunting above the fast water for emerging caddis of the vary same species found previously — the green rock worms that now dominated the trout's attention.

That incident also reveals a lesson: when it comes to sampling, don't stay fixed in time. A stream seined in April may show a host of organisms that will be long gone by June.

Second, don't stay fixed in place. Vary the water you investigate. Of course, you do wish to seine an area similar to the kind you wish to fish — the midge pupae you find in slow shallows won't always appear on the menu of trout in a deep run downstream. But if your angling results disappoint you, broaden the scope of your study. Maybe you *should* be fishing midges in slow water.

More examples: a rocky section of a river revealed almost nothing when seined late in the season, and produced nothing at all when fished. But a second sample, taken this time from a slower, sandy-bottomed location, showed enormous numbers of slender pink tubifex worms, the real reason behind the success of the San Juan worm. When a #16 deer hair caddis provoked only rainbows on a stream known for browns, a deep sample revealed a plethora of golden stonefly nymphs. When these were matched in a #6 tie, browns cooperated two of the first three casts.

All of these suggest that anglers should try not to fish blind or rely solely on the advice of absent experts (even those in guidebooks). Explore and inspect all waters, then vary your fly and fishing tactics according to what you find. Such study may not make you the "expert" you imagine, but only wiser and more successful.

# To Fight Again Another Day:
## The Federation of Fly Fisher's Catch and Release Guidelines

It is hardly an accident that most of the venues selected for this book are carefully regulated, with either zero fish limits or limits designed to minimize the impact of sport fishers. Such care is one reason the waters fish as well as they do.

The fortunate fact is that most released fish have an excellent chance of survival if handled properly...*if*. It's another fact that clumsy, ill-advised landings produce an unnecessarily high mortality rate — carcasses drifting downstream from the hand of a well-intended fisher who imagines he's left live fish behind.

The Federation of Fly Fishers hopes to reduce such waste. Among its diverse activities is the dissemination of information to anglers who would like to release their catch with the best chance for survival. To that end the FFF has distributed more than 10,000 copies of a booklet, *Catch and Release Guidelines* — a succinct, thoughtful, well-laid out piece of work, reviewed for content by more than a score of fishers known for their passion and commitment.

With the Federation's permission, *Catch and Release Guidelines* is reproduced here. Please note that the copyright belongs to FFF, along with credit for its creation.

## Catch and Release Guidelines

### Reviewers

| | |
|---|---|
| Robert Barnhart, Ph.D | Robert Behke, Ph.D. |
| Robert Black, MD. | Charlie Brooks |
| Willis Evan | Michael Fong |
| Rick Hafele | Roy Haile |
| Harry Kime | Lefty Kreh |
| Nick Lyons | Frank Richardson |
| Vince Ringrose, MD. | Terry Roelofs, Ph.D. |
| Marty Sherman | Mark Sosin |
| Spenser Turner | Ted Trueblood |
| Lee Wulff | Gordy Young |

First Edition Committee: Marty Seldon, Clyde Richie, and Dick Hall
Second Edition Committee: Starr Thurston and George Johnson
Third Edition Committee: Terry Lyons and Jim Abbs
(Drawings by Richard Bunse)

The Federation of Fly Fishers believe that "Catch and Release" regulations, and all forms of special regulations, are management tools to be used to improve fisheries' resources. We contend that these regulations are to be used to achieve improved fisheries, and are not an end in themselves.

By providing this handbook for your use we are emphasizing our dedication to the use of catch and release techniques to help improve and preserve our valuable fishing resources. For more information on how to get the most from your existing fisheries, contact your local government agency, affiliated club, or regional council of the Federation for help.

This handbook was first published in 1984 through dedicated efforts of members of the Federation of Fly Fishers. Those individuals and those responsible for subsequent editions are listed on the inside cover. We owe them a debt of gratitude for bringing the mechanics of barbless, no-kill, and catch and release fishing to sport fishers worldwide.

Due to heavy demand it is necessary to once again update this handbook. This is the third printing, with over ten thousand being distributed in the last year alone. Special recognition goes out to my predecessors, Marty Seldon, Starr Thurston, and George Johnson, without whose guidance this worthwhile project would never have happened.

Tight Lines,

Guy Tillotson
Executive Vice President, Conservation

# INTRODUCTION

### Lee Wulff, 1984

"Once upon a time, our wild trout fishing may have been the best in the world. Too many people took too many fish and the quality slumped. The private streams of the Old World where fishing was limited to a few, the take low enough to give high quality fishing, far surpassed it and represented good management. But the best fishing possible occurs when all the fish a good stream will hold are built up in that stream and maintained there. NO-KILL was America's answer to give the public of our country even finer fishing than the richest people of the world. No-Kill does not give us the seclusion that many of us dreamed of. The fishing of the future may very well be a companionable sport where anglers fish together, each with a wise, many-time caught fish to cast for, the most challenging angling known. It can be done in no other way!"

### Roderick Haig-Brown, *Fisherman's Spring*, 1974

"The fisherman's enormous advantage in the matter of bag limits is that he can limit his killing without appreciably limiting his sport, and he can also select what he does kill in a way seldom possible in other sports."

## Sport Fishing Institute, 1987

"An ethical angler realizes that fishing is fun. Fishing pleasure is not measured by the heft of the stringer, but by the angling difficulty offered by the particular fish caught — and often released — in an aesthetically pleasing environment."

## Catch & Release Fishing

From Alaska to West Yellowstone, from Sam Rayburn Lake in Texas to streams in New York and north to Iceland, size limits and creel limits have not been able to prevent the depletion of fish stocks in heavily fished waters. Larger faster-growing fish are cropped first, and the quality of angling decreases. The Federation of Fly Fishers supports catch and release fishing because, if used appropriately, it will usually produce fish of larger average size in the greatest possible numbers, resulting in increased catch rates.

Catch and release fishing, like any good concept, has its limitations. For instance, releasing fish in a pond of stunted bluegills will not improve the fishing. Nor will it help where habitat has been seriously degraded, but for many species, from largemouth bass to most billfish, and for most situations involving trout and salmon, the resource and the quality of fishing will only be improved by catch and release fishing. Remember! Be aware of the limitations and supportability of the particular habitat.

Catch and release fishing can be practiced by all anglers. The Federation of Fly Fishers would like to encourage all spin, bait, and fly fishers to join us in the preservation of more and larger fish for future generations. Catch and release fishing may be strictly no-kill or it may involve a combination of size and bag limits. But no matter how it is done, our goal is healthy, self-sustaining fish populations with proper distributions in all age classes.

Catch and release fishing works only if the fish are released, recover, and rejoin the fishery. This booklet has been prepared by the Federation of Fly Fishers to provide information on the proper techniques of releasing fish in streams, rivers, ponds, lakes, and salt water.

This information was compiled from inquiries to more than 100 fish management agencies around the world, from symposiums on catch and release fishing, and from a number of Federation members and friends. Catch and release fishing is important because it works! Please do your part.

## Fighting Your Fish

Don't fight or play your fish to complete exhaustion. Use a rod of sufficient strength so that the fish can be quickly landed. Use the heaviest leader possible. Even with light tippets, "hustle" your fish in. This is particularly important for cold water fish in warm water conditions, where mortality is higher because of higher temperatures. Be firm but gentle when handling the fish to avoid shock. Consider breaking the fish off if you're unable to land the fish quickly due to a light tippet or light rod.

Always treat a fish carefully. At times it may be necessary to "slide" a fish over weeds or thick cover to avoid having it burrow into heavy growth. A small fish sometimes can be "skimmed" across the surface rapidly by keeping its head up. But do not drag a fish with its mouth open.

## Landing a Fish

When ready to land your fish, try to avoid removing it from the water and keep it in water deep enough to protect it. Do not allow a fish to flop in shallow water or on the rocks. When fishing from a boat or float tube, or when fishing for large fish, use of a net can reduce landing time. Nets can be a disadvantage, however, with small fish or if you are using multiple hooks on your lure because both will tend to tangle in the net. Small fish should be landed by hand. Beware. Nets can damage eyes and remove protective slime from the body of a fish.

## Saltwater and Deep Lake Fishing

In salt water or deep lakes, a fish brought up from the depths will often suffer from over inflation of its swim bladder. This prevents it from diving in deep water and may cause suffocation. Under such conditions, you could attempt to puncture the swim bladder with a pin, needle, or if necessary, a knife point. This process may be fatal to the fish. With large fish, particularly in salt water, cutting the leader often is the best way to release a fish before it is exhausted.

Sharks are a menace in salt water. If one approaches while you are playing a fish, back off the drag and let the fish run freely. It may be necessary to let the fish escape by increasing the drag and breaking the line or tippet.

## How To Hold Your Fish

Don't hold a fish head up unless it is a spiny-rayed fish. Cradle it gently in your hands, holding the "wrist" just ahead of the tail section or with a gentle hand cupping lift. Do not hold it vertically.

Keep your fingers out of and away from the gills of any fish unless you intend to kill it. Do not put your fingers or thumbs over the eyes of any fish. You won't pacify it, but may cause serious injuries.

Never squeeze a fish in the throat or body cavity regions; vital organs may be injured. Pressure against a vital organ will often prove fatal. Professionals sometimes use woolen or cotton gloves to handle fish.

Bass may be held by carefully grasping the lower jaw with your thumb and forefinger. Small trout and some other fish may be handled with the same grip. If they are tilted upside down slightly, they are less able to "wiggle." Trout held upside down while removing the hook usually remain calm.

If you wish to photograph a fish, have a camera ready and do it quickly. If possible, get someone else to take the picture or hold the fish. Try to keep the fish in the water by cradling it, or by keeping it in a net beneath the water. If you wish to weigh a fish and have a net, weigh the fish in the net. After releasing the fish, get the weight of the net and subtract it.

### Reviving and Releasing Your Fish

Never throw a fish into the water. Grasp it gently and return it carefully to the water. Minimize the time any fish is kept out of the water. The longer a fish is out of water, the greater the probability it will die. Handling and time out of the water are the most important factors in the successful release of a fish.

Revive an exhausted fish by pointing its head into the current until the gills are working normally and the fish gains enough strength to support itself in the current. The fish will often surge out of your hands when it has recovered. The process may take some time.

Try to release your fish in low velocity water; particularly after a prolonged fight. Lead the fish to quiet water to revive it. Release the fish in shallow water so you can recover it if it is not able to swim. Use of stomach pumps to determine feeding of fish is not recommended. Without proper training, the pump may be fatal to the fish.

### Hooks

We strongly recommend the use of single barbless hooks on all flies and lures, when you plan to release fish. Small long-nosed pliers or curve forceps can be used to bend down the barbs on conventional hooks. The Federation of Fly Fishers urges that all anglers use bronzed steel, instead of nickel or stainless steel or gold plated hooks. If you break a fish off, or if you cut the leader when a fish is hooked deeply, bronzed hooks will corrode in a fish more quickly.

### General Fishing Guidelines

Occasionally, fish taken with trolled bait are hooked in the mouth and can easily be released using the same procedures outlined for flies and lures. Often fish taken on bait while still fishing will be deeply hooked. In this case, use a small wire cutter or snips to cut the leader as near the hook as possible. Use care not to let the fish beat itself against the boat, dock, or other objects. If you need to use a gaff, use a release gaff. Gaff the fish from the lower side of the jaw and from the inside out. To release the fish, simply unhook and pop out the gaff. Do everything you can to help a fish swim away on its own. If it seems disoriented, sometimes a slight push with the rod tip, a pole, or the gaff will stimulate the fish to move off.

### A Note from Lauren Bagley, Managing Director, Federation of Fly Fishers

The Federation of Fly Fishers was formally created in Eugene, Oregon in 1965. The purpose and objectives of the FFF today are still the same : To promote fly fishing as the most sportsmanlike and enjoyable way of fishing and the most consistent with the preservation and wise use of our game fish. This premise is based not only upon a dedication to the sport, but also the recognition that once a potential angler begins to consider imitating the form and behavior of aquatic life, a transformation takes place, and that individual — like most fly fishers — becomes a more dedicated conservationist.

The FFF also provides advice, suggestions and assistance to members in helping them to become more important and effective in their local areas. The FFF is founded on the belief that a local, grass roots organization is the best and most logical agency by which and through which to work for the preservation and improvement of the angling resources in its area. Effectively confronting catch and kill fishing regulations, hatchery displacement of wild and/or native fish, river degradation and agricultural pollution of ground water requires decisions and actions at the local level. The FFF is interested in restoration and conservation of all fish in all waters and feels that a broad ecosystem view is the only sound approach to fisheries conservation.

Join the FFF and lend your voice — and your support — to our efforts to enhance and preserve our fisheries resources into the 21st century and beyond. For membership information write to FFF, P.O. Box 1595, Bozeman, MT 59771 406-585-7592. E-mail. 74504,2605

# Appendix I
# Fly Shops

## Fly Shops at Hub Cities for Rivers

### East Carson River
- South Lake Tahoe
  *Alpine Fly Fishing*, P.O. Box 10465, South Lake Tahoe, CA 96158 / 916-542-0759
  *The Outdoor & Fly Fishing Store*, 3433 Lake Tahoe Blvd., South Lake Tahoe,
  CA 96150 / 916-541-8208

### East Walker River
- Bridgeport
  *Ken's Sporting Goods*, Main Street, Bridgeport, CA 93517 / 619-932-7707

### Feather River
North Fork above and below Lake Almanor: none dedicated. Some flyfishing tackle
can be found in Chester:
- *Ayoob's Sports*, 201 Main St., Chester, CA 96020 / 916-258-2611

Middle Fork: none dedicated. General tackle stores where some fly fishing tackle can
be found in Quincy:
- *Sportsman's Den*, 1580 E. Main Street E., Quincy, CA 95971 / 916-283-2733
- *Sierra Mountain Sports*, 501 Main Street (across from the Court House), Quincy,
  CA 95971 / 916-283-2323

### Fall River, Hat Creek, Pit River
- Burney
  *All Tied Up Fly Fishing Company*, 37026 Main St., Burney, CA 96013 /
  916-335-4732
  *Trout Country*, 38247 Hwy 299 E., Burney, CA 96013 / 916-335-5304
- Cassel
  *Clearwater Trout Tours*, PO Box 90, Cassel, CA 96016 / 916-335-5500
  *Rising River Fly & Tackle*, PO Box 30 Cassel, CA 96016 / 916-335-2291
- Fall River Mills
  *Shasta Angler/Intermountain Marine*, Fall River Mills, CA 96028 / 916-336-6600

### Upper Sacramento River, McCloud River
- Dunsmuir
  *Ted Fay Fly Shop*, 4310 Dunsmuir Ave., Dunsmuir, CA 96025 / 916-235-2872
  *Dunsmuir Fly Fishing Company*, 5839 Dunsmuir Ave., Dunsmuir CA,
  96025 / 916-235-0705

### Hot Creek/Lower Owens River
• **Mammoth Lakes**
  *Kittredge Sports*, 3218 Main St., Mammoth Lakes, CA 93546 / 619-934-7566
  *The Troutfitter*, Shell Mart Center #3, Mammoth Lakes, CA 93546 / 619-924-3676
• **Bishop**
  *Brocks Sporting Goods*, 100 N. Main St, Bishop, CA 93514 / 619-872-3581

### Lower Yuba River
• **Nevada City/Grass Valley**
  *Nevada City Anglers*, 417 Broad St., Nevada City, CA 95959 / 916-478-9301
  *Mother Lode Angler*, 13683 Day Road, Grass Valley, CA 95945 / 916-272-3474
• **Yuba City**
  *Bob's Fly Shack*, 488 W. Onstott Road, Yuba City, CA 95991 / 916-671-9628
• **Lower Sacramento**
  *The Fly Shop*, 4140 Churn Creek Road, Redding, CA 96002 / 800-669-3474

### Trinity River
• *Trinity Fly Shop*, P.O. Box 176, Lewiston, CA 96052 / 916-623-6757

### Truckee River
There are no dedicated stores in Truckee, but tackle can be found at the following:
• *Mountain Hardware and Sports*, 11320 Donner Pass Road, Truckee, CA
  96161 / 916-587-4844
• *Bud's Sporting Goods*, 10108 Commercial Row, Truckee, CA 96161 / 916-587-3177

### North Fork Yuba River
• **Nevada City** (closest available)
  *Nevada City Anglers*, 417 Broad St., Nevada City, CA 95959 / 916-478-9301
Some fly tackle may also be found at:
• *Bassetts Station*, Highway 49 and Gold Lake Road, Bassetts, CA 96125 /
  916-862-1297
• *Sierra Hardware*, 305 Main Street, Downieville, CA 95936 / 916-289-3582

## Fly Shops at Transit Cities with Commercial Air Service

### San Francisco Bay Area
• **San Francisco**
  *Fly Fishing Outfitters*, 463 Bush, San Francisco, CA 94108 / 415-781-3474
  *Orvis San Francisco*, 300 Grant Ave., San Francisco, CA 94108 / 415-392-1600
  *San Francisco Flyfisher's Supply*, 2526 Clement Street, San Francisco, CA
  94121 / 415-668-3597

- **East Bay**
  *A-1 Fish*, 517 8th Street, Oakland, CA 94607 / 510-832-0731
  *Creative Sports*, 1924 Oak Park Blvd., Pleasant Hill, CA 94523 / 510-938-2255
  *Fish First!*, 1404 Solano Ave., Albany, CA 97706 / 510-526-1937
  *Flies By Night*, 1015 B Street, Hayward, CA 94541 / 510-538-3861
  *Fly Fishing Outfitters*, 3533 Mt. Diablo Blvd., Lafayette, CA 94549 / 510-284-3474
  *Pacific Coast Anglers*, 2005 Crow Canyon Place, San Ramon, CA 94583 /
  510-830-8791

- **South Bay / Peninsula**
  *The Caddis Fly Shop*, 1538-D El Camino Real, Belmont, CA 94002 /
  415-508-0727
  *Emie's Casting Pond*, 4845 Soquel Drive, Soquel, CA 95073 / 408-462-4665
  *Mel Cotton's Sporting Goods*, 408-287-5994
  *The Midge Fly Shop*, 271 State Street, Los Altos, CA 94022 / 415-941-8871
  *The Ultimate Fly Shop*, 494 San Mateo Ave., San Bruno, CA 94066 / 415-583-1168
  *Upstream Flyfishing*, 54 N. Santa Cruz Ave., Los Gates, CA 95030 / 408-354-4935

- **North Bay**
  *Selective Angler*, 2215 Larkspur Landing Circle, Larkspur, CA 94939 /
  415-461-6655
  *Western Sport Shop*, 902 Third Street, San Rafael, CA 94939 / 415-456-5454

- **Sacramento**
  *American Fly Fishing Co*, 3523 Fair Oak Blvd, Sacramento, CA 94939 / 916-483-1222
  *Kiene's Fly Shop*, 2654 Marconi Ave., Sacramento, CA 95821 / 916-486-9958
  *Fly Fishing Specialties*, 9500 Micron Ave #129, Sacramento, CA 98527 / 916-366-9252
  Fisherman's Warehouse, 9035 Folsom Blvd, Sacramento, CA / 916-362-1200

- **Redding**
  *The Fly Shop*, 4140 Churn Creek Road, Redding, CA 96002 / 800-669-3474

- **Reno**
  *Reno Fly Shop*, 294 E. Moana Lane #14, Reno, NV 89502 / 702-825-3474

## Fly Shops on Major Routes

- **Chico**
  *Chico Powell Fly Shop*, 1154 West 8th Ave., Chico, CA 95926 / 916-345-9983

- **Stockton**
  *The Tobacco Leaf*, 123 Lincoln Center, Stockton, CA 95207 / 209-474-8216

- **Fairfield**
  *California Fly Shop*, 2201 Boynton Ave. Suite B Fairfield, CA 94533 /
  800-359-4811

- **Woodland**
  *The Belligerent Duck,* 1264 E. Gibson Road Space A119 (County Fair Mall),
  Woodland, CA 95776 / 916-666-3825
- **Ridgecrest**
  *High Sierra Flyfisher,* 337 W. Ridgecrest Blvd., Ridgecrest, CA 93555 / 619-375-5810
- **Oroville**
  *Valhalla Sports,* 4290 Highway 70 South, Oroville, CA 95965 / 916-533-2948

## Other Northern California Fly Shops

- **Wine Country**
  *Fly Fishing Etc.,* 7 Petaluma Blvd., North Petaluma, CA 94952 / 707-762-3073
  *Outdoor Pro Shop,* 6315 Commerce Blvd., Rohnert Park, CA 94928 /
  707-588-8033
  *Sweeny's,* 1601 Lincoln Ave., Napa, CA 94558 / 707-255-5544
  *Western Angler,* 532 College Ave., Santa Rosa, CA 95404 / 707-542-4432
  *Wind River Fly Fishing,* 1043 Atlas Peak Road, Napa, CA 94558 / 707-252-4900
- **Yosemite Area**
  *Yosemite Angler,* 49er Shopping Center, Mariposa, CA 95350 / 209-966-8377
  *Village Sport Shop,* Yosemite Park, CA 95389 / 209-372-1286
- **North and North Coast**
  *Eureka Fly Shop,* 505 H Street, Eureka, CA 95501 / 707-444-2000
  *North Coast Angler,* 260 N. Main Street, Fort Bragg, CA 95437 / 707-964-6598
  *Reel Fly Shop,* 614 S. Main Street, Yreka, CA 96097 / 916-842-6665

# APPENDIX II
## Other Resources

**Bureau of Land Management**
2800 Cottage Way
Sacramento, CA 95825
916-978-4400

**California Department of Fish & Game**
1416 Ninth Street
Sacramento, CA 95814
916-653-4576

**California Road Information**
( within California)
800-427-ROAD

**California Road Information**
(outside California)
916-445-7623

**California Office of Tourism**
801 K Street, Suite #1600
Sacramento, CA 95814
916-322-1397

**California Department of Parks & Recreation**
P.O. Box 2390
Sacramento, CA 95811
916-445-8513

**CalTrout**
870 Market Street, Suite #859
San Francisco, CA 94102
415-392-8887

**Friends of the Trinity River**
P.O. Box 2327
Mill Valley, CA 94942-2327
415-389-1300

**The Federation of Fly Fishers**
National Headquarters
406-585-7592

**United States Forest Service**
630 Sansome Street
San Francisco, CA 94111
415-705-2874

# APPENDIX III
# Photographers

The following people contributed photographs for this book; all rights remain with them.

- Victor Babbit, The Outdoor & Fly Fishing Store, 3433 Lake Tahoe Blvd., South Lake Tahoe, CA 96150 / 916-541-8208

- Chip O'Brien, 8501 Copper Drive, Redding, CA 96001 / 916-246-4700

- Herb Burton, Trinity Fly Shop, P.O. Box 176, Lewiston, CA 96052 / 916-623-6757.

- Kyle Giampaoli, Sunny Days Guide Service, 700 Panther South Lake Tahoe 96151, CA, 96151 916-541-7440

- Frank Holminski, Mt. Shasta Fly Fishing Guide Service, P.O. Box 128, Mt. Shasta, CA 96067 / April–November: 916-926-6648 / December–March: 415-661-5838 / Fax: 415-564 7719

- Kate Howe and Bill Howe, Classic Anglers, PO Box 16, Olancha, CA 93599 / 760-920-0267 / E-mail: clasang@inetworld.net / Website: http://www.inetworld.net/clasang

- Jim Mathews (through Kate Howe, at Classic Anglers — see above)

- Mike Mercer, c/o of The Fly Fish, 4140 Churn Creek, Redding, CA 96002 / 800-669-FISH

- Duane Milleman, c/o of The Fly Fish, 4140 Churn Creek, Redding, CA 96002 / 800-669-FISH

- Ken Morrish, Ashland Outdoor Store, 37 Third St., Ashland, CA 97520 / 503-488-1202

- Frank Pisciotta, Thy Rod & Staff, PO Box 10038, Truckee, CA 96162 / 530-587-7333 / email: cyberfly@hooked.net / Web: 222.cyberfly.com

- Edgar Yeechow (through Kate Howe, at Classic Anglers; see above)

- Ralph Wood, C&R Guide Service, 640 Kate Hayes, Grass Valley, CA 95945

- R. Valentine Atkinson, R.V. Atkinson Photography / 415-731-4385

- Seth Norman, 4721 Meldon Ave., Oakland, CA 94619n / 510-532-8908

# APPENDIX IV
# Contributing Authors

## Andy Burk

Born in Redding, California, Andy Burk began tying flies and flyfishing at the age of 12, interests that his parents encouraged. By 14 he was tying flies commercially. After graduating high school, he became a guide on two of the West's toughest spring creeks, Hat Creek and Fall River. For four years he guided and tied for Bob Brink's Spring Creek Angler's Fly Shop near Hat Creek.

Andy now works at the Fly Shop in Redding. He is a popular guest speaker and tying at clubs, conclaves, and shows, the fly tying columnist for *California Fly Fisher* magazine, and a freelancer writing for several national flyfishing publications. Andy is also a contract tyer for Umpqua Feather Merchants, of Glide Oregon, and many of his pattern designs may be found in flyfishing specialty shops nationwide. His new tying newsletter, "The Fly Paper," features informative articles on techniques, materials, and fly design.

Andy lives in Redding with his wife, Margaret, and his two stepchildren, Evelynn and Miranda.

**How to Contact:**    Andy Burk
3700 McHale Way
Redding, CA 96001
916-246-7932

## Herb Burton

Herb Burton is a resident of Trinity County, a professional guide and outfitter, owner of Trinity River Alps Angling Experiences and the full-service, year-round Trinity Fly Shop, four miles outside of Lewiston, where he also teaches flyfishing and fly tying. Both shop and home are near the banks of the river he's fished and guided for 25 years, on which he has logged tens of thousands of miles.

Burton is also a naturalist and conservationist. He has assisted in many of the resource studies and projects on the Trinity River, and written numerous articles for fish and outdoor periodicals: *Salmon-Trout-Steelheader, California Fly Fisher, Fly Tyer, California Angler, Fish Sniffer* and *Western Outdoors*. His current focus is on developing educational and instructional materials.

Burton is married to the former Patricia Daniels of Estacada, Oregon, who contributes her talents to running their business. They have two children, Kellie, 23, and Christopher, 10.

**How to Contact:**    Herb Burton
Trinity Fly Shop

P.O. Box 176
Lewiston, CA 96052
916-623-6757

## Jim Crouse

A native Californian, Jim Crouse grew up in the San Francisco Bay Area. He learned to flyfish with his father's cane rods on Zyante Creek during visits to his parent's cabin in the Santa Cruz Mountains. In his youth Jim learned the value of catch and release on backpack trips in the Sierras. He also started tying flies with his Official Boy Scout Fly Tying Kit.

After graduating from California State University at Hayward, Jim entered graduate school. During winter break in 1968 he took a vacation to South Lake Tahoe and, that same winter, moved there to become a ski instructor and permanent resident.

Jim has now been flyfishing alpine waters for 29 years. Demand for his popular local fly patterns and his love for teaching eventually led to a business license. Jim has been instructing and guiding for the last nine years. He is a professional guide for Fisher Fly Rods and a member of the High Sierra Fly Casters. He is also owner, head guide, and instructor for Alpine Fly Fishing, a Dan Bailey's authorized dealer in South Lake Tahoe, California. He has helped with many of the survey and stocking programs intended to benefit the East Carson River.

Jim has been married for 24 years and has two sons. He owns and operates a guide service and conducts mail order retail sales.

**How to Contact:**   Alpine Fly Fishing
P.O. Box 10465
South Lake Tahoe, CA 96158
530-542-0759

## Dick Galland and Clearwater House

Dick Galland has been flyfishing the West since the 1950s. He was a wilderness guide in the Rockies, the Southwest and the Sierra for 15 years, first with Outward Bound and then with his own wilderness adventure business in California. In 1982, he bought an old farmhouse on the banks of Hat Creek, California's first designated Wild Trout River, and opened Clearwater House, a flyfishing school and the only ORVIS-endorsed lodge in California. Dick's background in outdoor education is reflected in Clearwater's mission statement: to help each angler achieve the highest level of flyfishing skill that they aspire to. To this end, Clearwater offers more than 20 flyfishing schools for beginning, intermediate, and advanced anglers each season, and top rank guides selected as much for their exceptional people skills as their fine fishing abilities. The quality of meals and accommodations at Clearwater House demonstrate a total commitment to a quality fishing experience.

Dick has been involved with California Trout since the late '70s, serving as their Streamkeeper for Hat Creek, the Pit River, and Burney Creek. He has helped develop special regulations and habitat enhancement projects on these waters. He writes for regional flyfishing magazines. His is a strong voice for quality waters and wild trout in California's intermountain region.

**How to Contact:**    Dick Galland
310 Sunset Way
Muir Beach, CA 94965
415-381-1173
Fax 415-383-9136

## Dan Gracia

Although a native of California, Dan Gracia learned to flyfish after moving to Oregon. He acquired a rod rather by accident — and spent the next 11 years dedicating every spare moment casting for trout and steelhead.

In 1987 Dan moved back to California and met Dean Schubert, then the director of the Orvis West Coast schools. Shortly thereafter Dan took the position of schools coordinator; he has been teaching Orvis classes ever since. If Orvis is wise, they will keep Dan into his dotage: he gracefully combines enthusiasm, extraordinary expertise, and manifest good will. Readers visiting flyfishing sites on the internet will almost undoubtedly recognize his name and likely have had the chance to read his answers to inquiries — about as good a source of advice as you will find on the web.

Dan presents flyfishing programs at flyfishing clubs and shows and, during the fall and winter months, teaches fly tying.

**How to Contact:**    Dan Gracia
421 Williams Place
San Mateo, CA 94401
415-340-0560
Fax 415-348-8178
E-mail: dgracia@aol.com

## Frank Holminski

Frank Holminski is a San Francisco native who didn't discover the outdoors until high school. In college he became a horticulture major and studied forestry. After graduation, however, he pursued a career in business, spending 20 years in banking before "getting back on track."

He began flyfishing during a vacation to Sun Valley in 1975 and soon started hunting trout in Montana, Wyoming, and Idaho. For the first several years, he always used a guide: "My fishing time was limited, and a guide increased my chances of success. I used guides less often when success became less of an issue."

When he realized that flyfishing was now a passion, Frank determined to fish more often. It was then that he discovered the fishing of California, taking monthly treks to the north through the 1980s. "I found myself watching others and reflected back to my early years. I began to approach people and offer assistance. I found that I enjoyed helping people learn, because I was able to relive my first joys through them. It was then I decided to go into guiding."

With a fishing partner, Frank founded Mt. Shasta Fly Fishing Guide Service in 1988. That done, Frank quit his job, sold his house, and moved to Mt. Shasta.

**How to Contact:**    Frank Holminski
Mt. Shasta Fly Fishing Guide Service
PO Box 128
MT Shasta, CA 96067
April–November: 916-926-6648
December–March: 415-661-5838; Fax 415-564 7719

## Kate Howe

An angler for over 30 years, Kate began early, at the insistence of her mother — "She had me on the pier as soon as I could stay propped up in a grocery box." At nine Mom decided Kate should have a fly rod; now Kate's a highly regarded flyfisher and an internationally known tyer.

Growing up in California, moving back and forth between the San Francisco Bay area and the eastern Sierras, Kate received a diverse angling education, expanded by work as a licensed guide in California, Idaho, and Nevada, and through travels to Scotland, England, Japan, and Mexico, as well as the United States from Hawaii to the Midwest, Southern California to Alaska. She recently became one of the few women in the world to land striped marlin on a fly rod — a 112-pounder — and holds an I.G.F.A. 5 to 1 title.

Kate is a creative tyer with several commercially marketed saltwater patterns to her name. She has been featured as a Master Fly Tyer for the International Sportsman Exhibitions and as guest tyer at Federation of Fly Fishers Conclaves throughout the West. With husband Bill, she has written for *California Fly Fisher*, and their flies have been featured and photographed in a dozen regional and national magazines, including pieces by Nick Curciono, Dan Blanton, Tony Oswald, Dan Byford, John McKim, and others.

## Bill Howe

Bill Howe is the consummate flyfisherman, with over 40 years angling experience in fresh and saltwaters. His fishing travels have taken him from the Bering Straits to Ascension Bay, inland to Montana, Idaho, Wyoming, and Nevada; he has guided in British Columbia, on Silver Creek, the Bitterroot, Beaverhead, Musselshell, Green, Owens, East Walker, and Yellowstone. For many years he has also been an instructor of flyfishing and tying, a lecturer, and a Master Tyer at sportsmen's shows and conclaves. Bill considers fishing his vocation, loves the sport, and endeavors to teach and practice the skills necessary to catch fish under just about any circumstances.

A gifted designer, many of Bill's patterns have helped anglers set I.G.F.A records, in both salt and freshwater. Bill himself holds one of these, a record for Pacific bonito.

Kate and Bill own and operate their commercial fly tying business and flyfishing school in La Mesa, California. They are considered experts in the construction and design of completely synthetic ties, setting standards with their ALF (Anchovy Looking Fly) and FPF (Flashy Profile Fly), while garnering international attention. These and other patterns have appeared in *Fly Fishing for Bonefish*, by Dick Brown, *Saltwater Flies: 700 of the Best*, by Deke Meyer, *Bluewater Fly Fishing*, by Trey Combs, *Patterns of the Masters*, Federation of Fly Fishers, and (soon) *Innovative Saltwater Flies* by Bob Veverka.

**How to Contact:**     Bill and Kate Howe
Classic Anglers
10501 Enger Street
Bakersfield, CA 93312
E-mail: clasang@inetworld.net
Web: http://www.inetworld.net/clasang

## Duane Milleman

Duane Milleman has been angling northern California waters for 43 years and has hiked many of the state's rivers from the headwaters down. His passion to see and fish it all fitted (or perhaps directed) his education: he has a master's in PE and a BA in biology. Duane taught at the junior high, high school, and college levels, and began conducting flyfishing instruction in 1972.

After 11 years as a fencing contractor, Duane became a managing partner in Lava Creek Lodge. By the time he left in 1988, he had developed an interest in private waters, prompted partly by his long history with rivers and streams he had seen decline. Duane was in the main part responsible for the rehabilitation and development of what is now Hat Creek Ranch, the meadow section of Goodrich Creek, and that five-mile portion of Clear Creek running through the Kutras Ranch — just below the canyon he had fished extensively for years, "when the browns were as long as your arm." Duane now oversees those properties and others as manager of the Fly Shop Outfitters.

He has three children and four grandchildren, assuring himself a team of fishing partners for the future.

**How to Contact:**     Duane Milleman
c/o The Fly Shop
4140 Churn Creek Road

Redding, CA 96002
800-669-3474

## Chip O'Brien

At a young age, Chip O'Brien showed the telltale signs of carrying the flyfishing virus. Worse yet, he threw together a plan to write about it in hopes of infecting others. Alas, after earning a journalism degree, he was temporarily seduced by the senseless desire to make money.

Corporate sales brought him to Southern California in search of big bucks. Then one day, something in him snapped. Determined to put life on a different track, Chip moved his family to Redding almost a decade ago.

When he's not guiding for Clearwater Trout Tours or teaching flyfishing classes at Shasta College, he finds time to pursue his childhood dream. He is a columnist in *Western FlyFishing* magazine and contributes regularly to *California Fly Fisher* and others. He recently authored the Sacramento River edition of the *River Journal* series.

While a serious professional at both guiding and writing, O'Brien's smile is about as wide as his river; he laughs easily and often, and loves the sport.

**How to Contact:**    Clearwater Trout Tours
415-381-1173
E-mail at chip414264@AOL.com

## Frank Pisciotta

Frank Pisciotta is a native Californian who has pursued the state's trout from the lakes of urban Marin County across the myriad waters of the John Muir Trail. Altogether, he has over 40 years experience — time enough to learn and earn a reputation for competence. His guide service, Thy Rod and Staff, has operated out of Truckee since 1984 and is endorsed by Orvis.

Frank is also one of the sport's great hosts, about as generous, warm and enthusiastic a teacher as may be found on a stream — the kind of guide who enjoys a client's fish as much as any he catches himself.

**How to Contact:**    Frank Pisciotta
Thy Rod & Staff
P.O. Box 10038
Truckee, CA 96162
530-587-7333  /  Fax 510-798 8692
E-mail:  cyberfly@ hooked.net
Webpage:  http:// www. cyberfly.com

OR
The Reel School of Flyfishing
P.O. Box 10038
Truckee, CA 96162

## Ralph Wood

Ralph Wood spent his apprentice years in New Hampshire, learning his craft on the small freestone streams and brooks that predominate in "The Granite State." Here is the birthplace of his love for the myriad freestone streams of California.

For the last 40 years, Ralph has fished all across the Western states, especially northern California. He is a well-known guide, as well as a demonstration and custom tier, often appearing at conclaves and events for the Northern California Council, Fly Fishing Federation. He teaches fly tying for his local club affiliation. Ralph's collection of insect specimens is extensive; from these he adapts his ties to specific venues.

Ralph's writing and book reviews have appeared in *California Fly Fisher*. His other interests include his flyfishing sons, Chip and Jeff, and book collecting. He lives in the California Gold Country in Grass Valley.

**How to Contact:**     Ralph Wood
C & R Guide Service
640 Kate Hayes Street
Grass Valley, CA 95945
916-477-0780

# APPENDIX V
# Designated Wild Trout Waters

These waters are currently designated Wild Trout Waters by the California Fish and Game Commission (1996):

1. American River, North Fork, from Palisade Creek downstream to Iowa Hill Bridge (Placer County).

2. Carson River, East Fork, from Hangmans Bridge to Nevada state line.

3. Clavey River, upstream from confluence with Tuolumne River, excluding tributaries (Tuolumne County).

4. Fall River, from Pit No. 1 powerhouse intake upstream to origin at Thousand Springs, including Spring Creek but excluding all other tributaries (Shasta County).

5. Feather River, Middle Fork, from Oroville Reservoir upstream to Sloat vehicle bridge, excluding tributaries (Butte and Plumas counties).

6. Hat Creek, from Lake Britton upstream to Hat No. 2 powerhouse (Shasta County)>

7. Hot Creek, from Hot Springs upstream to west property line of Hot Creek Ranch (Mono County).

8. Kings River, from Pine Flat Lake upstream to confluence with South and Middle forks, excluding tributaries (Fresno County).

9. Kings River, South Fork, from confluence with Middle Fork upstream to western boundary of Kings Canyon National Park, excluding tributaries (Fresno County).

10. Merced River, South Fork, from confluence with mainstem Merced River upstream to western boundary of Yosemite National Park, excluding tributaries (Mariposa County).

11. Nelson Creek, upstream from confluence with Middle Fork Feather River, excluding tributaries (Plumas County).

12. Owens River, from Five Bridges crossing upstream to Pleasant Valley Dam, excluding tributaries (Inyo County).

13. Rubicon River, from confluence with Middle Fork American River upstream to Hell Hole Dam, excluding tributaries (Placer County).

14. Yellow Creek, from Big Springs downstream to confluence with the North Fork of the Feather River (Plumas County).

15. Cottonwood Creek, upstream from confluence with Little Cottonwood Creek, including tributaries (Inyo County).

16. Klamath River, from Copco Lake to the Oregon border (Siskiyou County).

17. Martis Creek Reservoir (Placer and Nevada counties).

18. McCloud River, from Lake McCloud Dam downstream to the southern boundary of Section 36, T38N, R3W, Mount Diablo B&M (Shasta County).

19. Deep Creek, from confluence with Green Valley Creek downstream to confluence with Willow Creek (San Bernardino County).

20. Middle Fork Stanislaus River, from Beardsley Afterbay Dam to Sand Bar Diversion Dam (Tuolumne County).

21. Truckee River, from confluence with Trout Creek downstream (excluding the property owned by the San Francisco Fly Casters Club) to confluence with Grays Creek (Nevada County).

22. Sespe Creek, a 25-mile section between the Lion Campground and the boundary of the U.S. Forest Service, Los Padres National Forest (Ventura County).

23. Merced River, from Yosemite National Park boundary downstream to Foresta Bridge (Mariposa County).

24. East Fork Carson River, from Hangman's Bridge near Markleeville downstream to the Nevada state line (Alpine County).

25. Bear Creek, Bear Valley Dam (impounding the Big Bear Lake) downstream to the confluence with the Santa Ana River (San Bernardino County).

26. Lavazzola Creek (Sierra County).

27. Laurel Lakes (Mono County).

28. Middle Fork San Joaquin River from the footbridge just above the confluence with Shadow Creek downstream to the footbridge just above the Soda Springs Campground (Inyo National Forest) and from the northern boundary of Devil's Postpile National Monument downstream to the Lower Falls (Madera County).

# APPENDIX VI
## Fly Plates

The fly plates shown on these pages were drawn by Barry Glickman, recognized nationally as a premier pen and ink fly illustrator. Barry is a consummate fly tier whose love for the art transforms three dimensional patterns into plates with contrast, depth, and drama. His illustrations have been featured in *Fly Rod & Reel* and run every issue of *California Fly Fisher*. His limited edition prints are displayed in both public and private collections.

Barry is currently involved in publishing a series of Master Flies by Master Tiers. His work is available by mail order: Barry Glickman, 1 Narragansett Cove, San Rafael, CA 94901, 415-456-9991.

*Caddis Pupa*

*Gray Ugly*

*Salmonfly Bucktail*

*Starling Pheasant*

*Beadhead Caddis*

*Sculpin*

*Peeking Caddis*

*Hunchback Infrequens*

*A Yellow Salty*

*Little Yellow Stone Nymph & Adult*

*Burk's Painless Baetis*

*Baetis Spinner*

*Bird's Nest*

*March Brown*

*Black Stonefly Nymph*

*Barry's Yellow Stone*

# Recommended Reading

*California Fly Fisher Magazine*, 12-A Guy Place, San Francisco, CA 94105

*Sierra Trout Guide*, Frank Amato Publications, Box 82112, Portland, OR 97202

*Freshwater Fishes of California*, University of California Press, 1984

*North Tahoe Trout: A Comprehensive Guide to Fishing the Truckee and Yuba River Drainages*, Dennis Pierce, Box 262, Rough and Ready, CA 95975

*California Fishing*, Foghorn Press, 555 De Haro Street, San Francisco, CA 95975

*California Blue Ribbon Trout Streams*, Amato Publications, Box 82112, Portland, OR 97202

*Western Hatches*, Amato Publications, Box 82112, Portland, OR, 97202

*An Anglers Guide to Aquatic Insects and Their Imitations*, Johnson Books, 1880 South 57th Court, Boulder, CO, 80301

*Caddisflies*, Lyons and Burford, 31 West 21st Street, New York, NY 10010

*Whitlock's Guide to Aquatic Trout Foods*, Lyons and Burford, West 21 Street, New York, NY 10010

# Index